'This excellent book features the lives of ... DFC and Rusty Kierath who were courageous and distinguished Australian fighter pilots, determined and innovative prisoners of war and daring "great escapers". Louise Williams tells their stories and reveals the impact on their families with great empathy, sensitivity and skill.'
— *Air Chief Marshal Sir Angus Houston AK, AFC (Ret'd)*

'It's a wonderful book and I thoroughly enjoyed it. It's the story of a Great Escaper, but it's so much more than that. It's an intimate portrait of a man who rose to every challenge that appeared before him, but also the tale of Louise Williams' quest to understand the uncle she never met. The characters are beautifully sketched, making this a totally absorbing story, written with empathy and insight.'
—*Professor Jonathan F. Vance, author of* A Gallant Company, The Men of the Great Escape

'Louise Williams' warm, wise, meticulously researched book traces the personal odysseys of two fine young Australians; taking them from the playing fields of Sydney's Shore School and the surf at Manly Beach, to their service as fighter pilots in the skies of North Africa, and on to their incarceration as POWs at the notorious Stalag Luft III. This book also offers fresh insights into the 'Great Escape' of March 1944, and its chilling aftermath, and has much to contribute on the subjects of remembrance, forgiveness and reconciliation.'
—*Peter Devitt, Curator, RAF Museum, London*

 **Louise Williams** is an award-winning writer, journalist and editor, and niece of John Williams. She has recreated John's story from family memories, letters, declassified documents, oral histories and interviews with survivors of the Great Escape.

She spent more than a decade as a foreign correspondent for Fairfax newspapers (the *Sydney Morning Herald* and *The Age*, Melbourne) based in Manila, Bangkok and Jakarta. Louise has written or contributed to a number of books and was the recipient of an Australia Council Asia Pacific Writers' Fellowship. Louise won a Walkley Award for Excellence in Journalism and the Citibank Pan Asia Journalism Award (in conjunction with Columbia University) for her work as a foreign correspondent. Louise is also a Research Associate of the Australian Centre for Independent Journalism (ACIJ) at the University of Technology.

A TRUE STORY OF THE

GREAT ESCAPE

A YOUNG AUSTRALIAN POW IN THE MOST AUDACIOUS BREAKOUT OF WWII

LOUISE WILLIAMS

ALLEN&UNWIN
SYDNEY·MELBOURNE·AUCKLAND·LONDON

Every effort has been made to trace the holders of copyright material. If you have any information concerning copyright material in this book please contact the publishers at the address below.

First published in 2015

Copyright © Louise Williams 2015

All rights reserved. No part of this book may be reproduced or transmitted in any form or by any means, electronic or mechanical, including photocopying, recording or by any information storage and retrieval system, without prior permission in writing from the publisher. The Australian *Copyright Act 1968* (the Act) allows a maximum of one chapter or 10 per cent of this book, whichever is the greater, to be photocopied by any educational institution for its educational purposes provided that the educational institution (or body that administers it) has given a remuneration notice to the Copyright Agency (Australia) under the Act.

Allen & Unwin
83 Alexander Street
Crows Nest NSW 2065
Australia
Phone: (61 2) 8425 0100
Email: info@allenandunwin.com
Web: www.allenandunwin.com
Cataloguing-in-Publication details are available
from the National Library of Australia
www.trove.nla.gov.au

ISBN 978 1 74331 389 3

Internal design by Phil Campbell
Set in 12.5/15 pt Bembo by Post Pre-press Group
Printed and bound in Australia by Griffin Press

10 9 8 7 6

The paper in this book is FSC® certified. FSC® promotes environmentally responsible, socially beneficial and economically viable management of the world's forests.

For our dear friend Michal Holy,

and in loving memory of John 'Willy' Williams and
Reginald 'Rusty' Kierath

It is a melancholy fact that escape is much harder in real life than in the movies, where only the heavy and the second lead are killed. This time, after huge success, death came to some heroes. Later it caught up with some villains.

– Paul Brickhill, RAAF officer, Stalag Luft III POW and author of *The Great Escape*

CONTENTS

Introduction		1
1	The Lost Letter	3
2	The Other Side of the Wire	7
3	How to Tell a True War Story	15
4	Great Expectations—the Making of a Young Man	17
5	The Next Leg	27
6	Introducing Michal	34
7	Paradise on Sea	39
8	In Search of a Decent Education	47
9	The Arrest	55
10	The Rise of an Aussie Icon	58
11	Choosing the Future	67
12	The Mother Country	72
13	Ivo Tonder—The Last Glimpse	77
14	In Search of the Elusive English Gentleman	81
15	Scotland, and the Brave	95
16	The first POW	104
17	The Australians Are Coming	108
18	Out in Africa	115
19	A Tale of Two Men and Two Messes	126
20	To War in the Desert	135
21	Reunion	146
22	Holding Your Nerve	152

23	Flipping the Bird	158
24	A Big Flap	161
25	While We Still Have Breath in Our Bodies	168
26	Down But Not Out	174
27	The Face of the Enemy	178
28	In the Bag	186
29	Big X	193
30	Second Time Unlucky	197
31	The Swimming Pool	200
32	Another German Friend	207
33	Cooking and Carpentry	211
34	A Ticket in the Lottery	220
35	Shuffling the Cards	223
36	The Bereaved Mother's Badge	230
37	In Memoriam	236
38	Surfing at Manly	244

Postscript—the Lost Letter, Found 247
Notes 248
Bibliography 272
Acknowledgements 275
Index 277

INTRODUCTION

I had never really expected to stand on the exact spot where the secret escape tunnel they called Harry came up 'outside the wire' of that infamous German POW camp, Stalag Luft III. Nor did I imagine I would ever have the opportunity to retrace the footsteps of my uncle, John, escapee number 31, and to put his story back together piece by piece.

I was born in 1961. My parents had lived through World War II and my grandparents had lived through two world wars. As family stories go, it's fair to say I grew up with John and his apparently extraordinary wartime experiences. However, despite the release of the movie, *The Great Escape*, and its popularity throughout the 1960s, the Hollywood version of the escape was so thoroughly Americanised that the real story remained distant, and largely inaccessible to us post-war kids, born into optimism and rapidly growing prosperity.

Europe was a very long way away from Australia's beaches. Certainly, we all embraced John's pre-war passion for surfing and his particular love of the southern corner of Manly Beach, a little pocket of paradise so sheltered and warm that it was always swimmable. At least that's what my dad claimed. My father, Owen, the tail-ender of the five Williams kids, and ten years younger than John, challenged himself, and us, to surf at Manly without a wetsuit all year round. It was much easier to relate to the history of surfing, and John's brief role as an early pioneer on a wooden board and as a champion surf-lifesaver at the local Manly club, than to distant former European and north African theatres of war.

And, to be honest, family history isn't for the young. When you are so busy planning ahead, there's never enough time to look back. We were so interested in where we were going, we didn't really pay much attention to where we might have come from.

By the 1970s war stories were fast going out of fashion anyway. Popular opposition to the Vietnam War, and to armed conflict in general, began to sour military homecomings. We began to re-examine the rights and wrongs of war from the safety of the affluent Australian suburbs, as though violence as a means to any end was a simplistic, moral issue; all bristling aggression, expansionism and military adventurism and never, in itself, an anguished response of last resort.

In the 1980s my father, mother and brothers travelled to Europe, then a major undertaking for a family of modest financial means. My dad stood at inquiry counters in London seeking information about John's war record to no avail. He hit one dead end after another.

The end of World War II had triggered some radical border realignments across Europe. Not only was Stalag Luft III now in Poland but Poland had fallen under the brutal Cold War purview of the Soviet Union and so was then firmly locked behind the Iron Curtain, the ruins of the camp left to the vagaries of nature.

And, the daily demands of life intervened. I became a foreign correspondent, a role that, ironically, enabled me to tell many other people's dramatic stories, featuring so many new and terrible types of conflict and cruelty that conventional warfare and the rules of engagement of World War II—at least as they were supposed to regulate wars to limit brutality—seemed almost naive.

So, for decades, John's story was (carefully) shelved.

Then in late 2011, an email arrived out of the blue from a complete stranger, a Czech pilot with a keen interest in military aviation history and, as it turned out, in John's escape route south. He'd picked up John's trail. Now, John's story was finally on its way.

THE LOST LETTER

14 May 1944

My grandmother, Mildred, always chose her words carefully. She had been practising for years. On that particular Sunday morning, she was confident that she could write a letter so utterly dull that it would slide, unmolested, across the desks of the various censors that stood between her and her eldest son, John. As she sat down with her thoughts, the early morning autumn sun was already retreating behind building clouds. The fine weather wouldn't last.[1]

There was a war on, as people never tired of saying. So few words to so tritely sum up such weighty wartime expectations. Mothers were, of course, expected to give their sons up to their fate in patriotic, good cheer. The way Mildred saw it, her pen poised, there were so few victories to be had over the distant enemy, so few outlets for that ferocious maternal love that fear and absence stoked, that to get every letter through was something worth bandying about with pride.

Collectively, Mildred's weekly letters to John painted a parochial picture of wartime life in the seaside suburbs of Sydney. By necessity they were little more than a bulletin of the comings and goings of family, friends and neighbours, these unremarkable characters buzzing around busily on the pages as though life went on as normal.

The instructions to the Australian families of prisoners of war or POWs were clear: mention anything at all of potential value to the enemy and risk a jail sentence or hefty fine. Many of Sydney's young men were gone; the city's famous beaches, formerly thronging with surfers and swimmers, picnickers and sightseers, now lay behind barricades and massive rolls of barbed wire[2] and the residents of many of the elegant mansions that fronted the gracious natural harbour had left for the perceived safety of the mountains to the west. Wartime rationing was, of course, in full swing.

Just a few hundred metres down the road from the Williams home a military detachment sat behind sandbags. Although the city had survived virtually untouched, save for the midget Japanese submarine attack of 1942 that had killed nineteen Australian and two British sailors,[3] recent developments to Australia's north were troubling. Exactly what the 'controversial political and industrial matters'[4] might be that could fall into enemy hands was so vague that Mildred gave anything beyond the petty domestic a wide berth.

No doubt John's letters from Germany, full of the camaraderie of cricket matches, football games, theatre troupes and study groups, and the ample leisure time the Germans afforded POWs of officer rank, were just as selective, even if he was, somewhat to the family's relief, 'down' and now 'just waiting out the war'.

None of which really mattered anyway. All Mildred's determination was focused on one goal: that the envelopes she so carefully addressed to Australian Prisoner of War no 848, Stalag Luft III, Germany—and the letters inside that she closed with her prayers for her beloved son—made it through. For all the years that John had been gone she had never stopped writing. Nor had he. It was more than six years now and sometimes she wondered what he looked like; the idealistic, fresh-faced new recruit of her memory was probably just that.

Such thoughts were, however, intensely private. Australian men were 'chin up' types. Whether they were large, loud, backslapping jokers or quiet, taciturn thinkers, they shrugged off the privations and pain of war and captivity and got on with the jobs at hand. By contrast, the women tended to quietly purse their lips or set their mouths in tight, straight lines. Adversity, it seemed, readily triggered that peculiarly female response of martyrdom. At the local shops, pointedly addressing each other with exaggerated formality and politeness, wartime mothers and wives were keen to recount their latest misery or woe, at least in part for the opportunity it afforded them to parade their strength to bear its burden.

Mildred was no different. She was extraordinarily proud of her son, and had feared for him, in equal measure. She 'idealised him', my Uncle David said, or was it 'idolised him'? I was never sure. Mildred liked to write out his rank in full, never omitting his DFC (Distinguished Flying Cross). At 23, John had become a squadron leader seconded from the Royal Air Force (RAF) to lead a Royal Australian Air Force (RAAF) squadron. This was not just because he had earned the right to lead, but also because the heavy death toll in the air war sharply accelerated every surviving pilot's progress through the ranks. Now, he was 24 years old and incarcerated indefinitely somewhere in Nazi Germany.

That the page she was writing would, sometime in the future, be held in his hands was the lifeline that linked mother to son.

Recently, Mildred's letter-writing schedule had become busier than ever. My uncles, David, her second son, then Barry, the third, had also signed up and gone. My grandfather, Llewellyn, whom everyone called Len rather than grapple with the difficult Welsh pronunciation, was working in northern Australia locating sites for new airfields and overseeing construction as the Japanese advanced south. It was only Mildred, my father, Owen, then a teenager, and Suzie, the oldest of the Williams siblings, and her baby at home. Suzie's brief wartime marriage had produced an engaging toddler, Stephen, whose progress Mildred happily recounted to John that day. Suzie's husband had returned to Asia, only to become a POW himself, so was now at the mercy of the Japanese in Singapore's Changi camp. Changi made the Nazis look humane.

It was Mother's Day that Sunday, 14 May. The weekend's newspaper had been somewhat reassuring. Enough of the news stories mentioned post-war plans to imagine an end might really be in sight. The tide had turned in the Allies' favour in Europe, although, for Australian troops facing the Japanese in the Pacific, David included, the future was far less certain.

Mildred wondered what news she might impart that day. There wasn't much she hadn't already mentioned, so she recalled a previous Mother's Day before the war. John, then an infectiously energetic, athletic teenager, was taking her to the pictures. The memory was bathed in that golden autumn light that seemed to reflect off the yellow sand of Manly Beach as the angle of the harsh Australian summer sun finally dipped and softened, signalling the cooler winter days and nights ahead. John had run ahead of her, along the beachfront near the small rented flat where they lived, and raced into the local milk bar. He came out beaming, bearing a box of chocolates, a sheer luxury. She still didn't know how he had managed to afford them.

This Sunday's letter was just a single page, closely covered on both sides. 'With all my love and prayers beloved son. May angels guard thee,' she signed off, as usual, sealing the letter and putting it aside to post the next morning.

That night a tremendous storm broke over the city, the lightning setting a building across the harbour alight, the hail and flash floods stripping the crops and fruit trees in the city's kitchen gardens and allotments that supplemented the spartan wartime rations.[5]

The postmark on the aged envelope shows Mildred's letter did, indeed, begin its slow journey towards Europe on Monday, 15 May 1944. We know, too, that it did get through, but not exactly when it reached Stalag Luft III.

John was, however, long gone.

For many decades, Mildred's letter was lost.

THE OTHER SIDE OF THE WIRE

If John was nervous, it didn't show. He'd always preferred to play the clown in life. Humour, especially in the recent years of air combat over the Western Desert in the Middle East and North Africa, and now in German captivity, had proved an effective antidote to adversity and its wartime derivate, fear.

Seventy years on, sitting at my desk at home with the familiar Sydney autumn sunshine warm through the windowpane, I still can't get past the first question that has always sprung, uninvited, to my mind. Even as a young child I turned this moment over and over again in my imagination, always wondering whether they were scared (and childishly hoping they weren't).

The more I have read since and the deeper I have delved into John's own story, the more naive that question becomes. The Allied POWs of Stalag Luft III were volunteer pilots and aircrew. They had survived dogfights, anti-aircraft fire, flak damage and the commonplace but often deadly handicaps of technical malfunctions, inadequate training and the resulting human error. They had crawled out of wrecked planes and bailed out mid-air, often over water or over empty desert sands, to make it back to solid ground alive and mobile, albeit behind enemy lines.

'It is almost superfluous to point out . . . aircrew were healthy young men who (almost daily) faced the imminent danger of serious wounding or complete annihilation', as the British book *The Flyer*[1] notes. At that time, fighter planes and bombers were the ultimate in modern war machines and therefore offered a new variety of terrifying and violent ways in which aircrew might meet their demise. Very many did. Surviving required every pilot and crew member to privately forge his own, intimate, personal acquaintance with fear.

By the time they took their allotted places to wait silently in the dark in Hut 104 of Stalag Luft III, the Germans' supposedly escape-proof prisoner-of-war camp, whatever complicated rationalisations and mental tricks they had mastered to fend off anxiety, they all knew exactly where they stood with risk.

But, already, things were not going to plan.

24–25 March 1944
It is an unseasonally cold spring in the eastern reaches of Nazi Germany. Snow still lies on the ground of the endless, uniform conifer forests that surrounded Stalag Luft III, hemming the POWs in, both physically and psychologically.

RAF Flight Lieutenant Leslie 'Johnny' Bull, as escapee number 1, should have already left John far behind. But his progress is hindered by a swollen trapdoor over the exit of the tunnel 'Harry' that runs, undetected, from under the wood stove in the corner of Bunk Room 23 to freedom, 'outside the wire'.

Leslie does go down and through first—lying pressed flat on one of the wooden trolleys of the ingenious mini underground 'railway' system that the carpentry team has built to speed the men through. The 9 metre deep, 105 metre long hand-dug tunnel[2] (as measured by the POWs' string) is barely big enough to accommodate a broad set of shoulders. At about 60 centimetres high and wide, the pressing, suffocating claustrophobia is only momentarily relieved by two underground caverns, or way stations, optimistically named Piccadilly Circus and Leicester Square. But when Leslie reaches the tunnel's exit, he discovers the soft spring snow has soaked the wood, sealing it firmly shut.

Working frantically with RAF Flight Lieutenant Henry 'Johnny' Marshall, another of the 'diggers' who has laboured underground for months excavating and shoring up the escape route, Leslie eventually prises the trapdoor open.

They have come up well short. They aren't in the forest at all. Anywhere between 3–5 and 25 metres short, depending on who is telling the tale.

After more than a year of operating a vast, secret network of hundreds of POWs assigned to every intricately planned aspect of the escape, they have made it 'out of the bag', as one of the many sayings went.

Their way home now lies within sight of the nearest watchtower and its rotating searchlight and is just as liable to be stumbled upon by the patrolling perimeter guards and their dogs.

At the same time, all those young, hyped-up men lying cramped up in the tunnel in wait are creating another unanticipated problem which might have been comical in any other circumstances. They are generating so much body heat that a steady head of steam is billowing, visibly, out of the exit shaft.

Leslie's solution to the shortfall, immortalised in virtually every account of that night, puts him further back in the queue. He should have been off first, heading quickly towards his train. Instead, he rigs up a line of string from the cover of the trees, his eyes closely tracking the sweep of the light. As the searchlight swings away, he jerks the string to alert the next man waiting in the exit shaft to rush out. It's slower than they'd planned, but it works.

By the time John finally pulls himself up and out of the exit it's around midnight; instead of one man every two to three minutes from the time the huts were locked down at 10 p.m., the pace has slowed to one man every fourteen minutes or so.[3] Close behind John is a fellow Australian, his closest friend, Royal Australian Air Force (RAAF) Flight Lieutenant Reginald 'Rusty' Kierath.

If there was one thing that had consoled Mildred about John's indefinite stint in Stalag Luft III it was that Rusty had shown up, having been picked up by a German boat after bailing out over the ocean, as his damaged aircraft plunged into the water. (True to form, Rusty's cheerful first letter home told it like a boy's own adventure, right down to the delight he took in sipping from his emergency brandy flask, savouring its warming effect as he floated adrift and alone for hours.)

Rusty is not just a fellow pilot from John's former squadron, the aptly named Desert Harassers (450s), although the camaraderie of shared wartime experiences was itself a sound foundation for many a strong bond. John first met Rusty at school when they ran out onto the oval together as keen Rugby players in pre-war Sydney, an era that seems a lifetime ago. As teenagers they were more affable sporting acquaintances, but their paths have since crossed, fortuitously, over many years and they have become allies and firm friends. As escape partners, they have not merely been thrown together by circumstances. From the moment they reorganised their allotted bunks inside Stalag Luft III to move into the same room, they have had each other's backs.

Now their fates are inextricably linked.

The men do not, of course, pause to take in this incredible moment as the sheer exhilaration of freedom collides with the first shock of wind so cold that it knocks the air out of their lungs. Later, this moment will be recalled by some as though it had played out in slow motion as, one after the other, they glance briefly back at the tunnel before disappearing into the darkness.

In the 1963 Hollywood version of the escape, the cameras and the bright lights follow the first group of POWs. With Richard Attenborough playing escape committee leader RAF Squadron Leader Roger Bushell, or 'Big X', the first group out are heading pretty much straight ahead from the tunnel exit. They have a relatively short walk through the trees to the back entrance of the main train station in Sagan where they are to purchase tickets for various distant destinations across Europe. Their forged papers describe them as businessmen of all sorts; their suits and fake suitcases look persuasive enough, at least at first glance.

Sagan, or Zagan as it is now known, was then a swarming, strategic military town, adjacent to the intersection of six major railway lines. Hundreds of thousands of Allied servicemen were incarcerated in numerous POW compounds nearby. Even late at night the main station was brightly lit and thrumming with activity.

Our group is going another way altogether. With Leslie's original group gone, he finds himself with John's 'party of foreign workers' when he finally passes responsibility for the string signal over to another escapee further down the line.

They're initially heading south-east and they have a very long, dark walk ahead. Disguised as a rag-tag bunch of Czech labourers, they are armed only with forged leave tickets purportedly from a local wood mill. Like the occupants of Stalag Luft III, they're actually a mix of nationalities—our group are British, Australian, Polish, Russian and Greek.

In retrospect it's difficult to gauge how much adrenalin sharpened their senses that night. By all accounts, at least some of the men, and likely John and Rusty included, regarded the whole thing as something of an extreme sport, which must surely come with its own measure of fun.

John leads off.[4] Even the sound of their own breath rings loudly in their ears, as they draw the ice-cold air in and out heavily, keeping up a solid pace. Around them the forest seems to vibrate with noise, none more alarming than the sound of their own boots crunching through the snow. As RAF Flight Lieutenant Bernard 'Pop' Green notes to himself: 'The frozen snow seems to make enough noise to wake the dead.'

The going proves heavy and at times the snow is up to the men's knees. Then a loud roar is heard in the distance, so they hit the ground, lying silent and flat. When a train finally passes nearby, it seems to be roaring and blazing with light.[5]

The jitters in the group prompt a few snappy exchanges, until John intervenes, his Australian drawl distinctive in the dark.[6] 'Okay, fellows, everyone relax . . . there's only kriegies [their expression for POWs, a shortening of the German] damn silly enough to be around on a night like this,' he says, reassuring everyone that they will hit the right train line if they just kept heading east.

As the hours wear on, their trek slows to more of a 'plod' through snowdrifts and slush. It's only 8 kilometres over flat territory as the crow flies, but how straight or otherwise they are walking in the dark is something even they don't know.

It's 4.30 a.m. or so when they finally come across the station they are looking for, at Tschiebsdorf. There's just one small brick platform rising a half-metre or so out of the forest floor, a modest waiting room–cum–ticket office and a handful of buildings, standing dark and quiet behind.

Now it's Jerzy Mondschein, a Flying Officer from one of the Polish squadrons flying under RAF command, who steps forward. His task is critical. They've all piled into the waiting room and it's Jerzy, a fluent German speaker, who brings out the money for the tickets.[7]

'*Zwölf?*', the ticket clerk barks incredulously, as though this tiny siding has never seen such a throng. 'Yes, twelve tickets,' replies Jerzy just as belligerently in German, as the rest of the group try to appear unconcerned.

The only people around so early are a local farmer and his wife. They poke their heads in and take one look at 'the pirate crew draped around the walls'[8] of the waiting room and withdraw quickly to stand in the cold outside.

The ticket clerk returns with no further questions and twelve tickets south towards the Czechoslovakian border in his hand, the first leg of the long overland journey to Switzerland.

The train steams in on time at 5 a.m. They are on their way.

❖

Over the decades since that night of 24 March 1944, various historians and writers have diligently tracked down every possible detail of the escape. Moving in ever tighter circles around the same set of facts, a long list of experts and amateurs has seized on any new angle, any newly declassified documents, to answer the who, why, what, when, where and how. Ultimately, their various questions come down to the same thing: could anyone have realistically expected things to have turned out any other way?

What transpired in Room 23 of Hut 104, and what followed, has been described and re-enacted many times over in books, in films and on television, all over the world.

The words audacious, courageous, daring, heroic and even reckless and foolhardy come to mind. Most dominant in our popular imagination is that big, bright, jaunty Hollywood blockbuster *The Great Escape*, in which Steve McQueen's largely fictional character, the American pilot Virgil Hilts, hogs the limelight among a band of talented, ingenious, irrepressible airmen in one of the most extraordinary wartime escapes of all time. (Although American POWs did play a role in the escape preparations, the USAAF prisoners were moved to another compound before the breakout).

More recent endeavours have, for example, followed contemporary pilots of Britain's RAF seeking to replicate the construction of the tunnel using only the makeshift tools the POWs had on hand, with mixed results. Others have featured the many long distance marches, walks and rallies in their footsteps and the numerous memorials and anniversary events that have sought to connect us, in some way, to the extreme challenges the great escapers faced.

The simple truth was that on that excruciatingly cold, moonless night, John was number 31, or perhaps 32, as accounts differ, in an escape that aimed to break 200 Allied pilots and aircrew out at the same time, the biggest mass escape effort of World War II.

Unlike many of the other POWs who had filled above-ground roles in the camp's clandestine escape organisation—forging travel documents, turning Allied uniforms into reasonable copies of local workers' clothing, scrounging extra food for escape rations, transforming razor blades into compasses—John had been directly involved in the construction of the tunnel.[9] He knew what to expect.

As head carpenter, he was responsible for every one of the thousands of planks of wood, mainly stripped secretly from the POWs bunks, that shored up the tunnel; something Steve McQueen handled in the Hollywood film. The carpenters also built the underground railway and turned bed boards into reasonably convincing fake wooden guns. And John's good-humoured demeanour had helped him befriend at least one key German guard who had been persuaded to take him on walks outside the camp, effectively reconnaissance missions for the escape committee. It would not be the first time he'd felt the sandy soil of the Silesian forest under his boots.

3
HOW TO TELL A TRUE WAR STORY

Everyone with even a passing interest in World War II history, or war films, knows what happened next.

In much the same way as our eyes are drawn to a burning wreck on a highway after a fiery crash, our imaginations tend to rush headlong towards the horror or the drama. Rarely do we take the time to appreciate those millions of ordinary moments that make up even extraordinary lives. All four men, and many of their fellow escapees, have long been defined by their fate. I have always wanted to understand what forces, within and without, propelled John through life.

War stories are especially hard to tell with any confidence because war, like crime and violence, simultaneously fascinates and repels. US writer Tim O'Brien, in his confronting 1990 short story based on his personal experiences of the Vietnam War, put it like this:[1]

> It can be argued that war is grotesque. But in truth war is also beauty. For all its horror, you can't help but gape at the awful majesty of combat. You stare out at the tracer rounds unwinding through the dark like brilliant red ribbons. You admire the fluid symmetries of troops on the move, the great sheets of metal fire streaming down from a gunship.

War is hell, but that's not the half of it, because war is mystery and terror and adventure and courage and discovery and holiness and longing and love. War is nasty; war is fun. War is thrilling; war is drudgery. War makes you a man, war makes you dead.²

All of which is undeniable. 'At its core, perhaps,' wrote O'Brien, 'war is just another name for death, and yet any soldier will tell you, if he tells the truth, that a proximity to death brings a corresponding proximity to life. All around you things are purely living . . . in the midst of evil you want to be a good man.'³

I don't want to let the ending swallow up these lives of these young men. I want to take a few big steps back.

GREAT EXPECTATIONS—THE MAKING OF A YOUNG MAN

My grandmother was a snob. This might seem like an unnecessarily harsh statement, casting Mildred, as it does, as an unsympathetic character so early on in the narrative. That's not my intention. Recounting John's story, with the many luxuries hindsight permits, does not entitle me to pass judgement on any of its players, let alone on someone who went through so much. But, as I rummaged around in the memories of older relatives and family friends, the same word seemed eventually to come to the fore to describe the manner in which Mildred steered the Williams family ship. Other softer words are, of course, offered first. She was 'particular' about things, she was very 'proper', she insisted on 'doing things a certain way'—which are merely euphemisms for the same thing: Mildred was a snob. But, whatever thoughts she had about her own station and status in life, whatever ambitions she had for herself, she had in spades for her family, especially her first son, John. That his mother believed so fervently in his character and capabilities, and fostered great expectations to match, likely imbued in John the belief that few of life's challenges were insurmountable.

That's not to say Mildred's own life was easy. Just like the rest of us, her early experiences largely accounted for her adult choices. Mildred was the only child of a young woman in service, as they used to say, in the upstairs-downstairs world that divided

Australia's wealthy pastoralists, industrialists and business leaders from their household help in the late 1800s and early 1900s. Young, convict-built Australia had none of the born-to-rule pretension of the hereditary class system of England's titled earls, lords and other various princelings but we had readily emulated the then-significant gap between the privileged and the rest. Although Mildred's mother, Martha 'Nellie' Eleanor Smith, was treated very well by her employers, for an extended period the Arnott family of the biscuit empire fame, she was definitely downstairs in the scheme of things.

Mildred's father was a labourer in the rugged central west of New South Wales. He abandoned his young wife and daughter in the rural town of Forbes early on and Nellie eventually filed for divorce on the grounds of desertion, an extremely unusual and courageous step for any women in the late 1890s. Nellie became a mythological family character in her own right. She was tenacious, hardworking and sharp, and determinedly made her way in life as a single mother in a world that offered women of any class few opportunities, let alone those not defined by a husband.

Relatives say she made a habit of rising at 6 a.m. every day, swallowing a raw egg whole and then reading the paper from back to front, having probably been among the first batches of girls to have learned to read and write when a new public school opened in Forbes in the 1870s. Later in life she devoted her holidays from toiling in other people's homes to helping out her sisters and brothers and their many children on small farm holdings in the district. Most remarkably she taught them water survival skills in rivers and dams in itchy knitted woollen bathing suits at a time when very few Australians, let alone women, could swim. That Nellie lived an active and healthy life for most of her 97 years seems entirely in character.

The young Mildred was just as determined. Conversely, what she wanted more than anything else was to fit in. At the time that meant aspiring to marry and then devoting her energies and intellect to family and community life. Men were the breadwinners and even female teachers had to give up their jobs when they married. Whatever steel Nellie had found within herself to tolerate a place on the social fringe in rural Australia, Mildred couldn't escape its confines quickly enough.

Mildred changed her surname, taking the family name of an elderly relative by marriage, disposing of her absent father and her early life in one fell swoop. She trained as a typist and moved to Sydney where she met and married my grandfather, Llewellyn, in 1915.

The new Mildred, Mrs Llewellyn Williams as was the naming convention of the time, would go to great lengths to keep her past at bay throughout her life. When Nellie came to visit, Mildred famously sent her mother around the back to the service entrance, instructing her not to knock on the front door in future. Nellie didn't mind in the least. She was thrilled Mildred had graduated; her daughter had home help herself.

Len too, was a terrific snob, but his aspirations were not a reaction against his childhood but a product of it.

His father, Edwin Williams, was a Welsh stonemason, like his father before him. As a young married man with three small children, Edwin and his beloved wife, Sarah, gambled everything on making their fortune when they embarked on that long ocean voyage to Australia. And they did.

Edwin went from skilled artisan to professional architect in Sydney, establishing an architectural practice in his own right that was responsible for a string of handsome sandstone churches and public buildings, including one of the finest examples of nineteenth-century sandstone architecture, Sydney's Australia Bank of Commerce.[1] The *Cyclopedia of New South Wales* of 1907, a who's who of the time, declares that Edwin's 'repute as an Architect knows no local boundaries' and sums up his career as a 'procession of success'.[2]

This might suggest that the roads of the emerging young Australian nation were paved with opportunity, if not gold. But, without connections, every newcomer paid their dues. Edwin worked like a Trojan. Then, personal tragedy struck. Sarah died of pneumonia at the age of 36, only two months after losing their eighth child, a baby girl. That left Edwin with six surviving children aged between two and twelve (their second son had died as a toddler). With no family support in their new country, the task of raising the children passed to Susanna, the eldest. She had written loving, heart-wrenching letters to her mother as she lay dying in hospital, promising to study hard and imploring her to come home, to no avail.

Somehow Susanna, barely into adolescence, managed to run the family house, forsaking her own prospects of marriage and children as the years dragged on. The family could afford some hired help but, for long hours every day while her father was at work, and later extended periods while he travelled to oversee building projects, it was Susanna who was in charge of budgeting, shopping and her siblings' education. Edwin never remarried. Instead he saved up to commission a stained glass window in Sarah's honour for the local church of her home town.

By all accounts, the kind young Susanna grew into an embittered and notoriously cranky middle-aged, then elderly lady. This is hardly surprising. Even when her own siblings had grown up, it fell upon her to take on her sister Fanny's children and household when Fanny died young. But her childhood empathy was not entirely consumed by her decades of personal disappointment and subjugation to the extended family's seemingly insatiable needs. Much later, she would play a pivotal role in young John's life, and that of his many cousins.

My grandfather was four years old when his mother died. He must have somehow muddled through his education at local schools with the help of his father and sister before going on to train within his father's architectural firm. Len then gained entry to study architecture at King's College, London, where he earned the Gold Medal for advanced construction and sanitation, concurrently qualifying as a structural engineer, before going on to the École des Beaux-Arts in Paris. I still have his collection of early photographs of Paris landmarks; the awe of a fresh-faced young man from a far-flung dominion of the British Empire viewing Paris with his own eyes is palpable, every image carefully marked with his name and preserved in a leather binder tied up with string.

So unusual were Len's academic and artistic achievements of that time that his return to Sydney in 1912 was reported in the *Sydney Morning Herald*. Len, it seems, was enjoying a charmed life, following apparently seamlessly in his father's professional footsteps.

With his marriage to Mildred, Len's talents and ambitions were cemented in a formidable team.

In 1917, the couple decided to move to Wellington, New Zealand. It was a still a young city, settled only in 1840 when its founders lured its first colonial settlers with their ambitious plans for building a 'Better Britain' or a 'Britain of the South'. In Wellington, the enterprising Wakefield brothers promised new settlers a society in which 'English class distinctions were preserved, but where industrious artisans and farmers could more easily work their way towards prosperity and respectability'.³

Len's story seems to flow a little too smoothly, skating as it does over the global turmoil of the time. World War I, or the Great War as it was then known, was raging when the Williams set off to establish their new life. Surely, this must raise some questions.

At the time, young men in Australia and New Zealand were under intense social pressure to sign up to fight for the Empire. In New Zealand, conscription had been introduced in 1916 and all men aged from 20 to 46 were legally required to register for war service.⁴ The bloody defeat at Gallipoli of the combined Anzac forces in 1915 had only hardened public opinion against those considered 'shirkers or disloyal'[5] and men not in uniform were shunned or singled out with the anonymous white feathers of cowardice. How then did Len's splendid career, and the comfortable family life it afforded, carry on regardless?

The story, as my uncle David told it, was that Len did, of course, report to the War Office in Wellington shortly after his arrival, as required. By this time Len was in his early thirties and he and Mildred had had their first child, Suzanne—Suzie.

Len turned up at the recruiting office in his outdated British khakis and putties—strips of fabric that soldiers wrapped around their calves, giving their trousers an odd look of jodhpurs—and produced his British territorial officer's rank. University students in England apparently took up officers' commissions in the territorial reserves when they graduated as a matter of course, so Len had too, almost a decade earlier. The Wellington War Office had no idea what to do with Len's old papers for a unit that might no longer even exist. They certainly had no provision for signing up pre-war British 'territorials' on the other side of the world. He'd have to start at the bottom with the rest, he was told.

'You don't expect me to fight with pimply faced bakers' boys do you?' he snapped before storming off.

New Zealand records do show that Len did in fact enlist but in the reserves. He had not been called up by the time the war ended in 1918. Consequently, unlike so many Australian and New Zealand men of his era who were killed and horribly wounded in previously unimaginable numbers, Len not only made it through the war unscathed, but his own professional 'procession of success' powered on uninterrupted. From New Zealand alone, of the 100,000 'sons' sent to fight for the British Empire, 17,000 died and 41,000 were injured.[6]

A year later, in 1919, John Edwin Ashley Williams was born.

The Great War, 'the war to end all wars', was over. The Williams' firstborn son began life as a new era dawned. All around, people were flushed with optimism. Both peace and prosperity seemed at last to be within reach.

New Zealand was about as far away from Britain as it was possible to travel on the globe, lying literally on the opposite side of the world, on the remote southern edge of the then expansive British Empire. Despite, or perhaps because of, this vast distance from the Mother Country, New Zealand's white Anglo-Celtic settlers set about building their fledgling nation in Britain's image, right down to the smallest details. (That they were imposing on Maori land is an issue that should be acknowledged but cannot be covered here in a few lines.) It was not only the political and legal framework that New Zealanders inherited, or the close and then lucrative trade ties they enjoyed with Britain, but also an apparent desire to cling to a collective love for a distant monarch and culture.

There was, of course, one very important difference. Britain's class system and its complicated social rules and mores were deeply entrenched. Although the British upper class would not prove immovable over the longer term, in the 1920s the English hereditary aristocracy was certainly not in the habit of throwing open its doors to working-class men made good.

In New Zealand and Australia, pedigree did not necessarily define an individual's future, just as the founders of the City of Wellington had anticipated. The Williams had made their own luck. A long line of Welsh stonemasons had finally sent a son to university in London, albeit via Australia. Now in Wellington, Len and Mildred were free to fashion their future in whatever way they saw fit. And just like many a nouveau-riche family, they aspired to just about everything their forefathers had not been able to enjoy or to offer their children.

The representative of King George V of England in New Zealand had some sage advice from the king himself for a nine-year-old John Williams and his school friends, their faces turned attentively towards the stage, their necks constricted in their regulation coats and ties.[7]

It was the school end-of-year ceremony of 1928, marking the beginning of the summer break and the liberation of the boys from the strict, busy schedule of the private Anglican boys' college the Williams had chosen for their sons. With its bracing winds off the water, large gardens and sports grounds, Wellesley College was modelled on Britain's private prep schools. Wellesley boys from the age of five were enthusiastically drilled to lead 'Godly', 'disciplined' and 'vigorous' lives. The school believed that academic excellence and physical prowess went hand in hand, so all sports were compulsory. Wellesley boys swam long distances and learned how to save lives in the brisk Tasman Sea, they boxed, they marched and handled muskets, played competitive Rugby and cricket, ran cross-country, raised money for charities and, of course, attended church.

The Governor-General, Sir Charles Ferguson, confided in the boys that King George kept a list of ideals on his wall 'that His Majesty believes should be hung up in every school in England'. That the sentiment extended to the schools of the British Empire which was then at its zenith is, of course, implied. By the mid-1920s Britain oversaw a worldwide empire that covered a fifth of the land on earth and British global naval superiority meant Britannia really did rule the waves.[8]

The Governor-General warmed up with some general points, exhorting the boys to aim high in whatever they did. More specifically, he quoted from King George V's list. There was obedience 'to the rules of the game', there was winning if they can but being a good loser if they can't, there was 'not crying over spilt milk' and learning to distinguish sentiment from sentimentality and avoiding 'cheap praise'. Then there was sacrifice, usually for one's country but in this case, as New Zealand is a dominion, that loyalty was ceded to Britain.

'Teach me that if I am called up to suffer, to go away like a well-bred beast, and suffer in silence,' recounted His Excellency. Above all, he counselled, 'be manly'.

What the boys made of this list—or whether they took it in at all—can only be conjecture. It may have been only the parents and teachers who nodded approvingly in the audience, the somewhat abstract notion of a distant king going right over the young boys' heads. Newspaper reports of various Wellesley school events of the era reveal similar, constantly repeated themes of self-control, discipline, responsibility, citizenship, as well as sacrificing oneself for others, one's country and one's heritage.[9] These young English gentlemen in training had a lot to live up to.

But unlike the English adage that 'children should be seen and not heard', Wellesley College had gone out on a limb by inviting the close involvement of parents in the school community. It also instigated various then unusual school prizes, for achievements like 'effort' and 'improvement', to ensure their boys felt encouraged and valued[10] and believed they could make a difference in the world. The Williams embraced this ethos wholeheartedly, sponsoring a prize for academic improvement in Mildred's name and the 'Llewellyn Williams' cup for cricket, convinced that education mattered above all. By 1928, there were two Williams boys at the school, John and David. Son number three, Barry, was still a toddler at home.

Meanwhile, Len's professional fortunes continued on a steady upwards trajectory. After initially serving as a junior partner to an established Wellington architect, Len had gone out on his own, soon making a name for himself for his Art Deco designs, then the epitome of forward-looking modernity. In particular, he was known for a string of cinemas, including the lavish De Luxe Theatre in central Wellington, with its grand white Sicilian marble staircase, daring black marble bathrooms, tiled walls and Grecian-style bronze fittings. The roaring 1920s, the golden age of cinema, was everything the austere war years were not: flashy, extravagant and opulent.

Throughout the 1920s the family lived on the steep hill that overlooks Wellington Harbour in a large house, run by Mildred and her tireless house help. They holidayed in their cottage on Lake Taupo. Len embraced motoring and posed the family for photographs in front of various large family vehicles, like their four-door Bentley. Len branched out into local politics and commerce too, assuming a position as one of the founding directors of, and first major shareholders in, the Australian and New Zealand Banking Corporation Limited, the predecessor of today's international ANZ Bank.[11] But, perhaps, he was over-extended.

When the new year of 1929 ticked over my father, Owen, was born. It was as though, with each new addition to the family, someone turned the volume down. If John was larger than life, a strapping athletic boy who relished every challenge in his path, Owen was, from the start, quiet and shy, a listener. As it turned out, he was also largely ignored. Global events soon unfolded that overshadowed all else.

By October that year, the world's stock markets were in free fall. The family's stock holdings were virtually worthless and so too was Len's architectural practice; with no money circulating, building sites stopped dead. The Great Depression had begun.

Bit by bit, every asset the Williams owned was liquidated, at fire-sale prices. Len scrambled, but soon they lost the family home.

Mildred found herself standing on the docks in Wellington Harbour with the children at her side, a modest collection of suitcases their only remaining possessions.

THE NEXT LEG

There were many sound strategic reasons that Stalag Luft III had been built just outside Sagan (Zagan), in the heart of Germany's eastern Silesia region.

For a start, the camp was—for any POW who happened to make it out—located about as far away as possible via German and German-occupied territories from the freedom of neutral or Allied nations. It was also sited, most inconveniently, on a largely flat plain of sandy soil, which meant that any escape tunnel, the favoured way out, was constantly at risk of caving in on itself and its occupants.

Stalag Luft III was specifically constructed to corral the officers of the various Allied air forces in one place, under especially watchful eyes.

Pilots and aircrew were valuable because their training soaked up time and money, and their skills were critical to the prosecution of the Allies' military strategy. Warfare had moved on from the cold, fetid trenches of World War I; victory this time round would be decided in the air. The Allied air forces wanted their pilots and crew back up in the air behind the controls of bombers and fighter planes and their guns. And air force personnel were mostly ambitious, driven types. They took their 'duty' to escape seriously, at least partly because they craved both being part of the action and making a difference. They did not want to sit the war out, impotently, while their mates continued to carve out their personal legends in daring bombing runs and mid-air dogfights.

Extra security measures at Stalag Luft III included heavy trucks that rumbled regularly around the perimeter to hasten the collapse of any hidden tunnel that might be inching its way towards the high barbed-wire fence and microphones buried under the surface of the sandy soil to pick up reverberations caused by digging. Nevertheless, about 100 tunnels of various dimensions were attempted during the camp's lifetime.

The prisoners' bunk huts were relatively sturdy. The Germans went to the extra trouble and expense of building them up off the ground so that any underground exit could be easily seen from outside, as well as constructing them of reinforced double walls of pine slats.

Although many varied factors came into play in the escape, the Germans' overriding strategic error was to herd such a large number of well-educated and highly motivated officers—with a formidable mix of leadership, organisational and technical skills between them—into the same compound, then to leave them sitting around twiddling their thumbs.

Unlike other POW ranks, Allied officers were not required to join the work gangs that formed up every morning in the other local POW camps. Meanwhile, there was only so much sport that the often under-nourished POWs could enjoy, especially in the freezing winter months. Consequently, the collective creativity and determination of many fine, under-occupied minds was channelled into a clandestine network that plotted to outsmart the Germans to achieve the biggest mass POW breakout ever seen.

While the men knew pretty much everything they needed to know about the challenges they faced on the inside, and worked out some extraordinary ways to circumvent them, they knew much less about what they might encounter on the outside.

In addition to its sheer distance from the various Allied

frontlines and the closest neutral territories of Switzerland and Sweden, Sagan was, from the Nazis' point of view, an ideal location. The Silesia region bordered Poland. Here, local authorities had been enthusiastically rounding up POWs from the moment Germany launched its invasion of Poland in the early hours of the morning of 1 September 1939, from the cover of the same Silesian forests that would later conceal the progress of the great escapees.

The region's history, too, was not unimportant; both events leading up to and during World War II, and events long past.

The decisive 1939 invasion of Poland had followed various crudely staged Nazi provocations and propaganda campaigns used to justify Germany's building aggression against its Polish neighbours. On the night of 31 August 1939, the Nazi news service announced the Polish Army had launched an unprovoked cross-border attack on the Third Reich, striking in Silesia.[1] In truth, as the Nuremberg trials would hear in detail after the war, the SS (Schutzstaffel), the Nazis' elite paramilitary force or 'black shirts', had faked the incident. Exploiting drugged German political prisoners from the nearby Dachau concentration camp, the SS had dressed them up as Polish soldiers and forced them to stage an attack on a German radio station and then to sing the Polish national anthem on air, before mowing them down in cold blood,[2] their usefulness at its end. Three days later, Britain, France and their allies, including nations of the British Commonwealth and South Africa, finally declared war on Germany.

But competing territorial claims over the rich Silesia region dated back as far as written records go. Although the Polish dynasty of the Piasts contested the territory from the tenth century, its petty princes eventually carved the region up into small fiefdoms and encouraged immigration from Germany to help increase agricultural productivity and to develop the local coalmines and the textile industry, giving the region a distinct Germanic character.[3]

Silesia later fell variously under the control of the Bohemian

Crown (now largely the Czech Republic) to the south, the Hungarians and the Austrian Hapsburgs, German royals and then the German Prussian expansionist, Fredrick the Great. Silesia remained within Prussia until the end of World War I, when much of Upper Silesia—home to most of its profitable coal-mines and steelworks—was granted to the newly independent nation of Poland under the Treaty of Versailles. Consequently, Silesia stood as a symbol of the great humiliation of Germany that followed World War I—and such humiliation helped fan the nationalist Nazi movement. This coincided with the rise of what today may seem like ludicrous notions of the Germans' superiority and consequently their need for, and right to, territorial expansion. Hitler not only exploited exaggerated claims of the poor treatment of ethnic Germans living within the 'lost' Polish regions of Silesia but also harked back to the notion of *Lebensraum*,[4] living space.

The *Lebensraum* theory of the late 1800s, proposed by the German geographer Friedrich Ratzel, argued that the survival of any species, including humans, depended on emigration and adaption in a constant cycle of territorial expansion. Indeed, for humans to remain healthy—operating collectively as various peoples (*Völker*)—one *Volk* would need to conquer or colonise another, to secure 'living space'. To Hitler this meant the constant expansion of German power and territorial control eastwards. After the German invasion and annexation of Czechoslovakia of 1938–39, Poland, and especially the coveted Polish region of Silesia, was literally next in the firing line.[5]

At the height of the war some 300,000 Allied POWs were imprisoned around Sagan, including more than 10,000 air force officers incarcerated in Stalag Luft III. Much of the local population was German speaking and sympathetic to the Nazis' nationalist expansion. POWs could expect little sympathy 'outside the wire'. Local hostility would only intensify as escapees headed south into the parts of Silesia that had enthusiastically expelled ethnic Germans only a few decades earlier after World War I, but had since been reclaimed by Germany. This was exactly the direction our group was heading in.

25 March 1944
It is still dark when the early morning train from Tschiebsdorf steams in. It is a plain collection of old carriages, each with an aisle down the middle that divides the space up into sets of facing, bare wooden benches.[6] John and his party crowd into three pairs of seats, taking up all the space to avoid interaction with any other passengers. But there are no other passengers; the train is virtually empty as it pulls out to a quiet, collective sigh of relief.

Sagan lies within a thatch of strategically important train lines. But our group are off the main network, and largely out of sight. The only disadvantage is that the 'all stops' train south is moving excruciatingly slowly.

Everywhere they look, the men see snow on the ground; first lying in patches around the small rural villages on the flat and gradually deepening in the hills. Soon, the train fills up with chattering German schoolchildren. The men are mute. They haven't slept all night, their sullen faces are appropriately grubby and unshaven, their eyes mainly closed, their heads nodding, as they doze on and off, onto their chests.[7]

Suddenly, a wave of panic silently tears through the group. A stout German conductress is bearing down on them, shouting and pointing. Her target seems to be Rusty. His thick blond hair might suggest he's local (in fact his family are of distant German descent), but he has no chance if he's forced to speak.

The woman reaches the men, scowling and pointing at Rusty's cigarette. Jerzy jumps in, while the others continue to feign sleep, which, if the conductress had been paying attention, might have seemed very strange, if not suspicious, given the noise.[8] It's a non-smoking carriage. But, the 'Czech workers' charade holds up under her cursory scrutiny. The conductress isn't interested in scruffy foreign workers. As soon as the cigarette is out, she struts off.

For more than four hours the train picks its way towards the Czechoslovakian border. No one bothers with our group. There is nothing more to report. The train is going on further, but they've chosen the tiny station of Boberröhrsdorf to get off.

'Gentlemen, it is now snowing heavily,' remarks Johnny Dodge, a British Army major who had found himself, inexplicably, in an air force officers' POW camp. They are the only passengers to alight. Apart from the small station, there are only fields and farms around. From Boberröhrsdorf, the snow-covered Jizera mountains that divide Nazi Germany from Nazi-occupied Czechoslovakia—and their chance to connect with the Czech resistance—are usually within clear sight. On that morning, the mountains are moving in and out of the thick clouds.

Even on a clear day, both distance and altitude are notoriously easy to underestimate. What the tired, cold men can see of the range doesn't look too steep, but the twenty-five kilometres or so to the border promise to be harder going than any of them could ever have imagined.

Jimmy James, in one of two long conversations we had in 2006, a few years before his death, explained the group's determination simply. He paused, took an audible breath and said: 'We were just push-on types of chaps, really.'

But not everyone did push on from Boberröhrsdorf.

The group's carefully laid plans were at their end: the men were to disperse into less obvious pairs or to set off alone. Of the twelve, only four chose to hike over the mountain range, despite the impossible weather and their inadequate clothing. They were John, Rusty, Jerzy, and Leslie.

The rest, including Jimmy, were so buoyed by the success of their train journey and so bitterly cold after a couple of hours on the road that they decided to risk another train ride. They converged in various configurations on a larger station instead.

Jerzy had a wife and young daughter, Małgorzata, in

Nazi-occupied Poland. His letters home regularly reassured his daughter that he would see her soon. Leslie had a son, a toddler living in London with his wife, his sister and her young daughter, named Leslie after him. They were fiercely motivated: they were heading home no matter what. And so were John and Rusty.

Armed only with their home-made compasses—fashioned ingeniously by another Australian, Warrant Officer Al Hake, from melted-down bakelite gramophone records, slivers of magnetised razor blades, glass and solder from the seals of tin cans—tiny maps drawn on silk handkerchiefs and a small supply of odd, home-made high-kilojoule escape rations, they really are pushing on.

They set off separately in pairs. As they walk away, their footprints fast disappear under falling snow; they, too, fade from view, into the white.

By late that afternoon, all eight of their former travel companions have been arrested.

Our group is down to four.

What none of the twelve men yet know is that around 5 a.m., just as their train had pulled out, a perimeter guard at Stalag Luft III was homing in on the tunnel's exit in the pre-dawn half-light. He'd probably noticed that steam was rising, strangely, from an indentation in the snow.

As the guard swung his rifle off his shoulder and pointed it in the direction of the tunnel exit, the men stopped dead. They lay flat on the snow or crouched, silent, in the trees.[9] It was over.

RAF Squadron Leader Laurence Reavell-Carter, escapee number 76, jumped up and revealed himself. The oft-repeated tale—which may or may not be true—goes that Laurence was no linguist. In his panic, he shouted, '*Nicht scheissen*'—do not shit—instead of '*nicht schiessen*'—don't shoot. It is even funnier when you consider that an earlier moment of anxiety had featured another guard taking a very long time to empty his bowels just near the exit.

Fortunately, the guard did neither but the alarm had been raised.[10]

The man hunt was on.

6
INTRODUCING MICHAL

My dad always insisted that fact was stranger than fiction, no matter how creative or imaginative the author might be.

That I found myself, in 2012, stumbling around thigh deep in soft spring snow alongside Rusty's nephew Peter Kierath, in the same Czech mountain range the four had trekked across—68 years to the day after the Great Escape—was one such unexpected true tale.

How many small twists of fate had to play out over decades, and how many stupendous political and technological changes had to come to pass, for us to reach this point, especially given that the region's Cold War isolation and then active hostility to all things 'Western' had so effectively severed the story's thread? Even with the relatively new-found power of the internet it was extraordinary enough that the right Williams family had ever been singled out from the millions of the same name on the other side of the world—and only because my youngest brother, David, had happened to have stumbled upon and had signed up to a particular Facebook group.

Peter and I had only known each other for a couple of days when we discovered, firsthand, the perils of the wet, spring snow that collapsed suddenly into deep holes, taking us with it. We'd both flown out from Australia separately and had met in Prague, me with my brother, mother and step-father, all on our first trip to the Czech Republic. With Peter we had also just met Jerzy and Leslie's relatives for the first time.

Our host was Michal Holy, the Czech commercial pilot responsible for that first unsolicited email we had all received sometime in late 2011. He had no personal connection whatsoever to any of us or to the escape; he was far too young to have experienced the war and, only a few years earlier, he hadn't even realised that any of the escapees had made it into wartime Czechoslovakia.

Many emails followed, backwards and forwards, their vapour trails of unresolved emotions criss-crossing the globe. Our unlikely group of perfect strangers had mostly been born after the war. But the escape and its haunting consequences—just like the personal experiences and losses of any war or conflict—had been passed down in various guises from one generation to the next. For the Australians, so distant from the British-led post-war investigations, little accurate information had ever reached the next of kin.

Presumably, the first rash of colourful, popular adventure stories the escape spurred owed much of their gripping pace to the creative licence their authors employed; they were not particularly helpful in setting any one participant's story straight. I wanted to test our own larger-than-life family myth of John the fighter pilot against whatever truth could still be assembled, so many years after the events.

In March 2012, we finally met Michal in person. He walked towards us beaming, his hand outstretched.

The chosen rendezvous point in the old town centre of Prague seemed almost ridiculously picturesque, with its medieval cobbled streets overlooked by its imposing Palace. That we Australians were still blinking, disorientated, buoyed only by that vaguely nauseating effervescence of jet lag that only truly long haul flying can induce, just made the occasion seem all the more surreal.

Michal had not only managed to track down the families of the four men for the first time, but had organised the funding and unveiling of a solid handsome granite memorial to them on Czech soil, complete with a Czech air force fly past, plenty of Czech dignitaries, various international diplomats and military attaches and a smattering of locals old enough to have survived the war.

Then, he'd invited us to walk—or at least step out of the mini bus at strategic locations—in their footsteps, backtracking along their route, as far as it could be determined, all the way to what is left of Stalag Luft III. As Silesia had been returned to Poland after World War II, and the Germans again expelled, the camp's ruins now lie in Polish territory.

Why? That's both a short and a long story. I suspect the longer version is still evolving, or at least my understanding of it. I also suspect Michal's quiet generosity is not unrelated to his childhood experiences in post-war Czechoslovakia as the rise of the Soviet Union trapped much of Eastern Europe in yet another authoritarian nightmare, the Communists pretty much taking up where the Nazis had left off by way of terror, repression and persecution.

But, that's not where we will start with our introductions. Firstly, there's something that needs clearing up immediately. Michal's family name 'Holy' does not denote any kind of moral or spiritual authority or superiority. In fact, he laughs, in Czech his name means 'a bald man', which he isn't.

Michal tells the short version like this. He had always been fascinated by planes and aviation history, especially the stories of World War II he'd heard as a child. As it happened, one of the most ferocious mid-air battles of the war, the Battle of Ore Mountains, took place about 120 kilometres from Prague over the town of Kovarska in September 1944. The Nazis' hold on power was slipping and US Air Force heavy bombers, B-17G Flying Fortresses, were flying daring daylight bombing raids deep inside German-held territory. Over the Ore Mountains bombers of the 100th Bomb Group, known as the 'The Bloody Hundredth' because of the heavy losses they had suffered, were flying escorted by US P-51 Mustang fighters of the 55th and

339th Fighter Group. The American planes flew directly into a formation of German Messerschmitts (ME 109s) and Focke-Wulf 'Shrike' (FW 190s) intercept fighters.

More than 50 planes were shot down in less than an hour.[1] Townspeople still tell of the rain of aircraft parts, parachutes and men. Men jumped from low altitude and hit the ground before their parachutes opened. Some were impaled on trees and one dead airman even landed in a shop in the town's main street. There was carnage everywhere. The Americans lost 143 aircrew killed, wounded or captured and the Germans 23.[2] Those US Air Force personnel who survived bailing out were promptly incarcerated, some at Stalag Luft III.

Even today wrecks and plane parts are still being uncovered locally and over the years a museum has been built up by some of Michal's friends, giving him a chance to help with some amateur aviation archaeology. In 2009, he decided to pursue a personal research project into the fates of those surviving pilots who ended their war inside Stalag Luft III, which lies about four hours from Prague by road. But the American pilots never really got a look in. During Michal's first visit to the remains of Stalag Luft III, his focus shifted entirely.

'It was freezing, literally, about zero degrees. The vast area of ruins was empty so I was entirely alone, surrounded by pines trees,' he told me, early on, not entirely without emotion.

'Of course, I knew about the escape, it was famous, and I had read whatever I could find before I embarked on the trip. I knew the Americans weren't actually involved despite the Hollywood film and once I was standing in the camp in the cold and the silence it dawned on me that this was what I wanted to know more about.'

That our four had made it to Czechoslovakia—and another small group to another Czech region—was something he'd never previously heard. That made the escape all the more intriguing.

'There were lots of things. As a pilot I knew what it must have meant to go into combat with so few hours of flying experience.

In modern aviation we just train and train and train and a lot of flying involves memorising responses.

'But, how did they single-handedly fly Kittyhawks, that were so clumsy and slow compared to Messerschmitts, and shoot and dodge the guns firing at them at the same time?

'Or maybe it was thinking about what it took to build the tunnel by hand?

'Or maybe it was that they kept walking through the snow with no end in sight. My own shoes were soaked and I was absolutely freezing but I had my car waiting nearby.'

Whatever it came down to, Michal believed it was something very special that had come together on that exact spot in the wet, cold, gloomy Silesian forest. He put the Americans on the backburner.

In Prague sometime later, Michal applied to view documents held by the Czech National Archives, expecting to find references to British and Canadian escapees. He was handed a large, thick file, stuffed with aged papers, mainly in Czech.

What he hadn't expected to fall out were the original Gestapo documents with POWs Williams, Kierath, Bull and Mondschein clearly named.

PARADISE ON SEA

The Great Depression hit Len and Mildred with all the force of a crash tackle. Momentarily, they found themselves pinned to the ground, stunned and winded, wondering what their world might look like when they dragged themselves back onto their feet and dusted themselves off.

But, Len wasn't easily defeated. With the family back in Sydney and ensconced initially in a cheap boarding house in the Sydney seaside suburb of Manly, then crammed into a two-bedroom flat nearby, he tenaciously sought out work. Any work. In his mid-40s, Len became a cleaner by night and a draftsman by day, helping out with technical drawings for a local engineering and construction firm. Mildred retreated. All around her the social order that had so recently prevailed was collapsing, taking many with it. It seems it took all of Mildred's energy just to maintain her precarious hold on the pretentions she had worked so hard to fashion.

I often imagine that this was when Mildred set her mouth in that tight, thin line of determination that so often defined her as the years progressed. Or was it actually disappointment or disapproval?

But for the Williams kids, Manly Beach was about as close as they could have possibly imagined to paradise. 'We were kids, we really didn't think about it,' said my uncle David of the drastically reduced circumstances that had all the boys sleeping on a row of camp beds on the covered verandah of their small rented flat. When it rained, or during winter, they pulled down the canvas awning to keep out the elements. They couldn't quite see the ocean but they could smell it—and they could feel the unfamiliar, pulsating warmth of Sydney's summers. What sheer luxury after a childhood of rigorous school sports, endurance swimming and lifesaving in the frigid, grey New Zealand waters. They just had to walk out the door; only two other properties were closer to the sheltered southern corner of Manly Beach.

Money worries were for adults. Much more interesting were the throngs of local kids and the wonderland of the local beaches and bush. School principals had temporarily dispensed with school uniforms. They were too expensive, and so too were shoes. The Depression kids of Manly swam, explored, fished for their supper and ran gloriously free.[1] Some of them lined up for their family's allotted billy of free soup and a small paper bag of bread at the local theatre that had been converted into a soup kitchen, or found themselves living 'doubled up', as they used to say, with relatives or friends. All around shanty towns of tents optimistically named 'Happy Valleys' were springing up along the waterfront where fish and eels could be pulled out of the sea and cooked over fires lit in empty metal drums.[2] Many of the camping families had saved a few favourite pieces of good furniture. When they pulled back their canvas flaps their old living rooms had been re-created inside, complete with lounge set and carpet.

The Williams' experience of a terrible comedown in life was hardly unique and hardly extreme; Len still managed to amply feed, clothe and educate (although that was a bone of contention) the five kids and they always had a decent roof over their head. They never queued for handouts or came even close to finding themselves on the streets. At the time, the menial work gangs formed by local councils were filled with everyone from unemployed barristers and solicitors to tradesmen. Everyone hefting large rocks or sealing roads with hot bitumen, as part of job creation schemes, did the same tough, tiring work, regardless of their past lives.

When Manly Council had sought in 1929, the same year the world's stock markets collapsed, to raise funds from the national government for a major beautification project for 'the playground of Australia', it was rapped sternly over the knuckles. 'It is doubtful if Australia can afford to play on any ground at present. If there had been more work and less play she would not be in the position in which she now finds herself,' Manly Council was told in rebuff.[3]

Ironically, the project's rejection ensured there was, in fact, even less work in Manly, triggering the collapse of the local building trade. 'Your builder mates were out of work, so your plumber mates were out of work . . . when building went out that was the end of everything you might say because there were so many associated trades,' said local Charles Goodman[4] of the circumstances that Len, the architect, had found himself in.

Local oral histories of the Great Depression recount tales of parents crying and fighting and speaking in whispers, often not even bothering to retreat behind closed doors. But many kids still regarded Manly as 'the best place to live in the world'.[5]

Commentators worried in the pages of magazines about the 'moral development' of these free-range seaside children of Manly and the surrounding waterside settlements, the campers and those with parents still in work, alike. But, some went out on a limb to welcome a new era, a clear break from the inherited constraints of English-style indoor parlour lives of reading and playing quietly. 'Even if the parents . . . do allow their children to run about on the beaches unattended, what will they see that will have a demoralising effect on them?' wrote well-known commentator Enid Delalande in the *Australian Women's Weekly*.[6] M. Truby King concurred: 'One could hardly think of a healthier existence'.

Neither could John and the rest of the Williams kids. Life could hardly be more exhilarating amid all the economic gloom, could it?

Then John met Hans Wicke, or Harry, as he later called himself and has since been known. But John always called him Hans.

Hans Wicke was a few years older than John. That, in itself, would have been sufficient to impress a boy only just on the cusp of adolescence but already intent on rushing, headlong, towards manhood. John looked up to Hans, both literally and figuratively. In the almost impossibly athletic teenager, John saw his own aspirations for the future. With thick white-blond hair, bright blue eyes, a perpetual tan and his heavy wooden surfboard, Hans seemed like the quintessential popular beach boy, the ultimate role model for the new arrival from New Zealand.

Hans was much more than that. Like John and the other Williams kids, he was not actually local. He too was an outsider, albeit an outsider who was a decisive couple of years ahead of John in making his mark and in fitting in. Arriving from Germany with his family in 1927 with only what they could carry, Hans had skilfully read the social currents of his new environment. He understood exactly what had currency with his peers as a peculiar new macho beach culture was emerging along Sydney's beaches that cast young men as something between an Adonis and hero, the manly protectors of the coastline.[7]

There was no need for the two boys to talk about their family's money troubles, they were common enough. Hans insists that he and John never did. In any case, both had been brought up to consider any discussion of one's financial circumstances crass and impolite in the extreme. But, like the Williams, the Wickes had washed up in Manly because they had fallen on hard times. Hans's father was German and his mother Australian, but Hans had been born and raised in Germany. The Depression was still a couple of years off, but Germany had been reeling for almost a decade from the humiliating reparations imposed on its economy after World War I. The Wickes had once had interests in steel factories and chains of newly popular cinemas, as had Len, Hans said. They had lived in a large home with household help and a driver. But, when the swirling undercurrents of nationalism and socialism collided in the rise of a man called Adolf Hitler throughout the 1920s, they left it all behind.

Hans's earliest memories of Manly and the Depression years that soon followed feature his brother and their bikes, as they rode around in seemingly endless circles, a wooden crate piled high with their mother's home-baked Berlin buns. This was the very first income they made, he said. In Manly, they had to start again, at the bottom.

Enlisting the kids in informal family ventures was not at all unusual, especially once the Depression hit with full force. In fact it was Mildred's determination to hold herself above all this creative make-do activity that was out of place. Either way, it didn't seem to disrupt John and Hans's pursuit of virtually every adventure Manly had to offer.

'Just what did that mean?' I asked Hans, many, many decades later. What were the two inseparable friends like? By way of an answer he suggested this story. 'Of course, it was a ridiculous thing to do when you look at it now,' he said.

Long before anyone had heard of extreme sports, or the marketers who have managed to turn them into businesses, kids were more than happy to rely on their own resources to hunt down danger.

Hans and John's favourite flirtation with risk in the early days of their Manly friendship involved the sheer sandstone cliffs that drop dramatically into the Pacific Ocean from North Head. At low tide the rock shelves below offer local fishermen temporary refuge from the swell, but first they must manage to pick their way down safely to the water. At high tide the rock shelf and its rock pools largely disappear, leaving only the odd boulder shorn off the cliff in the distant past above the waterline.

I went looking for the boys' particular vantage point on a clear windy winter morning. The sun was barely up, just a red orb over a vast expanse of shiny cobalt water. The wind was sufficiently biting to imagine it was blowing off a distant snowdrift somewhere in the southern Australian Alps and the sky was a vast, empty, cloudless soft blue. Manly Beach is a morning place, all year round. As always, the swimmers were stroking their way collectively around the rocks towards the inlet known as Fairy Bower, the sand and rocks below magnified in their goggles so the stingrays and fish appear to jump up off the sea floor.

The main settlement of Manly occupies a narrow flat spit of land: to the south lies the ferry terminal and the still, calm waters of the beaches and coves that front Sydney's sheltered harbour; to the north lies a long stretch of ocean beach where the surf rolls in.

It's only a five-minute walk between the sheltered harbour-front and the waves. From the flat, North Head rises up gradually out of the water like the knobbly back of a lizard's head. As the close, humming huddle of humanity recedes, the waterfront path winds up into the stunned, salt-blown bush that covers the headland right down to the cliff's edges. Scrambling with youthful enthusiasm to peer over that sheer drop has always been among the many local rites of passage the area offers; the heady combination of untamed bush and the surrounding waters provides a veritable smorgasbord of potential dangers and corresponding childhood dares.

I love the Australian bush with a passion that probably exceeds any objective assessment of its beauty. Along the coast it is especially scrubby; the vegetation is every bit as meagre as the poor sandy soil that sustains it, the prickly bushes are bent and the twisted trees permanently lean in, away from the constant wind that blows off the water. The bush is full of dry branches that look like snakes and lizards, and snakes and lizards that look like dry branches.

Beneath this tatty, dull veneer there are little gems of colour: the tiny purple flowers, soft grey leaves and emerging white buds of the flannel flowers and, on this particular morning, a gathering of black cockatoos feasting noisily in the gnarled tops of a giant banksia, its cylindrical flower heads full of huge seeds.

The cockatoos are chatting in discordant tones, bent, consumed by their task, a flash of yellow on their heads, the odd streak of yellow revealed as they stretch their giant black wings. They aren't quite close enough to touch, but almost. Unlike their smaller white cousins who seem willing to rub shoulders with humanity, these majestic black birds are much shier, and now increasingly rare. To be up so close is such a rare privilege that I can't help but feel a new lightness in my step.

All my way along the track, I pass only one other person. He's walking head down and purposefully the other way.

These days this path is dotted with all the requisite warning signs about the dangers of the nearby cliffs. Alone on the track, the cool wind finding its way through the poor cover, I am surprised to find myself feeling almost jumpy. I have no idea how far I need to climb, just a vague idea of where I should be heading. I am looking for the thick sandstone wall that was supposed to maintain the isolation of the novitiates and the seminarians holed up in the palatial St Patrick's seminary and its vast grounds that overlook Manly from North Head. It has been here since 1885 and so, by the 1930s, it had long stoked that familiar allure of the forbidden, at least for the local kids.

I've looked at the solid stone boundary wall many times from the road myself, but never right up close and never where it stops abruptly at the cliff's edge, apparently unbreachable due to the sudden drop.

And then, suddenly, it's there. The boys' challenge was not to try to climb over the thick wall, which would have been difficult enough: it was to find even the smallest foothold and shimmy around its edge on tiptoes, hanging out over the cliff and the rock shelf below. There are no obvious handholds, and barely a toehold of precariously sandy soil underfoot. The solid sandstone is so thick that not even the most strapping of lads could have possibly reached around to secure their hold.

I am both stumped and amused. So, that's what they did for fun. I can't help laughing, especially when I run my eye back along the wall to the doorway-sized hole that has since been cut out to let everyone and anyone through.

IN SEARCH OF A DECENT EDUCATION

When the Williams first arrived in Manly, the kids all traipsed off to the local public school a block away, just like everyone else. Although Mildred privately vacillated between resentment and despair, education was compulsory and public schools were free.

In the early 1930s Manly Village Public School was much like a young child's drawing; a simple block of a building, a triangle of a roof, the structure plonked thoughtlessly in the middle of a small flat piece of bare, cleared land. Although it was noted for its inadequate outdoor space and the punishing lack of shade, it was not the unsuitability of its British design that was of most concern. Proper provision had not been made in Manly for the throngs of people who came and went, and their children, particularly during the Depression. The school's own official history describes it as 'overcrowded, sometimes grossly so' in the 1930s. Virtually no other area was 'so poorly served by the public education system', the history says; 'most other Sydney suburbs and large country towns had received better government support for the formal education of children'. Consequently, 'the school environment was not nearly as stimulating or attractive as the outdoor surroundings'. Non-attendance and truancy were major problems for the school authorities.[1]

If Mildred and Len were determined to provide their children with the best possible education, they soon discovered they had come to one of the worst possible places to do so, sharpening their unfamiliar sense of powerlessness to a keen edge. Despite Australia's early commitment to universal education and its mostly high levels of literacy, the school's history notes that public education in Manly at the time 'never seemed completely satisfactory due to overcrowding'. In fact, 'sometimes it was much less successful than elsewhere despite centralised control of the curriculum'.[2]

None of which bothered the Williams kids, my uncle David said. Everyone was in the same boat and the failure of the school to engage the local boys, in particular, in academic pursuits only fuelled their outside interest in sport. Locally, swimming, surfing, cricket and Rugby thrived.

Then, everything changed. The Williams kids were unceremoniously plucked out of the Manly Village School. The boys were measured up for grey suits and Suzie for a long drab skirt and a dowdy shirt and tie. They were going to the Sydney Church of England Grammar School. The girls' school was a little closer than the boys' school, but for all of them it meant a long tram ride, there and back, every day. How they were going to pay was a mystery. The answer came to light only recently.

My uncle David thought my grandfather might have managed to sell something left over from their heyday in New Zealand, perhaps the holiday cottage at Lake Taupo. But, the answer came from my cousin once removed, Judy, who had grown up with John, Dad and the other Williams kids.

All the Williams cousins, including Judy, had a secret benefactor. That same cranky Aunt Susanna who had raised Len and his siblings was still looking out for the extended family. She had inherited the family home and assets, in recognition of her lifelong sacrifice. She was a good manager and had been very careful with her money. Now she was quietly doling it out to ensure her many nephews and nieces could still go to good schools, no matter how tough the times. She had 21 nephews and nieces to consider, and she would continue to help for as long as she could afford to. She obviously didn't expect any thanks. None of the Williams cousins knew where their school fees had come from.

On the weekends and long summer evenings, John and the Willams kids still tore around Manly, happily rubbing shoulders with kids of any circumstance. John still slept on the verandah of the Williams' cramped Manly flat with his brothers, all lined up on cot beds like sardines. But on weekday mornings he now put on his new grey suit and straw boater and headed off as a day boy to join the sons of professionals, businessmen, graziers and merchants at 'Shore', as the school was better known due to its prime location overlooking the harbour and city from Sydney's affluent north shore.

'Yes, we were about the only ones living in a flat,' laughed my uncle David. Most of the other Shore students of the era came from huge stately homes on Sydney's leafy north shore, or rural properties, he said. The Williams boys made friends with the Horderns, heirs to the retail empire epitomised by Sydney's grand Palace Emporium, once the largest department store in the world. From the Manly flat, they went to stay at the Horderns' mountain retreat. 'Maybe, the various parents cared [about family income]. But, we were only kids. It didn't matter [to us].'

It is tempting to make some kind of sweeping statement about the significance of this particular junction in John's life.

It is true that when he first walked through the substantial wrought-iron gates of Shore in 1931, at twelve going on thirteen, the kinds of opportunities my grandparents had envisaged for their children before the Depression seemed to open up again, not least of which was the chance to pursue the academic subjects that would allow him to aspire to a university education. But, as much as being 'a Shore boy' did mean—and the influence of the old school tie was not insignificant—it was still up to John to chase his own future.

The school was originally founded by the Church of England in New South Wales in the late 1800s with the express purpose of fulfilling its duty to provide education of a high standard in conformity with its religious principles. Its stated goal was to turn out graduates with a 'clear understanding of the obligations expected of a Christian gentleman'[3]—a Christian gentleman of the Church of England, that is.

That Shore enthusiastically cast itself in the mould of Britain's elite public schools was merely a reflection of that mission. It chose its school colours to match the college of Cambridge University that its first headmaster had attended. In the early days, its masters (teachers) swanned around in full academic robes and it boasted someone called the sergeant major who, for the apparent purpose of organisation and discipline, swaggered around wielding a cane and subjected the students to regular marching drills. Boys also vied for promotion to the senior ranks of the school Cadet Corps, a kind of quasi-military junior Home Guard that practised with real guns. Conditions in the dormitories for boarders were rudimentary and 'rough behaviour' that would nowadays be called bullying was common, if not rife. Masters were quick to give any errant boy a box on the ears, but not to wade in when it came to shielding the younger, or less robust, of students from the over-enthusiastic pranks, or naked aggression, of their peers. And prefects, who made up a large proportion of the older boys, were quite within their rights to give the younger boys a paddling with their sandshoe.

Originally, English-born headmasters had been enticed to Sydney from various renowned British universities, bringing with them their codes and creeds, especially, their belief that 'games formed the character of boys'. The 'instinct of sport' had helped create the British Empire, speech-day guests were told in 1901. On the sporting field, parents could expect their sons to develop those virtues that marked the real man: courage, chivalry, vigour, straightforwardness. Later, even the fine conduct of the gallant

Australian troops on the terrible battlefields of World War I was put down to sport and its role in teaching boys to play for their side, not for themselves[4]: that is, to sacrifice 'personal convenience' for the good of the team, the house, the school or the group. Sport also let boys discover how hard it actually was to become good at something.[5]

By the time John enrolled at Shore in the early 1930s, a subtle shift was taking place. The first Australian-born headmaster had been sought out, in recognition that 'rather than seeing themselves as loyal citizens of the British Empire' this was a generation who saw themselves as faithful, 'independent Australian Britons.'[6] L.C. Robson, the successful candidate, had come through in the 1920s like the proverbial new broom and had made it abundantly clear to masters and students alike that he would have it his way at the school. As a former military officer who had served in World War I, he believed firmly in 'service and sacrifice'. He stamped out the worst of the 'barbaric' bullying and demanded 'humility, chivalry and unselfishness'. In a school of almost uniformly privileged boys, Mr Robson attempted to shine a light on social inequality. His first efforts in the mid-1920s resulted in a Shore Club in the working-class Sydney suburb of Erskineville that promoted a spirit of service, an understanding of social responsibility and a 'broad view of life and responsibility'.[7] In 1930, the effects of the Depression brought hardship and need right to the school's doorsteps. Many students had to be withdrawn due to lack of funds. At the same time, the press accused Sydney's so-called 'Great Public Schools', of which Shore was a founding member, of producing 'thoughtless citizens actuated by short-sighted selfishness'.[8] In response the school conceded somewhat vaguely that its students did need 'to be better prepared to stand up before men'. On a practical level that meant the formation of new outward-looking organisations, like Scouts, to ensure students could 'act out a conscious social role in the community'.[9]

Such small steps towards an emerging sense of Australian identity and a concern for social issues, however, were not inconsistent with either conservatism or elitism. When Shore launched its Jubilee Appeal in 1936, it framed its own responsibility in this way: an editorial in the school magazine, *The Torchbearer*, declared Shore 'must become one of the powerhouses which shall produce Australia's leaders'. As an established school, 'known and respected' across the Empire, 'the burden of leadership should fall heaviest upon us'. That task involved promoting among their students the 'high personal character' and 'the ideal of service' upon which no less than 'the nation's future depends'.[10]

To what extent such idealised ethics and morals were actually embraced by the students is unclear. Chapel, too, was compulsory, yet a number of oral histories suggest the school's Christian message was mainly endured, not embraced, in large part due to the droning manner in which it was delivered. But the message of 'service and self-sacrifice' was consistent with Australia's role in World War I, a trauma that still cast a long shadow over daily life. As international tensions again began to intensify, it was a message that fell on receptive adolescent ears, always keenly attuned to the prevailing expectations of impending manhood. For John, it was very much in keeping with other important influences in his life.

This doesn't mean the teenage boys of the pre-war 1930s consciously carried the weight of the world on their shoulders. They were no less buoyant than any other generation. On the contrary, the earnest posturing of the adults around them was probably experienced much like the constant din of the cicadas of an Australian summer. At first we listen, remark on their arrival, and smile. But soon their noise disappears into the background. It goes on and on, for weeks or months. We no longer hear it but it's still there.

The waters of Sydney's Middle Harbour were deceptive. White sandy beaches and calm, shallow turquoise waters along the northern shoreline suddenly gave way to very deep colder channels favoured by some of Australia's largest, wide-roaming sharks. The tiger, the whaler and the bull shark were often reported along this northern reach of the main Sydney harbour in the 1930s and 1940s, mostly when a fisherman lost a dog,[11] but occasionally when a swimmer disappeared in waist-deep water.

With no local Olympic swimming pool yet built, Middle Harbour was where Shore, and many northern Sydney schools and swimming clubs, went to compete. The pool was the tidal Spit Baths, a stretch of harbour enclosed in shark netting strung between a series of wooden pylons stretching out from the southern shore. A wooden walkway gave swimmers access to the opaque green water and the starting blocks that never seemed to sit quite right. They were always either partly submerged at high tide or way above the water when the tide was out, exposing a thick oyster and barnacle crust that readily shredded hands and feet.

Wading in from the shore wasn't popular either. The grey, silty muck underfoot was dotted with rocks and shellfish and often swarming with crabs. Kids used to say they learned to swim quickly at the Spit Baths so they could avoid the scratchy silt between their toes and dive into the deep water from the walkways instead. That the baths produced a long list of champions was also often put down to the many obstacles lurking in and about a harbour pool. 'One would swim across the pool quickly to avoid the jelly fish that floated in on the tide and got trapped,' recalled one local resident.[12] To feel a swarm of jellyfish slide across your bare skin mid-race was enough to shave seconds off anyone's best time.

John was fourteen when he stood on the starting blocks at the Spit Baths alongside Shore's older, fastest swimmers. That year, he had decided not to stay in his age group but to enter himself in all the open events for the annual swimming carnival. In his line of sight stood Snow Swift, already seventeen and a school sporting icon. Snow was swimming captain, boxing captain, a rower and a

First XVs Rugby player.¹³ John chased him over 440 yards (400 metres), the longest distance event on offer, and came in second. By the next year, Snow's last at school, John had beaten him.¹⁴

Snow's close friend was Reg 'Rusty' Kierath. Rusty was also a sportsman to watch. Rusty was a boarder from that state's hot, dry rural west, so he wasn't a competitive swimmer. He and John were on nodding terms. Rusty was in the Rugby First XVs; only the representative rowing team was more prestigious. John, two years behind Rusty and Snow at Shore, was in the Rugby Second XVs. Over winter the two teams trained together, the younger Seconds deferring respectfully to the older boys like apprentices hungry for every scrap of wisdom that would help secure their turn at the top of the pecking order. The Seconds were also allowed to tag along to various social events. Rusty was 'a splendid player, a fine tackler and always on the ball'.¹⁵ In other words, he was driven.

At fourteen, John was a good, but not exceptional, sportsman. But he was also driven, and he was fit and big for his age. He was close enough to the leaders of the pack to be able to imagine the view from out front. He constantly challenged himself, snapping eagerly at the heels of the older boys' success.

THE ARREST

We know that John and Rusty and Leslie and Jerzy struck out on foot in two separate pairs, heading towards the Czechoslovakian border. It was a long slog, uphill most of the way. By March the snow should have melted. The forest should have been passable. The trees should have concealed their progress.

Instead, the wet spring snow melt and endless trip hazards that lay just beneath likely slowed them to a crawl. Here, we lose them. They are simply gone, missing off everyone's radar, except perhaps each other's.

We assume they cross each other's paths or are forced back onto the road where they join up. Their disguises are reasonable enough. Their jackets are shiny with grime. Their faces are aged by stubble and fatigue and their shirt collars are as tatty as their immigrant workers' identity might suggest. But, underneath, both John and Leslie are wearing ribbed turtle-necked woollen jumpers, just the kind of precious garment that was hand-knitted with such care for POWs and sent over from home. Maybe they are too new or too thick?[1]

What transpired when the Nazi ski patrol stopped, apparently near or just over the Czechoslovakian border, can only be assumed. Author Alan Burgess, in his unattributed 1971 account, described them floundering around, bitterly cold, up to their waists in snow. He extended this apparent dramatic licence to sketch a compelling scene. 'On the afternoon of the second day, they saw a military patrol, on skis, travel[l]ing swiftly towards them. The Germans had rifles slung over their shoulders. The four airmen were stuck in snow as securely as flies on wallpaper.'[2]

Other accounts put it more simply. They were apprehended by a mountain patrol.[3]

We do know their trek did end in the basement of a handsome terraced row of Art Deco offices and apartments in a town called Liberec, occupied by the Nazis and known as Reichenberg. They had made it out of Germany, but there was still little chance of a sympathetic reception.

The prosperous, elegant northern Bohemian town of Liberec could hardly have been more beautiful. Surrounded by mountains forested with spruce and beech trees and dotted with fine historic churches, it was the kind of regional European town that lends itself to syrupy clichés. At the time, it was the administrative centre of Sudetenland, the name the Nazis gave to the border regions of Czechoslovakia populated by ethnic Germans. Without bothering to consult Czechoslovakia, the British and French had ceded Sudetenland to the Nazis in 1938, in exchange for a non-aggression pact. The British Prime Minister, Neville Chamberlain, famously called the crisis 'a quarrel in a faraway country, between people of whom we know nothing' and went on to prematurely declare 'Peace in our time'. When the Nazis marched into Reichenberg, locals lined the streets cheering. The rest of Czechoslovakia would soon be swallowed up by an expansionist Germany, this time without Chamberlain's nod, as his policy of appeasement failed.

How did the four men feel as they were shuffled into their basement cells at the local Gestapo headquarters? No one knows—but I did get some idea from Jimmy James. Scared? Not in the least. They had been treated reasonably fairly in Stalag Luft III by their German captors. They expected nothing less. Disappointed? Yes, but there is always the next escape. More than anything else, Jimmy said, they would have been physically and mentally exhausted, beyond anything that even combat had previously thrown up. 'I think you can understand how cold and wretched we (all) were if I tell you that when I was thrown into a toilet cubicle in the police station, I immediately collapsed onto the floor and fell fast asleep.'[4]

10
THE RISE OF AN AUSSIE ICON

In Manly, the kids knew their place. Literally. Younger boys aspiring to join the ranks of the fabulous, bronzed young men who manoeuvred heavy wooden surfboards through the waves had to prove themselves first, Hans told me.

Everyone had a relationship with the water. Children learned to swim before they could walk,[1] mostly at the Manly Cove harbour pool, formed by an expansive shark proof net strung across much of the still water bay. A generation of Manly kids learnt how to keep their head above the cool, salt water alongside various swimming stars like Australia's first individual Olympic gold medallist in swimming, Andrew 'Boy' Charlton. Charlton's coach, Harry Hay, himself a silver medallist, taught and trained the kids too. This free 'wonder pool', the largest at the time in the southern hemisphere, kept locals and visitors 'fresh and fit' and was a powerful antidote to economic hardship.[2] What Manly didn't have in jobs or money, it had in sport, producing many of the nation's crack swimmers of the time.

Apart from school swimming, John competed diligently and determinedly with the local Manly Amateur Swimming Club at the pool and by 1935, he was part of the New South Wales Junior Championship team. But he had long set his sights on something even more alluring than the company of swimming champions.

'If you wanted to join the surf club, you waited until you were tapped on the shoulder,' said Hans.

John was fifteen when he was finally talent spotted. He was moving beaches. From the kids' club on the habourside, he was joining the young men of the Manly Life Saving Club on the surf beach. John and Hans trained for and passed their surf-lifesaving Bronze Medallion exams in 1935, qualifying them for patrols and, just as importantly from their point of view, for competing in the popular surf carnivals. The training manual that was—and still is—known among lifesavers simply as the 'Blue Book' became one of John's most treasured possessions.

Once John had stepped across the threshold of Manly's old wooden club-house he had joined the most desirable coterie his teenage self could possibly imagine.

A funny thing had apparently happened to the physique of Australians, the corpulent and stick-thin alike, when 'surf fever'[3] first broke out in Sydney at the turn of the twentieth century, thanks largely to the much celebrated act of civil disobedience by William Gocher, the editor of the local Manly paper.

In 1902 Gocher had dared to bathe during daylight hours, an activity banned since the 1830s, apparently to preserve the morality and modesty of the young colony. His defiance was widely recognised as the tipping point that finally ushered in daylight siwmming. By the following year, Australia's beaches were open all hours.

The siren call of the surf gave rise to much flowery language. C. Bede Maxwell in her early history of Australian surf-lifesaving described the 'sea's caress' as 'delaying as the arms of a gay, exciting mistress'.[4] The following year one correspondent, writing in the *Sydney Morning Herald*, hit on something else that would begin to shift Australia's self-image.

> One strange fact that may seem hard to believe, but is nonetheless true, is that corpulent people get rid of their loose unnecessary flesh by regular surf bathing, while thin people put on flesh—not loose, flabby, unhealthy stuff, but good sound firm flesh.
>
> Their muscles are hardened, and the blood corpuscles of the skin improved . . . surf bathing is helping to build up a race of fine young Australians.[5]

With surf bathing, however, came a new challenge. At Manly Beach, the local Sly family used their fishing boat to rescue bathers who had overestimated their swimming ability and underestimated the waves and rips. But, by 1907 as crowds flocked to the beaches, such makeshift solutions were clearly inadequate. A formal volunteer surf-lifesaving movement was formed. There's still passionate argument as to which surf-lifesaving club was actually Australia's first. Manly was, however, among the nine founding clubs of the Australian Surf Life Saving Association.[6]

Beach going in general and surf bathing, in particular, were cast as desirable, even patriotic activities that transcended the pursuit of personal pleasure, despite that heady, even hedonistic, thrill of diving through clean, cool waves and 'shooting' them back to shore. 'Future generations of Australians will be the better for the sun and surf which their fore runners enjoyed,' claimed *Surf in Australia*. All of which depended, at least in part, on the success of the surf-lifesaving movement. By the 1930s, tens of thousands of people had been rescued and not a single life had been lost while lifesavers were on duty.[7] The surf teemed with dangers for the unwary and the uninitiated. The Surf Life Saving Association, with its discipline, fitness, surf training and new methods of rescue, 'provided the public with a means of safety and confidence in surf bathing'.

If early colonial Australia had been epitomised by the rugged pioneering bushman, then by the Anzacs in the trenches of World War I, by the time John and Hans took their places on patrol at Manly Beach the Australian surf-lifesaver was emerging as the national icon of their generation. That characteristic mateship forged during the early years of colonial settlement—in which survival often depended on standing by each other through thick and thin—and the ability to see humour in life no matter how trying the circumstances—the so-called larrikin spirit—fitted in neatly with the lifesavers' self-image.

> The lifesaver was regarded as typically and distinctively Australian ... [They] embodied many of the values that Australians believed were national traits ... [and] strengthened Australians' sense of themselves as innovators, as people who could devise new ways of doing things, instead of habitually looking to the 'mother country'.[8]

'A brown bodied Manly boy', wrote C. Bede Maxwell in her early history of Australian surfing, 'was almost every Sydney girl's target.

'Each one that strode past, magnificent and colourful, was in her eyes a mighty surf-swimming hero, the breakers his steeds, the ocean his broken foe.'[9]

As the Depression slowly loosened its grip, it seems everyone was full of the promise of the future. While Shore was busy grooming Australia's next generation of leaders at school, the surf-lifesaving movement was being credited with being 'largely responsible for the building up of this new and virile nation that is Australia'.[10]

Surf-lifesavers were expected to be 'good blokes', to take part in sometimes elaborate pranks and to drink with the best of them (although, as pubs closed at 6 p.m. and money was tight, alcohol consumption was actually lower in the 1930s than during many other decades[11]). But, at the same time, they were also expected to be up early, to turn up reliably for their voluntary patrol shifts, to be fit, capable and competitive, and to be always ready and able to save lives. That is, to make a difficult job look easy.

Surf-lifesaving was physically and mentally challenging. It was a movement based on paramilitary discipline and the need for sometimes formidable teamwork, displayed in various famous mass rescues over the decades that instantly transformed those familiar groups of sun-bronzed lifesavers, who seemed to lounge languidly as they cast a cursory eye over the swimmers, into an effective, well-oiled machine.

It went without saying, of course, that lifesavers were expected to honour the 'larrikin', maverick tradition. But those who were unable, or unwilling, to discern where that invisible line lay between irreverence and the dereliction of their duty quickly found themselves expelled.

When John joined Manly Life Saving Club it was a tight, elite unit but not in any social or economic sense that he might have recognised from school at Shore. In the 1930s, the wooden billiard and recreation room of the club-house was often crowded. Over that decade, 'probably more than half of the club's active members were unemployed for long and varying periods' and the club gave them a place to meet and socialise, a clear sense of identity and purpose and even a small income-generating button-selling business; that is, until it was discovered that most of the profits had been drunk. Members also 'clubbed in' to cover expenses for surf carnivals and to ensure that after winter football matches 'everyone had a beer in their hand'.[12]

The powerful, unpredictable and sometime treacherous ocean was a great leveller. 'Princes, peers, paupers and bums—are all equal in the surf', the early Manly club surf pioneer, Charles 'Snow' McAlister, used to say. This new 'gladiator caste, envied by all men and adored by all women',[13] these 'sun-tanned southern Vikings',[14] was not defined by class or wealth. It was also internally democratic. For many members it was their first experience of influencing how something was run via a vote. It was as though by shedding their regular day clothes at the beach, Australians could escape the pigeonholes to which established social hierarchies would otherwise have confined them.

But elitism was the club's defining character. Surf-lifesaving was a highly physical, ultra-masculine movement of white Australian men who were required to put the group before the individual, and service and self-sacrifice before themselves. That they had privileged access to the best view of the waves, a place to store their surfboards and were supposedly so irresistible to girls were coincidental perks.

Boardriding had arrived in Manly on a pine ironing-board. At least that's how one of the best stories goes. Shortly after the Hawaiian surfing legend, Duke Kahanamoku, visited Australia in 1915, Snow McAlister had taken an unusual interest in his mother's ironing.[15]

Secreting her pine ironing-board out of the house, Snow regularly wagged school and took it out into the Manly surf. He was eventually caught because he couldn't explain his sunburn when he came home in the afternoons but the ironing-board had already proved extremely useful in building his initial skills. Snow won the Australian surfboard titles of the 1920s four years in a row and is still widely regarded as the father[16] of Australian boardriding.

For Hans and John the surf club was their entree to the fabulous new world of boardriding. The heavy boards were kept at the clubs. Surf-lifesavers were the pioneers to emulate, and the physical strength and the knowledge of the ocean that lifesaving training offered laid the foundations for understanding how to manage, if not master, the waves, on such unwieldy lumps of wood. The sheer joy of getting successfully to your feet as you shot forward on a wave was just 'wonderful', Hans told me, his eyes shining. Even more so if you were lucky enough to find yourself sharing a wave with a pod of dolphins.

Hans wanted to follow in Snow's wake. His eye was on winning the Australian surfboard championship for Manly and he needed John. Surfboard riding was then an exhibition event among the many team events that pitted the Australian surf clubs against each other in various tests of skill and speed from lifesaving techniques to surfboat races, sand races and ceremonial marching. Surf carnivals were great entertainment; the high drama of man versus nature drew large crowds.

The standard equipment for the boardriding event was three metres of solid redwood that weighed about 27 kilograms, and was wider than could be easily carried under even a large man's arm. The winner was the boardrider who managed to propel his heavy board the fastest, first paddling out through the waves, then around the deep water buoy, before riding the waves back to shore. It was both an extreme endurance event and a test of surfing prowess. But there was always an element of chance in how the waves rose and broke that everyone called the 'luck of the surf'.

John spent most of the daylight hours during the week at school, playing school sport or just getting there and back; Hans was already working as an apprentice aircraft engineer at the Sydney factory of de Havilland. If they wanted to train together, they would have to innovate.

The answer lay at the northern end of Manly Beach in the large shark-free lagoon fed by the local creeks draining into the ocean. By day its sandy bottom and its darting schools of fish could be easily seen through crystal-clear waters. By night, the local fishermen took over its shores.

Everyone knew not to swim in the ocean after dark, not only because sharks preferred the cover of darkness, but because of the risk of becoming disoriented. Instead, John and Hans built their strength at night by paddling up and down the safe waters of the lagoon to the point of utter exhaustion. John pushed Hans. Just when he thought he couldn't pull his arms through the water one more time, John was on his tail and so he did. The local fishermen looked on, perplexed and slightly annoyed.[17]

❖

These unusual night training sessions also helped push John forward at the surf club for the so-called 'marquee event', the real crowd-puller: the surfboats. He was taller than most teenagers his age and increasingly stronger, exactly the kind of tough athlete they needed. The joke about the selection of boat crews went like this. Line all the aspiring 'boaties' up against a wall and throw bricks at them. Take the guys who don't flinch.

Australia's wooden surfboats were originally built as rescue craft, based on a modified open whaleboat. Their popular appeal lay in the spectacle. With only four men on the oars—and their sweep, or skipper, standing precariously upright in the stern, steering, like a misplaced gondolier—they must pull desperately up the face of huge breaking waves or attempt to shoot a wave to shore without being swamped. Photographers and cinematographers relished the chance to capture a boat tumbling down a breaking wave, spilling oars and crew, or only just making it up and over the top of a wave, hanging momentarily suspended in mid-air before collapsing into the trough behind.

'To watch a surf boat race in large surf, as determined crews stroke manfully to their doom is to witness a glorious triumph of optimism or blind courage over common sense', wrote surf historian, Tim Baker,[18] noting the absolute faith the oarsmen must have in their 'sweep' as he steered, them facing backwards, into the waves. A visitor to Australia suggested another description: 'mountaineering in boats'.

The bigger the forecast waves, even gale conditions, the larger the crowds that flocked to revel in the Roman holiday atmosphere of crashing boats and injured men. When big storms whip up the large ocean swell off Manly, a bombora forms out to sea over an offshore reef, offering the biggest waves the area ever experiences. For surfboat crews those waves—'looking as high as a three-storey building' towering over them—were irresistible. In other words, John thought the surfboats were terrific fun.

In retrospect, John's entree into surf-lifesaving, and the new sport of boardriding, played a role in later securing him a spot in the escape from Stalag Luft III. This might seem unlikely, but one of the skills required of wooden board surfers was carpentry. There were no commercial surfboards available. Large pieces of wood had to be sourced and shaped and they had to be regularly maintained. John and Hans even went to the trouble of painting John's board in his school colours. Then there was the challenge of getting the boards to the lagoon, when carrying them that distance was beyond even the fittest of young men. Hans had a small car, and so he and John carved, sawed and hammered together some wooden 'roof racks' in Hans's garage.

What few people knew was that Hans and John also used their time on the water to speak German. John was studying German at school and it was a good chance to practise.

'In the lifesaving club we would never talk in German because in those days it looked like Germany was going the wrong way, but we could at practise at night,' said Hans of the ripples of concern already reaching Australia over Hitler's intentions. He didn't think much of John's pronunciation, but John did know what was being said. Hans reckoned John would have been able to listen to, and communicate with, his prison guards.

Hans wasn't exaggerating about his talents in the surf. By 1939, he was indeed Australian surfboard champion. John did okay, too. In a glass cabinet in my living room is a small, somewhat tarnished silver trophy engraved with his name as an Australian junior boat champion of 1935. The waves were relatively small the day John's crew won the national junior title at Dee Why Beach, much to the disappointment of the crowd.[19] My dad used to say: 'Your uncle John was a national champion surfer, you know.' But he wasn't. The boats were a team event; there was no individual glory to be claimed. He was just a member of a group of young men who knew how to work together.

CHOOSING THE FUTURE

Hans didn't much like Mildred, but he was far too well brought up to let it show. A formidable figure with exacting standards, Mildred, to a young Hans, seemed to stand guard like a glowering watchdog at the Williams' front door. This was probably less by design than circumstance. Len was, by then, virtually an absent father. He was taking work wherever he could find it, so was often away, and it was Mildred who had to carry on at home.

Regardless, Hans found himself turning up even more frequently on the doorstep of the flat, hoping to be invited in.

Hans's surf training and his job were going well. He and John were now regular drinkers at the newly rebuilt Art Deco Steyne Hotel, its large plate-glass windows looking directly out to sea. That John was under-age caused some occasional ripples of anxiety. One late afternoon when the police burst in to haul the many errant 'youngsters' out by their ears, John and Hans had looked nonchalantly into their beers. The police walked past without a second glance at the tall Williams lad. In those days, said Hans, by way of explaining the potential seriousness of getting caught, 'the police would give you a good clip over the ear if they heard you say as much as "bloody" in public'.

Hans also had something else on his mind. He was very keen on Suzanne (Suzie), John's sister, who was closer to his own age than John. Seriously keen, he said. Not that the boys ever talked about girls or romance. You just didn't. And Suzie was very close to Mildred. So Hans found even more reasons to visit the flat. Life seemed to have found a comfortable rhythm within the idyllic surfside bubble of Manly Beach.

For all their boys' own adventures, John and Hans were ordinary, as much as anything else. They beat well-worn paths to and from school, work, the beach, football training, church and the pub. They rebelled predictably against the strictures of their parents' era, revelling in the relative freedom of the beach, and they aspired to push themselves to the absolute limits that modernity offered. Yet, like every generation, they did so while absorbing those same conservative values, like diligence, resilience and stoicism through every pore of their skin.

That I can look back now and imagine the 1930s in bright, vibrant colour is merely a function of the manner in which stories take shape. That a brilliant summer sun seems to illuminate the intensely masculine world they inhabited is the result of the passing of time, which has rendered it unfamiliar, and so new, to me. John and Hans's world stands out only because it contrasts so sharply when set against the backdrop of my own, very different childhood, growing up as I did in the 1960s as the fabric of Western societies and institutions was being torn up and remade.

All of which means that it is relatively easy for me to recognise the cracks that were starting to appear, from the ominous shifts in geopolitics to the tensions inside the surf clubs, and even the new strains on the boyhood friendship that erupted just when Hans was beginning to imagine marrying Suzie and becoming part of the Williams family for good. But I imagine that change crept up on John and Hans so slowly that they only really noticed it when it was already there.

In 1936, as Hitler geared up for the Berlin Olympics, sports-loving Australians didn't know quite how to react. The *Sydney Morning Herald* raised some serious concerns, despite simultaneously acknowledging Germany's 'gigantic transformation for the better' over the preceding three years. Hitler's string of achievements, especially his 'triumph' over mass unemployment, had only come by 'spending the entire liquid resources of the country' and borrowing so heavily, even from his own people, that many citizens would be paying their future taxes with promissory notes. The Nazis' violence and discrimination against German Jews and other minorities, too, was already known in Australia and its consequences feared.[1]

Some influential Australians seemed bedazzled anyway. Harry Hay, one of the Manly club's best-known lifesavers and a long-time Australian Olympic swimming coach, reported back to the local surf-lifesaving community after returning from the Berlin Games, his fifth as competitor or coach, that he had never seen anything like it. *Surf in Australia* reported his speech in its January 1937 issue:

> Mr Hay was particularly impressed with the Hitler Youth Movement. He was given access to several camps. There are no unemployed in Germany, every lad being drafted into the Youth Camps for 12 months training.
>
> My Hay's comment that these camps could well be instituted in Australia is not without ultimate possibility. Mr Hay remarked that in Australia there are too many loafers living on the Government, and we are regretfully compelled to agree with him.[2]

The magazine was presumably referring to those young men not in the surf-lifesaving movement.

A few months later, in April 1937, the magazine reported remarks made at the Manly Jubilee official dinner by Brigadier-General Lloyd, MLA, who, apparently having seen cinema newsreel footage of the Hitler Youth in action, had concluded 'that the physical fitness of Australia's youth (relatively) was pitiful'. The only remedy, he told Manly's official guests, was to be found 'in the introduction of the Fascist development plan'.[3]

Such public remarks seem extraordinary. But those enthusiastic proponents of surf bathing and surf-lifesaving in Australia, which reached its zenith in the 1930s, had long skated perilously close to the purported goals of the eugenics movement. The Surf Life Saving Association, through its official magazine, had gone as far in 1936 as to suggest a 'stronger race' was emerging from the water.[4]

Eugenics had been invented in 1883 by the geographer and statistician, Sir Francis Galton, who borrowed from his cousin, Charles Darwin, the theory of evolution as the foundation of his new pseudo-science 'of improving racial stock' by regulating marriage and, thus, procreation. His so-called 'positive eugenics' was aimed at artificially producing a better human race by 'encouraging the physically and mentally superior members of the population to choose partners with similar traits'.[5] In 1904, he presented his ideas to a large audience of physicians and scientists in London and the ensuing worldwide publicity spawned 'eugenics groups' in Europe and the United States during the first half of the twentieth century.

In Australia, senior scientists even claimed that through our sun-loving, active outdoor life 'Australians were becoming distinctly different to our British forefathers not only in height, weight and build, but also in chemical composition and nutrition' in a lecture entitled 'The Adaptation of Man to Australian Conditions'.[6]

The true horror of the application of eugenics by the German Nazis through the elevation of the 'Aryan race' above all others, so legitimising the extermination of Germany's, and then Europe's, minorities was, as yet, unimaginable and, likely, incomprehensible.

As 1937 dawned, the two friends were apparently increasingly at odds. Hans had been in Australia since he was thirteen years old, but he was still, in the eyes of many, German. The Nazis were flexing Germany's military muscle. They had joined Mussolini's Italian fascists in lending military support to Franco's fascists in the Spanish Civil War and although Britain desperately wanted to avoid another war, international volunteers were banding together to fight fascism. *Surf in Australia* soon found itself scrambling to formally disassociate itself from that brief gush of admiration for the Nazis that had appeared so recently within its pages.

John, my uncle David said, was following events in Europe seriously. He believed that Britain, and therefore Australia, would have to take a stand. He expected his generation would have to go to war. I don't know what happened when Hans and John, and consequently the entire family, fell out over their regular beers at the Steyne Hotel. The Williams always claimed that Hans said something along the lines of: 'Just wait until the Nazis get here, they'll sort the Australians out'. Such a direct provocation seems both unlikely and out of character, having met Hans several times and talked this through. By contrast, Hans remembers the decisive conversation as a very animated discussion about what John should do next, given international developments. John had passed the university entrance exams but he wasn't sure that was the right direction to go in.

As an aircraft engineer, Hans believed aviation was the future, in peace or conflict. He advised John to join the air force, something he says he has always regretted. That's exactly what John did.

12

THE MOTHER COUNTRY

Pilots aspiring to join the fledgling Australian Flying Corps during World War I were asked one particular question first: 'Do you ride?' The theory was that an outstanding horseman had a sense of balance and a light hand, attributes considered essential for handling early aircraft.[1] Among the elite group of only 158 Australians who became World War I pilots, the famed Light Horse Regiment was considered an ideal apprenticeship for taking to the air. Many a horseman found himself trading in his lavish emu plumes, bandolier and that familiar weight of a bridle in his hands for a plain brown tunic jacket and a modest set of 'wings'.[2]

Two decades later, as war again appeared imminent, what might distinguish one fine young man from the rest?

Since the Great War, as it was still then known, aviation had developed dramatically. The early wood and fabric biplanes had morphed into metal structures capable of carrying a worldly new elite of glamorous, well-heeled air passengers. Individual aviators were making heroes of themselves, challenging and breaking distance records. Previously unimaginable speeds were being chased and attained.[3]

Magazines and newspapers pored over every detail of the lives of the 'sky-pilots', who 'conquered space and distance, laughed at the perils of night and storms and unknown lands'.[4] In an age before flight became a routine form of mass transportation, Hollywood stoked the myth with fabulous new releases like *Test Pilot*, featuring Clark Gable as the dashing 'devil-may-care' pilot at the controls.[5] In Australia, families crowded around their radio sets waiting for regular instalments of *Howie's Way*, breathlessly billed as 'a thrilling aviation saga'.[6]

Much popular and political debate also focused on Australia's aviation future. Were we sufficiently 'air-minded' in this dazzling new era to take full advantage of the potential for flight to end our geographic isolation? Had our gallant pioneers of aviation, like Charles Kingsford Smith, already shown the world we could punch above our weight in this most modern of pursuits? By 1937, as tensions built in Europe, the world's industrial powers were weighing up their relative strengths in terms of the performance and numbers of their aircraft. The Australian government announced the production of the first Australian-built warplanes in Melbourne and the modest Royal Australian Air Force (RAAF) was considering its immediate future.[7]

Britain's air force expansion was already in full swing. But even the doubling of places in the service in fewer than two years could not keep pace with popular demand. In 1937, more than 17,000 young British men applied for 3850 pilot traineeships.[8] The RAAF had routinely sent 25 or so of its own cadets to train with the RAF every year. In addition, the RAF took a small number of young men directly from the dominions, lads they considered 'overseas British', part of the extended family. That year, four places would go to New South Wales.

By the late 1930s air force recruitment had been transformed. Psychological testing was still some time off, but advances in science and technology meant complicated physical and mental examinations played a significant role in selection. There was one characteristic that really stood out. Every successful candidate was in perfect physical nick.

'In virtually no other endeavour was a man required to keep so many groups of antagonistic muscles in a state of "wakefulness" or perform such a variety of constant co-ordinated leg and arm movements as in managing high speed war 'planes',[9] an aviation medical specialist explained, also noting that such scientific insight was beyond ordinary doctors of the day. Such feats of dexterity were not achieved in isolation; a pilot simultaneously endured rapid changes in altitude, air pressure and temperature and, often, was also aiming and firing guns, or bombs. To assess an individual's resilience to such forces one somewhat-less-than-scientific early RAF test was to spin an aspiring candidate very fast in a chair then ask him to walk along a straight line painted on the floor.[10]

Modern air forces wanted 'young men in their physical prime passing through that period in their lives when they are prepared to take risks to achieve a certain objective'. That didn't mean young chaps 'who laughed at danger, but those who laughed at the fear of it'.[11] That such a fine line divided zeal, courage and bravery from recklessness and foolhardiness did complicate matters but that was something the initial stage of training could sort out.

Of course, the small RAF advertisement that caught John's eye in a Sydney newspaper listed only the standard conditions of eligibility. Theoretically, all that was required was proof of age (over 17 and a half but under 25), proof of pure European descent and proof of completion of the requisite level of mathematics and physics. In Australia, it was the Air Board that made the pick.

There may have been significant differences between what Australia's Air Board and the British local recruiters in England had in mind. For a start, Australians liked to think of themselves as somewhat more egalitarian and, so, less influenced by the old school tie. Anyone who had the necessary intellectual and physical prowess could aspire to becoming an RAAF pilot, so too, presumably, a locally selected RAF officer. But, in practice, it was elite schools that emphasised maths and science, ran military cadet programs and prided themselves on their rowing and Rugby teams. The Depression, too, had disrupted the education of an entire generation of young men who were now coming of age.

In Britain, however, the RAF was unashamedly selective. 'The accent was on quality . . . cadets were well educated (public school, preferably), came from higher social backgrounds, and were good at sport'.[12] Or as one applicant was told brusquely:

> The RAF was not for people to join to escape the army, because they didn't like the uniform, or the navy because they couldn't swim, but was really an exclusive club for those of higher intelligence and above average physical fitness who were, in addition, dedicated to the service of their country.[13]

From the time John had been old enough to struggle into a suit and cap, he had been dressed up like an English public school boy, albeit with first a New Zealand and now an Australian accent. At expensive schools modelled on the British public school system, he had been drilled in the values and mores of the Mother Country. He was a good, if not exceptional, student and in his first year of medicine at the University of Sydney, he had more than the requisite level of maths and science. He had spent years practising for the armed forces as a school cadet. He was both a proven team player and a relentlessly competitive individual. Probably more than anything else, he was also very good at sport.

When the letter arrived offering John one of only four RAF short service commissions for New South Wales, no one went about crowing. But, the entire Williams family quietly puffed out their chests. Suddenly, the cramped Manly flat was filled with the energy of organisation and anticipation. There was the ship voyage to consider. There were photographs to commission.

To most people, the threat posed by Hitler's sabre-rattling still seemed decidedly remote. For the moment, Mildred could at least savour John's success. And it was at least partly hers to enjoy. She had ferociously guarded her children's opportunities, lately against the odds. In many ways, John's RAF commission was Mildred's vindication. At eighteen, her eldest son was well mannered, well spoken, well read and infectiously enthusiastic about life. He knew when to stand up straight with his broad shoulders back. That she was 'incredibly attached to John', as my uncle David said, and would be terribly affected by his departure, was something to keep to herself.

John left Manly and his beloved beach at the height of summer. On his last night at home, my father Owen, then eight, ran around bug-eyed with excitement, weaving in and out of the crush of big tanned young men that seemed to fill every corner of the flat. Hans was conspicuously absent. The tide was turning. Important surf club officials were asking questions about what it meant to be a German in Australia. They were already manoeuvring ominously behind the scenes against one of the finest boardriders that Australia had ever seen.

David, then fourteen and still one of the kids, was out in the kitchen frantically cutting tomato sandwiches with Mildred and Suzie, trying to keep up as the party wolfed them down with beer.

'I was younger, so I suppose I was just a bloody nuisance really,' David laughed. 'But, I used to half-worship John and lean on him a bit when I needed help. I can still remember all of his friends from that night.'

The next morning, just before John stepped out the front door, he pressed two quid into David's hand. 'That was a lot of money,' David said. Astonished, he didn't know quite how to feel. Happy, touched, proud and sad, all at once. Four years later, the war in full swing, David too enlisted. He, too, pressed two quid into his younger brother Barry's hand as he left the house.

13
IVO TONDER—THE LAST GLIMPSE

I've taken many lovely sunny days for granted throughout my life. The psychology of light and warmth, so important in northern Europe, is something Australians rarely have cause to consider. But, visiting Sagan and the surrounding countryside for the 70th anniversary of the escape in March 2014, I came to appreciate the optimism that a bright day might unexpectedly inject into an otherwise bleak tale.

The day of the 70th anniversary broke dark and sombre. It rained and sleeted and rained. The downpours came at us sideways, driven by the wind, so it seemed that there was nowhere to hide. The clouds hung so low they scraped the ground. The gathered families and dignitaries were fortunate enough to be huddled under a canvas marquee. The ceremonial military formations of RAF and other officers were out in the elements. In the forest surrounding the ruins of Stalag Luft III, the dirt tracks and the clearing marking the tunnel's exit quickly turned to puddles and mud.

It wasn't snowing, like it had been in the harsh spring of 1944, but, the wet, freezing cold was gradually defeating the guests. We were, of course, a stoic, respectful and deeply appreciative audience, determined to rise above the bad weather, but many of us were visibly shivering violently. How the escapees managed in thigh-deep snow seemed almost too distressing to contemplate.

The following day, when the sun broke through in the late morning, it seemed like a gift. The countryside looked so fresh and green that the mental weight of the previous day began to lift. We drove south on quiet country roads, past small farms and modest rural buildings with our Czech pilot friend, Michal Holy, and a new acquaintance.

We had met the quietly spoken Petra Tonder in Sagan and were travelling back to Prague together. Her father, Flight Lieutenant Ivo Tonder, a Czech RAF pilot, was escapee number 21. By sheer chance, it seems, his fate and that of John's escape group were inextricably linked. What followed for Ivo Tonder had set Petra's own life on a particularly challenging course from the moment of her birth after the war.

Ivo and his escape partner, British Flying Officer John 'Johnny' Stower, should have been on an 11 p.m. train that night. But the delays had meant they stayed back to help haul the men through the tunnel on the wooden trolleys to try to make up time.[1] No other train was running until 6 a.m., so they set off on foot.

'My father didn't talk too much about it, but he did tell me about how incredibly cold and tired they were, that they walked all night, and that they dug a hole to sleep in the next day,' Petra said.

'What I remember particularly is that, even in these conditions, he told me they felt exhilarated to be free.'

Ivo and Johnny Stower had a difficult time dodging civilians and dogs, walking by night and hiding among the trees by day. As they had been among those selected for train travellers' disguises, they weren't adequately dressed for hiking but they kept going. By the third night, Tonder said, they had walked more than 50 kilometres, and had passed the town of Kohlfurt. They had no idea a *Grossfahndung*—a national hue and cry—had been authorised mobilising tens of thousands of local and national police, Gestapo, soldiers, Hitler Youth and civilians in a massive manhunt.[2] Extremely cold, hungry and tired, they decided to double back to town to board a train.

Ivo spoke good German and the pair had no trouble getting on a train heading toward Reichenberg, where John and his group were already being interrogated by the Kripo (the police) and Gestapo officers.

During the journey, Ivo and Johnny were asked for their papers. Their forged documents passed the scrutiny of two plain-clothed policemen from Reichenberg who were earnestly embracing the *Grossfahndung*, casting their eyes particularly keenly around the carriage. Then the gaze of one of the officers stopped dead on the pair. Something had registered. It took a moment for him to process the realisation. He had seen trousers like theirs somewhere else before. Then he remembered where: on John and the others in the Reichenberg cells.[3]

We drove south from Sagan for about 45 kilometres then pulled into the modest Polish town of Wegliniec, formerly the German town of Kohlfurt. Its expansive, dated railway station suggested that nowadays the town is very much a shadow of its former self. The clouds had dispersed; the sky was clear blue, the wind crisp and cold. I climbed up the stairs of the pedestrian overpass that leads to the large Art Deco waiting rooms and platforms, now mostly boarded up.

I stood with Petra at the top of the rise, looking down on the many empty tracks. It was easy enough to imagine a thronging railway junction patrolled by German troops. What seemed more extraordinary was the fact that we had met at all. It had taken me much of my own lifetime to pick up John's trail and on that day I was standing with the daughter of the only eyewitness to what happened next.

Ivo and Johnny, too, were incarcerated in the cells of the Reichenberg police station. Once they had been questioned in the basement, with no apparent menace, they had been taken upstairs where they met John, Rusty, Leslie and Jerzy, and heard of their capture by the ski patrol near the border.[4]

There were two Gestapo officers wandering around the station; this wasn't something to be left to the local police. Ivo saw our four sign statements but they didn't say anything more sinister than that the answers they had previously given to the Kripo were correct. But something else had changed.

'During this time, I had the impression that Squadron Leader Williams had learned something about his fate,'[5] Ivo told war crimes investigators after the war. It was only John, not the others.

'He was not normally a nervous man, but he was clearly pale and scared.

'I have no reason to suppose that he had behaved in a provocative manner during his interrogation or that there was any cause for him to be more alarmed than the others.

'After this they were taken back to their cells . . . I never saw the four again.'

14
IN SEARCH OF THE ELUSIVE ENGLISH GENTLEMAN

John arrived in England in mid-winter in January 1938. He was embarking on a new chapter of his life in the land of that mythical creature, the English gentleman, a man not only of good humour, good manners and good nature, but one who understood the meaning of all those familiar words like courage, duty, gallantry, sacrifice, honour and humility and the rest. A gentleman was intellectually and morally equipped to navigate his way successfully through the minefields of life with the minimum of fuss.

There is no doubt John stepped off the boat with lofty expectations. He had been surrounded by adults keen to nourish a colonial chip on his shoulder most of his life. Ironically, it was learning to fly in England that brought him crashing down to earth.

John's first stop was RAF Prestwick, near Glasgow in Scotland. With the other new short service commission trainees he moved into a hotel just near the airfield where basic training took place. From now on he would be messing with the elite. In the RAF, officers and the rest didn't mix. If the handful of dominion boys had no idea what the social norms of the RAF might be it was up to them to learn fast.

'I would describe it [the RAF] as one of the best clubs in the world,' said RAF Wing Commander Robert Helm, who also did his basic training at Prestwick the same year.[1]

'You had the prestige of a commissioned rank, you were also a pilot—and in those days flying an aircraft was unique. It just put you head and shoulders above other people of your age.'

The daily basic training routine, said Helm, was initially reasonably relaxed. Mornings spent studying theory, afternoons in the air, or vice versa. There was enough free time. 'We played golf, we went drinking in Ayr [a nearby town], we chased girls. You name it, we did it.' Splendid. The new RAF recruits walked with a spring of superiority in their step. They were impudent and indulgent. They prided themselves on drinking hard, playing hard and still getting up in the morning sufficiently clear headed and keen eyed to pull a stalled single-engine plane out of a spin. These invincible young men saw themselves as the vanguard of a new era of modernity and advanced technology. They were contemptuous of the stuffy sea-dogs of the navy and the stiff conformists of the army, many of whom were just as appalled by the young RAF.

Flyers were a new breed. They left their top button undone and 'took malicious pleasure' in arriving 'slightly scruffy' to dine in upmarket London restaurants. None of this seemed to dent their popularity and allure. Indeed, once war had broken out, the RAF's 'bomber boys' and 'fighter boys' were forgiven just about any social transgression. 'The general public remained wedded to an affecting image of fresh-faced young men living life to the full in those precious intervals between active duty, [they were] reckless sensualists under constant threat of death.'[2]

All of which is, of course, a sweeping generalisation. No stereotype ever does justice to the true heart of the many different individuals within any apparently uniform group. But, first impressions are important. The new boys arriving from the dominions found themselves stunned, even winded, as though they had walked unexpectedly into a closed door. They 'had to negotiate a RAF culture which appeared to them class-ridden and hidebound' and which represented their 'growing estrangement from the mother country'.[3]

John had no complaints. But neither did his early letters home mention a single new friend or any modicum of fun.

In retrospect, said Wing Commander Helm, 'It is surprising how confident we were. We had amazing confidence in our own ability.'

In fact, said the renowned RAF Squadron Leader Billy Drake, who crossed paths with John in 1938 and later befriended him as a fellow fighter pilot in the Middle East: 'We were a very amateur organisation in the 1930s, right up until 1939. The air force was a new arm of the services . . . we had no real doctrine, everyone who had taken part in World War I was either dead or retired.'

By contrast, he noted '[The Germans] were very thorough; they had more up-to-date aircraft and they had operational experience.'[4]

That the RAF and the British government were inadequately prepared for the looming war, and the decisive role air power would play, seems obvious enough in retrospect, particularly with today's easy access to declassified documents. Behind the scenes, the RAF had been scrambling since its first major expansion was approved in 1934 after a damning inquiry by the Defence Requirements Committee.[5] Prior to 1935, the RAF was 'turning out pilots with the bare ability to fly an aeroplane' and only the briefest of introductions to the military aspects of flying. At the time, more advanced training was supposed to be carried out within an inadequate number of operational units that had no experience of combat.[6]

Meanwhile, in Germany a highly skilled professional officer class, well versed in mechanised warfare, had long been building in competence and strength despite the Allies' order for the disbanding of the Flying Corps and the prohibition of the production of military aircraft after World War I.[7] Under the guise of fostering a successful civilian aviation industry, German governments had been subsidising aircraft manufacturers since the 1920s. The lessons and knowledge of World War I had been fruitfully applied to develop new and advanced aircraft designs.

When Hitler came to power in 1933, Hermann Göring, a World War I German ace, was made air minister and the expansion of military aviation became a priority. Both Hitler and Göring would later play decisive personal roles in the lives and fates of John, Rusty and their fellow escapees.

In 1935 the Luftwaffe was formally announced. By 1936 many of the high-performance German aircraft that would participate in World War II were already in prototype form and undergoing testing. The outbreak of the Spanish Civil War in mid-1936—which provided the Nazis and the Italian Fascists with the opportunity to side with Franco's Nationalists—gave the Luftwaffe, and its Condor Legion, the chance to put its aircraft, pilots, tactics and doctrines to the test.[8] The Condor Legion was modern and fast; it was experimenting with planes such as the Messerschmitt Bf 109. Among its targets was Guernica. The Legion's bombing of the local market killed over 1600 civilians, an atrocity immortalised by Pablo Picasso in his painting of that name that depicts the carnage.

During a ferocious debate in the British Parliament on 25 May 1938, serious criticisms were levelled at Prime Minister Neville Chamberlain. Sir Archibald Sinclair, who would later become Britain's wartime secretary of state for air, warned:

> The gravamen of our charge is that while the Government undertook at the beginning of this expansion scheme to close the gap which was then widening between our air strength and that of the strongest air force within striking distance of our shores, that gap has not been closed but has continued to widen and is still widening . . . That is the cause of our anxiety at the present moment.[9]

A motion calling for 'a complete and searching independent inquiry' into the state of Britain's air defences was defeated.

Although Chamberlain conceded various 'delays, disappointments and checks' in the expansion program, he was confident that, if put to the test, the RAF 'would prove to be one of the most formidable fighting machines in the world'.

Within months, Chamberlain was handing over Sudetenland in Czechoslovakia to the Nazis, still downplaying the threat. But that crisis did trigger an intensified expansion within the RAF.

'Following Prime Minister Chamberlain's return from his meeting with Adolf Hitler [September 1938] . . . there were some immediate and ominous changes in our lives,' wrote Drake after the war.

'We went at once on a war footing. Our aircraft were painted in camouflage colours, our guns were kept loaded. In rotas pilots slept in the hangars at night.'[10]

But merely recruiting 'large numbers of untrained men was no answer to the problem of effectively manning an increasing number of units'.[11]

Throughout 1938, John excelled as a trainee pilot. The basic training routine consisted of 'just getting in and doing as you were told'.[12]

Even in peacetime, flyers received danger money because aircraft were fallible, and trainee pilots even more so. Training accidents were common, and sometimes fatal.

Pilots needed, first and foremost, to learn how to fly safely. Given that aircraft stall was virtually inevitable, much time was spent working out how to swiftly correct the resulting, and potentially catastrophic, spin. Aerobatics were introduced too, as well as frequent repetitions of forced landings. Elementary training gave the young students some warning that their instructor was going to cut the trainer plane's engine. Later, without any notice, an instructor would shut the engine down, requiring the student to respond quickly and find a safe way in. 'You always flew with an idea that you would have to force land, so you always had a field or something in mind,' said one of John's contemporaries.[13] In the south of England, one group of RAF trainees located a nudists' camp, so, to keep things interesting, they always tried to head that way.[14] In Scotland, no such landmarks broke up the day. In the evenings, trainees wandered into town to drink, talking loudly about their exploits in the hope of impressing any local girl within earshot.

John's RAF service record notes that after nine weeks he was a 'smooth and accurate pilot, who has made good progress, above the average'.[15] In his theory, too, he was above average in all subjects. His probationary period was over. He was permitted to wear his wings. The next move was to Uxbridge, just west of London, for uniforms and kitting out. Measuring up required a trip to Savile Row, London, and Gieves, the exclusive British tailor ('What side does sir dress on?'),[16] then to RAF Ternhill for more advanced training in the English countryside.

If initial training at Prestwick was relatively relaxed, said Wing Commander Helm, the next stage was anything but. It was time for toughening up. The physical drills were constant and difficult. Long marches, plenty of square-bashing (military drills) and absolutely no allowances for dawdlers. Lectures now included 'conduct and behaviour befitting an officer', the so-called finer points of life.

> What we mainly learned was mess etiquette. Things like never mentioning women, what constitutes honourable behaviour, how to recognise ranks, how to pass the sherry and the port—most of us wanted to know this anyway. And, no gambling, of course, only bridge.

All of which only exacerbated John's sense of never quite fitting in. The best thing to do was to put his head down and concentrate on his flying.

By the time John had been flying for nine months, he was

singled out. Every trainee was desperate to be posted to an operational unit. John was going to the Central Flying School in provincial England instead.

For a nineteen-year-old, it was an extraordinary tap on the shoulder. John had neither the experience nor the pedigree normally required; places were usually limited to British officers with at least 1000 hours flying in their logbook. But by 1938 the RAF had realised that what it needed even more desperately than competent pilots were pilots skilled enough to instruct.

That bible of modern aviation of the time, *Aircraft* magazine, advised its readers that selection lists for the CFS 'should be read with awe by everyone connected with the flying Services'.[17]

'There is no higher testimony to supreme excellence in flying ability.'

To John, it felt like a crushing disappointment. He would not be sleeping in his kit in a hangar with his peers ready to go if, or more likely when, war broke out.

In addition to regular recruits, the RAF expansion program in the late 1930s was counting on other sources of men to fill the ballooning deficit of pilots.

There were a growing number of 'weekend flyers' in training: both a Volunteer Reserve Force that began to take candidates from a range of backgrounds from 1936 as well as that particularly distinct arm of the RAF, the Auxiliary Air Force and the related university squadrons. The AAF dated back to the 1920s and had been envisioned by Lord Trenchard, the Commander of the Royal Flying Corps in World War I, as 'an elite corps of civilians who would serve their country in flying squadrons in their spare time'.

If the regular recruits John had met regarded themselves favourably in the scheme of things, the AAF pilots were something else again. The AAF:

was characterised by the most extreme kind of social exclusiveness to be found in Britain in the 1920s and 30s. To be an AAF pilot was to belong to a jealously guarded elite, access to which was barred by social and financial hurdles which were impassable to many who might have wished to fly with them.[18]

So exclusive was this club that some members owned their own planes and various society mentors entertained them at their country estates. Cambridge and Oxford universities, then later London University, boasted squadrons similarly conceived to smooth the path into the RAF for the crème de la crème by providing flight training on site.

The part-time AAF pilots of No. 601 Squadron were especially well known as the Millionaires Club. Among them was the South African-born Roger Bushell who, while an outsider, was considered 'marvellously amusing' by Britain's socialites, was an exceptionally talented skier and something of a cad, although rake might be a more accurate term. The young men of 601 drove fast cars, lined their flying jackets with red silk and considered themselves above those codes of behaviour that applied to the rest, other pilots included. Bushell had limped his way through law at Cambridge University, putting skiing ahead of his studies. But he was sufficiently well connected to find a place as a barrister, while flying at the weekend.[19]

He would prove a passionate and determined pilot, and later a talented, if arrogant, escape artist who would hold the fate of many at Stalag Luft III, including John, in his hands.

The Volunteer Reserves of the RAF, on the other hand, brought in the radical idea that, although there was an educational hurdle to clear, there were, theoretically, no social barriers to enlisting for flying training.[20] Bringing in thousands of potentially middle-class men was still done cautiously, given institutional concerns about 'compatibility and competence'.

While the AAF members were all commissioned officers, the reservists were not. They filled the non-commissioned (NCO) ranks of Sergeant, Flight Sergeant and Warrant Officer. This clear division in the ranks was deliberately engineered to avert an upper-class outcry. The AAF was made up of 'officers who expected to share their lives with men who appreciate their outlook on life and know how to fit in'.[21] In other words, men who believed they had been born to rule, or at least to run, the British Empire and who could not imagine that things might work in any other way (or that the end of empire was already looming). Officers, therefore, were assured of their own superior mess, better facilities and batmen to keep them comfortable. The new class of sergeant pilots dined together in decidedly less salubrious surrounds.

It had taken considerable pressure to push the AAF elite to accept that the 'pilot establishment' should be opened up to non-commissioned ranks. But, by the time war broke out, every man was needed. As the war progressed, much more profound challenges to old models of power and position would build, and the Australians would play a significant part.

John was homesick, chronically so. He was weighed down by an odd kind of malaise. Nothing physical. He didn't look any different but it took more energy than he had ever imagined to keep up the constant good-humoured banter that station life demanded.

'You talk of missing me, but there is only one of me and six of you. So how do you think I feel?' he wrote home in mid-1939.

Britain, and its armed forces, had been on a knife's edge for month after month, resulting in exhausting bursts of intense training and readiness exercises. 'This international situation is making me sick. In fact, I think it's worse than war,' he counselled, with the naive impatience of a boy who has strayed no closer to a real military front-line than a spirited Rugby brawl.

John diligently maintained his weekly writing schedule. The exchanges from one post day to the next were often as detailed and intimate as a family conversation in the living room. Mentally, he was following life in Manly as though he was still there.

Backwards and forwards the family discussed books, music and news and opinions. Mildred filed every letter away in order to be re-read. Every aspect of John's new life was like a fascinating, unfamiliar bauble, to be carefully picked up and turned over in her hands, again and again.

In March 1939, Mildred had passed on the news that Hans had finally done it. He had won the Australian Surf Board championship, giving the Manly club its first Australian board title since the reign of Snow McAlister in the 1920s. Moreover, he had done it in front of his home crowd; it was the club's turn that year to host the national titles on Manly Beach.

The 1939 carnival was more important than ever because the selectors were there to pick the first surf team to represent Australia internationally in the glamorous new Pacific Surf Games to be held in Hawaii later that year. The publicity surrounding the event was unprecedented, largely because the rapidly rising Australian media magnate, Frank Packer, and his new populist *Daily Telegraph* newspaper, were sponsoring the team.

Hans stands beaming with his enormous wooden surfboard in the early publicity photographs.[22] Then his name and his image simply disappear.

Although he was by then an Australian citizen, Hans had been denied a passport to travel. Frank Packer's influence was reportedly such that his reluctance to have a 'German' on the team was noted. Australian officials would help Packer leave the country's best surfer behind. Soon Hans found himself ostracised at the beach, then expelled from the Manly Life Saving Club altogether.

'I am sorry to hear Hans has fallen from grace so badly, but it will do him a lot of good,' John wrote, suggesting their own parting was, indeed, not on good terms. John was worried about Hans, nonetheless. Neither John nor the family knew exactly what the surf club had against him. John suggested my grandfather, Len, try to find out. Events would soon overtake any polite inquiries from the Williams family.

About his new life as a flight instructor, John was lukewarm. His students were progressing well and that was gratifying enough, even if they did seem 'a bit scared' of him.

By mid-1939, John had been posted to the Cambridge University Squadron (CUS). Ironically, Len, to whom an English university education had been the ultimate privilege and a symbol of both social standing and success, could hardly have been prouder.

On the other hand, when John was offered a permanent instructor's position with the CUS within a month of arriving in Cambridge, he had no hesitation in turning it down. He asked to be put on the list for a transfer to a new RAF training base in north-east Scotland instead.

The magnificent 800-year-old university was then in the throes of expanding access to poorer students through scholarships and bursaries. There were concerns, even within its own upper echelons, that the considerable cost of a Cambridge education was limiting access to a very particular elite.[23] The cost of a single year's education was then more than the average male wage of about £200 a year. The university's demographics were reflected in the 'serious problems' caused by the burgeoning 'motor habit'. 'The alarming increase in the number of motor vehicles', particularly students' cars, driven onto the fine lawns within which the ancient, sandstone buildings and gardens were set had been worrying administrators since the 1920s. 'The aeroplane had also arrived on the scene', a lengthy history of the university notes, prompting a 'prohibition on undergraduates flying without their tutors' permission'.

At the annual CUS gala dinner, the vice-chancellor, Professor H.R. Dean, proposed the toast with the quip that:

> the members of the Squadron could look down on all England [sic], from John o' Groats to Land's End—except on their own university town, as it is forbidden to Cambridge men to look down on Cambridge itself.

John motored into London in an old Bentley with other instructors and attended many a splendid Cambridge party. But, he told Mildred, with no apparent regret, that he could not afford to buy the requisite tails for formal events. Without a private income to supplement his modest air force wage, and relentless peer pressure to drink and be merry, he was constantly broke.

Many starry-eyed new recruits envied the sophisticated 'long-haired' or 'Brylcreem boys' who filled the Cambridge, Oxford and London university air squadrons, and the extra latitude they seemed to enjoy despite their antics.[24] John bemoaned the constant company of a 'bunch of Philistines'.

Coincidently, the same term is used by the Australian-born but British-raised Richard Hillary, later a famous RAF fighter pilot, although in quite a different context. 'We radiated an atmosphere of alert Philistinism', he wrote in *The Last Enemy* in 1942, describing his path to becoming a Battle of Britain ace, via one of John's later flight training units.

'We were cliquy, extremely limited in our horizon, quite conscious of the fact and in no way dissatisfied about it.' His Oxford College, Trinity, was 'a typical incubator of the English ruling class before the war', a haven for well-to-do kids who barely bothered to study, but were assured of securing cushy positions in the civil or colonial service.

For the more recent arrivals to the great 'Oxbridge' establishment, those serious, industrious, bursary types of the professional middle classes, the 'long-haired boys' like Hillary had little time. Not, he argued, 'from plain snobbishness', but more because 'we did not speak the same language'.

'Through force of circumstance they had to work hard; they had neither the time nor the money to cultivate the dilettante browsing which we affected'. He almost seems to have felt sorry for these striving, middle-class intellectuals: 'they were balanced precariously, and with irritation, between a despised world they have come out of, and a despising world they couldn't get into'.[25]

This early chapter of *The Last Enemy*, as eloquent and insightful as it is, and as skilfully as Hillary critiques his own, makes it hard to look at the treasured portrait John had mailed to Mildred without feeling at least a twinge of humiliation, on his young behalf. Standing proudly in a London park in a stylish new outfit and overcoat that the family could ill afford, he had, the family thought, 'looked the part'. But he had made it into the RAF only to find himself surrounded by overconfident young men mocking virtually everything he had ever been taught to respect.

The ground must have felt as though it was constantly shifting beneath his feet, no matter how many times he regrouped in search of a firm toehold—especially as a 'colonial' in their British midst. Recounting an undergraduate debate over the 'folly of patriotism', Hillary quotes a fellow student as saying: 'We have been exhorted ever since [seizing nations all over the world] to love not only our own country, but vast tracts of land and people in the Empire whom we have never seen and never wish to see'.

On most training days John trod a well-worn path. He ploughed up and down the local swimming pool, played darts, had a drink at the 'the local' at the end of the day. 'That's all life consists of in England. It's easy as hell to get in a rut . . . but I am not there yet.'

But his discomfort was palpable: 'Tell Suzie [his older sister was then undecided about a new romance after Hans disappeared from the scene] I don't mind who she marries, so long as he isn't an Englishman.

'The longer I stay here the more I realise that the English gentleman is a very rare gem—but I'll admit that when you do strike one he rings true', he wrote.

More than anything else he was looking forward to finally getting back home on leave before Christmas. He didn't.

One weekend, he ventured into London's Soho district, the magnetic epicentre of a bohemian mix of foreign eateries, brothels and pubs frequented by novelists, artists, poets and cinematographers, an antidote perhaps to the relentless CUS snobbery.

John had only recently turned twenty. Upright and out of place in his stiff blue RAF uniform, he peered through the haze of cigarette smoke, nursing his beer, with a group of fellow flight instructors. He leaned discreetly in towards huddles of drinkers, trying to pluck as many words as possible from the general racket. John was transfixed.

'We sat in a pub for three hours just watching and listening—it makes you think.

'They live in a world of their own. No rent paid for eight weeks or more until they sell a picture or a play, or something, and then a big party, then back to poverty again. All struggling until the production of their masterpiece.

'In many ways', he told Mildred and Len wistfully, 'they are to be envied.'

15

SCOTLAND, AND THE BRAVE

When John woke up on the morning of 18 January 1940 it was dark and bitterly cold. He reached over to grab his jug of water. Overnight, as his room's fire had died in its grate, the water had frozen solid.

It was a brutal winter across Europe,[1] that first winter of war. John was in Kinloss, Scotland, a remote RAF base so far north that the training planes only just got airborne before the men saw the last stretch of British soil disappear beneath them, to be replaced by the heaving, cold waters of the North Sea.[2] Gloriously remote and raw, John had thought over the past few weeks. On that Thursday, the 140th day of a still-distant conflict, the station's personnel scurried around the snow-bound base like crabs, darting from one building to the next, trying to avoid the sharp bite of the icy wind.

John had been drilling his students to fly at night in the driving snow. When a waxing moon and the northern lights coincided, the night sky was as luminous as day. It was like a 'fairy land', John wrote, an 'unforgettable' spectacle, comparable only, perhaps, to the pure joy of the flash of silver fish through a clear, turquoise wave. The airstrip ran right up to the edge of a fine sweeping bay. Its waters, too, glowed, a curious phosphorescent green.[3]

'It hasn't been above freezing for a long time now and one gets quite used to it. It makes flying fun too.'

John was in his element. He had the new perils of ice on the wings and windshields and the danger of running into snowstorms, 'and getting covered in the stuff', to overcome. 'When that happens you just wind down the window and put your head out and come in with frostbite on your nose . . . a marvellous experience. I still prefer the sun though.' John's scheduled home leave had, of course, been cancelled.

When war had finally been declared on 3 September 1939, nothing and everything had changed. After those many long months of drills and preparation, the young RAF boys finally had a clear sense of purpose, if not yet a clear mission. On the ground in Europe, the horrifying, wholesale destruction of Poland unfolded. The Nazi invasion that brought Britain, Australia and other Allied nations into open conflict with Germany had merely been Hitler's opening move. The Soviets, too, then moved on Poland, like the second claw of the pincers, then on Finland. The Nazis surged forward, invading Denmark, Norway, France, Belgium, Luxembourg and the Netherlands, as though they were working their way methodically through a list tacked to the inside of the turrets of their Panzer tanks. One by one, European nations surrendered to Nazi occupation.[4]

Instead of a ferocious and widely anticipated air war, the Luftwaffe and the RAF initially flew mostly defensive patrols, buzzing tentatively around the edges of the fighting, peering down from on high on naval ships, engaging intermittently before retreating home. Although the Luftwaffe was ready to be unleashed against France and England, Hilter held his planes back. For Londoners who had expected to hear Luftwaffe bombers massing overhead, the quiet normality of daily life had a 'strange, somnambulistic' quality,[5] a sense of foreboding in the lull before the inevitable storm.

Neither the RAF nor the French air force was yet strong enough to strike out pre-emptively with any prospect of success.[6] The RAF was scrambling with even greater urgency to increase its strength. Many of the pilots it desperately needed in the air were still feverishly learning how to fly.

After idling briefly on standby the long-haired boys of the Oxford University Squadron, with their rudimentary weekend flying skills, were posted to Kinloss for advanced flight training. Hillary and his friends motored on up.

Their cosy pre-war bubble had burst. Kinloss was heaving with new, ruddy-cheeked young recruits from many walks of life, all of whom were striving to excel and all of whom 'wanted to be an Ace of some kind'.[7] Those who had been selected as non-commissioned officers were crammed into hastily constructed Nissen huts. 'They were very crowded, and the bigger and stronger chaps among us got the beds nearest the coke stove—it was a poisonous thing, it's a wonder we weren't all asphyxiated,' said one of those NCOs, Nigel Rose.[8] Hillary's young officers' group was billeted in a small, unheated stone cottage, more austere and plain than they could ever have imagined.

It was less than two years since John's own arrival in Scotland as a naive trainee. Now just twenty, he was ensconced in his own room, batman on call, gramophone and pool table at his disposal. With no operational experience, he and many other similarly inexperienced instructors found themselves responsible for turning out the pilots the war was waiting for.

Like John, many of the new arrivals were struck by the splendid isolation of the village that apparently owed its name to the loss of the ancient Scottish king, Duff MacMalcolm. 'Tradition bears', says an account written in 1842, that Duff was assassinated in the region in 962 and 'his body was for a short time concealed under the bridge in this parish . . . its name, as if commemorating this tragic event, is by the less educated classes in the surrounding district sometimes written as Kingloss'.[9] The extensive ruins of a once grand abbey, founded in 1150, cast weird, mesmerising shadows as the sun went down 'like a flaming ball', painting the inland mountains purple and gold.[10]

As a late RAF expansion-period airfield, Kinloss was short on facilities but it did have something more important: big, relatively stable, clear skies. In a nation of persistent fog and rain, the RAF could not afford to have its planes frequently grounded by bad weather. And it was as far away from the anticipated area of operations, East Anglia, as possible; a Nazi invasion of Norway had not been imagined, so the potential vulnerability of the far north of Britain had not been taken into account. Training on single-engine Harvards and twin-engined Oxfords, the next generation of RAF fighter boys and bomber boys was taking shape.

'I shall never forget the first time that I flew really high', Hillary wrote of north-east Scotland, 'and, looking down, saw wave after wave of white undulating cloud that stretched for miles in every direction. I dived along great canyons, the sun threw the reddish shadow of the plane on to the cotton wool walls of white cliff that towered on either side. It was intoxicating.'[11]

Something just as important as the honing of technical skills was also unfolding.

The melting pot of the expanding RAF meant the long-haired boys were no longer huddled together slapping each other on the back within their own elite squadrons, so they no longer dictated how things were done. 'At the beginning of the war there was definitely a prejudice ... we were to have the nonsense knocked out of us', Hillary noted. As it happened, this apparently didn't prove necessary, at least at Kinloss.

The camaraderie of isolation, coupled with the intense experience of flight training, and the shock of the first deaths in training accidents, began the essential process of assimilating men, so diverse in their lives and habits, into something bigger than themselves. That this transformation went largely unnoticed by the embryo pilots themselves, who 'lived together, laughing, quarrelling and rapidly maturing in the incubator of that station',[12] wasn't important. It was evident enough in the likes of Hillary extending his respect and friendship to instructors and ground staff alike. He had come to 'speak the same language' as even the sergeants, he wrote.

In *The Last Enemy*, Hillary laughs at one of his peers who had announced disdainfully on arrival:

> You must understand in our service we have a number of uneducated louts from all over the world, none of whom can speak his own language properly. It becomes necessary to invent a small vocabulary of phrases, equipped with which they can carry on an intelligible conversation.

At the time this particular chap was a very poor pilot, with a very impressive vocabulary. Within three months he was an excellent pilot, but his vocabulary was 'pure RAF' slang. He jumped just as quickly as the next man onto anyone caught 'shooting a line', drink in hand.[13]

Anyone who has ever embarked on a long-distance love affair understands the passion and bitter determination with which those precious threads that connect us to a significant other, or others, are guarded, whether that love is for a romantic partner, a family, friends or even a place. Others will fail, but we will not. We also know that those threads stretch and strain regardless, despite our best efforts. As the RAF boys began to find some cohesion, support and an unspoken mutual understanding within their own ranks, the bright colours of their peacetime lives began, slowly, to fade into the background. The social divisions did not, of course, dissolve. But, importantly, the lines did begin to blur. Although John remained just as diligent in his correspondence, he no longer seemed so dislocated. He was looking forward not back. It was just as well he was no longer counting the days until he could get home.

There was one complication. A girl named Doreen. Only weeks after turning down the position with CUS in mid-1939, John had told Mildred: 'I have found a nice girl here at last . . . she is very beautiful, with very dark hair and brown eyes. I seem to prefer brunettes, somehow.'

By the time the transfer to Scotland came through John was romantically entangled. Doreen shared his love of classical music. She was even keen to marry. 'But, it is hopeless', John wrote, despite managing to get leave to meet her in London, at least on one occasion.

What were the options for a flyer in love? Some thought love was essential, as important as aviation fuel to a fighter pilot. But, within the RAF there were those who thought the business of war left no time for romantic love, or that romance was a dangerous distraction that diminished combat effectiveness, as though the heart could be subject to the same rigid discipline as all other aspects of military training.[14]

There also were those who thought that 'the harsh reality of war and the ever present threat of physical annihilation made romantic sentimentality seem inappropriate or even absurd'. As Francis notes in *The Flyer*: 'If the flyer could not guarantee being able to protect himself from the cannon fire of a Messerschmitt 109, he could at least prevent himself being downed, instead, by Cupid's arrow'.[15]

The famous wartime photographer Cecil Beaton went as far as to claim that the flyers of the RAF represented the 'finest elements of the British character, not least because they were able to exercise appropriate self-restraint when faced with the siren song of female sexuality'. Francis also quotes an RAF liaison officer, Rom Landau, as saying: 'When faced with a conflict between the call of duty and the call of sex—often interpreted as a call of love—he [an RAF officer] fights a far less difficult inner battle than do most of his foreign colleagues'.[16]

Others simply believed that succumbing to love's pull just wasn't fair. On the one hand, it was unfair to a young woman at risk of being left grieving over her fallen lover. On the other, it was unfair to a flyer's fellow pilots who would be troubled by a broody, lovesick colleague in their midst and would fear, now he was focused so intensely on a young woman back home, he could jeopardise their collective safety by avoiding the risks essential to success in combat.[17]

All of which seems a little too dramatic and serious for a twenty-year-old Australian in a Scottish village, his Doreen still back in Cambridge. After meeting Doreen in London over Christmas of 1939, John told the family she had 'written a pleading letter, asking for the real reason I wouldn't marry her'.

Here I am stumped. As Hans said, he and John never talked openly about relationships, no one really did. My access to John's letters, too, is dwindling. Many were unfortunately damaged beyond rescue when my uncle's basement was flooded decades ago, so I am missing some of the context. The family is clearly supposed to understand. I suspect the real reason had nothing to do with gallantry. The most promising theory is Mildred's disapproval, perhaps based on his youth, but also possibly because Doreen, in Mildred's eyes, didn't measure up. Or, of course, John might have had cold feet.

I can only really guess. John's first wartime romance is over.

By mid-1940 Britain was in a state of shock, 'like a wounded soldier who feels no pain'.[18] After the fall of Paris on 14 June 1940 and the capitulation of the French, the Allies' westward retreat was followed by the evacuation of British forces from Dunkirk, in which the RAF suffered heavy losses: 106 RAF fighter planes were shot down as they attempted to provide cover. 'They (the British) knew that the situation was desperate, if not catastrophic, with almost all the army's weapons and vehicles abandoned on the other side of the Channel', wrote Anthony Beevor, in his substantial history, *The Second World War*. 'A self-comforting belief developed that although the British always did badly at the beginning of a war, they would win the last battle, even if nobody had the remotest idea how.' Britain was now facing the Nazis in Europe alone, protected only by the moat of the Channel.

The RAF training operation at Kinloss had been relocated further south once Norway was in Nazi hands, allowing bomber squadrons to take over the closest base to the Norwegian coast. The first days of the Battle of Britain were only weeks off.

When the war broke out, there had been 450 Australians dotted throughout the RAF.[19] Within a week, the British government had informed Canberra that 'the main weakness of the Allies vis a vis Germany was in air power'. The Australian government, then confident that no immediate threat was looming in the Pacific, prematurely approved an expeditionary force of six Australian squadrons. That Australia neither had the aircraft required nor could afford to dispatch so many of its finite numbers of experienced flyers who were needed to train new recruits soon became apparent. By October 1939, a new proposal for Australia to supply 20,000 pilots, 20,000 air gunners and 12,000 navigators was unveiled, representing an instant tenfold increase in its pre-war training commitments.[20]

Then the Australian prime minister, Robert Menzies, announced that the 'British, Canadian, Australian and New Zealand Governments had agreed to combine in the training of the skilled personnel of a vast air force, the scale of which is literally without precedent'.[21] This was the Empire Training Scheme, in theory an elegant and simple model to build air strength by exploiting each of the Allied nation's comparative advantages. For a start, the large numbers of pilots needed couldn't possibly be trained under Britain's grey skies.

Of the tens of thousands of recruits from the dominions who would rapidly swell the Allied air ranks, about a third would perish in training accidents and operations, their risk of dying rising, at times, to one in two on the front-line.[22]

In the meantime, the British were reeling. In the first major battle initiated in the air, the Luftwaffe launched its assault on

London and southern England in July 1940, seeking to destroy Britain's air defences and so lay it open for invasion and occupation. RAF fighter squadrons, piloted mainly by young men barely into their twenties, were outnumbered. They held the line over more than three terrifying months. On 17 September 1940, when the Nazis 'postponed' the air offensive and the planned invasion in the face of their own considerable losses, the RAF's reserves were almost entirely depleted.[23]

Hillary and his batch of young Kinloss trainees were among the first into the air; like John, a few of the 'sober, sensible types' had been held back to be trained as instructors.

Hillary flew with exceptional bravery and skill, but was horribly burnt when his damaged plane exploded in flames. He survived by landing in the water off the English coast, the cold water providing the first relief, and the initial treatment, for his terrible burns. He then endured excruciatingly painful and experimental reconstructive surgery, during which time he wrote his famous book. In 1943, the gifted young writer and pilot was killed in a training accident, having implored the RAF to put him back up in the air despite his debilitating scarring.

The Battle of Britain proved the Allies had an impenetrable base, turning Britain into 'the world's most unsinkable aircraft carrier' and so providing a platform 'for the sensational growth of Allied air power'.[24] Churchill famously declared of the RAF: 'never in the field of human conflict was so much owed by so many to so few'. The RAF lost 1023 planes; the Luftwaffe 1887.

The RAF had also won some crucial breathing space to rebuild its depleted ranks. And the Australians were coming. Lots of them. Again, John was on the move and, again, he was stepping into a role he had never even imagined.

THE FIRST POW

In Sydney in mid-1940, Mildred and Suzie were subpoenaed to appear before a secret court.

Nervous and formally dressed, they came face to face with Hans in the makeshift dock in an anonymous room somewhere in the city. Hans was accused of being 'a threat to public safety'. The Williams had been identified as long-time family friends and were required to give evidence.

Under emergency wartime legislation, Australian authorities had extensive powers of surveillance and control over 'aliens', those people residing in Australia from enemy nations. The contradiction of sending Australians to fight fascism overseas in the name of democracy and freedom but resorting to draconian security measures at home was not lost on many commentators of the day. Prime Minister Robert Menzies had promised that the internment of enemy aliens was to be restricted to the 'narrowest limits consistent with public safety and public sentiment'. Short of incarcerating aliens, other measures like alien registration and a permit system controlling places of residence and travel and bans on the ownership or possession of guns, signalling equipment, planes and even motorcycles and cars were in force.[1] Of the 45,000 or so 'enemy aliens' then living in Australia, more than 10,000 were incarcerated at the height of the internments in 1942, considerably more than had been originally envisaged.

When war had been declared, Hans had immediately lost his engineering job at the de Havilland factory, where he had previously certified planes as airworthy. He then limped along with a bit of teaching and some contract work. But, on 20 June 1940, as his records show, he was 'captured' and listed as a POW.

With no corresponding wartime infrastructure in suburban Sydney for POWs, Hans's 'capture' involved him being arrested and taken by police to the local station where he was locked up in a regular cell, just like a criminal—but not before a malicious desk sergeant had asked him to turn out his pockets. The sergeant made a show of counting out Hans's one pound and two shillings and records it as 'one pound', telling him he can have his one pound back when the Allies win the war. With ten or fifteen other young German men rounded up on that same day, Hans is then transferred to Long Bay jail, the state's maximum security prison.

'Imagine, slammed into Long Bay jail for nothing—you no longer feel like a human being, you think, is this where you are going to spend the rest of your life? I was pretty naive in those days, I saw a bloke go completely mad, he went off his head,' Hans said.

The closed court hearing was the due legal process internees were afforded. Today, the allegations against him seem fanciful, almost hysterical. But Australia was gripped with paranoia and fear as the Nazis pushed their way across Europe in the first half of 1940. 'The fear of a British collapse, lurid accounts of fifth columnists undermining resistance [to the Nazis] in Europe and Italy's entry into the war [on 10 June 1940] all led to a surge in the numbers of aliens being interned.'[2]

Hans had, out of curiosity, visited the German club in Sydney and was taken aback when the evening ended with a sharp 'Sieg heil', he said. But, that didn't seem to be the problem. Nor was it his earlier expulsion from Manly Life Saving Club on vague and spurious grounds. It was that Hans's family had gradually rebuilt their fortunes following the Depression and had purchased a piece of land in a new housing subdivision high on the hill above Manly, with a panoramic view over Sydney Harbour. With their family home now built, the Wickes could look straight out to sea to the harbour's mouth, where two sheer sandstone headlands marked the entry to the extensive, sheltered harbour waters. It was, in fact, an ideal vantage point for a German spy to monitor shipping movements in and out of Sydney, or to signal enemy forces in the waters off shore. Even the family's oil heater for home heating was suspected of being intended for use in refuelling German submarines.

After a stint in Long Bay jail, Hans and his batch of fellow German POWs were trucked inland to the rural town of Orange where they slept locked in the unheated local sports club on sacks filled with straw. Then, onto the rural town of Hay to the south, until that camp was needed to house the Japanese.

Hans finally ended up in Tatura in northern Victoria, where a sizeable number of the German internees were, in fact, pro-Nazi. Viewing their detention as 'a form of sacrifice for the German nation, they insist on speaking German, run a German school for their children behind bars, preserve German cultural practices and (with the tolerance of the Australian authorities) even maintain Nazi rituals', according to historical accounts.[3]

What role did Mildred and Suzie play in Hans's fate? As little as they could under the circumstances, my family have always believed.

'I'll admit Sue didn't speak against me, but she didn't speak for me,' Hans said of the young woman he had hoped to marry. By that time, he said: 'I felt they [the Williams family] were against me.'

Hans's internment was confirmed regardless. He would spend years behind barbed wire, and suffer discrimination and restrictions for decades after his release. But he would never ever let anyone know what had happened to him during the war.

❖

More than 70 years later, as I slowly waded through document after document, gradually piecing together John's life in Manly in the lead-up to the war, I came across a number of references to this extraordinary 'German' surfer who featured prominently in the Williams' life. Then, I stumbled across a reference that suggested he was still alive. Astoundingly, he was an active, alert 97-year-old who had only recently swapped his early morning laps in the pool for a more leisurely daily walk.

In 2012, I nervously made a call to a retirement village on the water south of Brisbane. I left a message that I was John Williams' niece. Hans was quick to call back.

'It's been more than 70 years since I have heard from anyone from the Williams family,' he said, clearly emotional. We arranged to meet. After that court case in Sydney, he had never seen Suzie again. Would I mind, he asked, bringing a photo of Suzie with me?

17

THE AUSTRALIANS ARE COMING

At 25, Rusty Kierath was 'a pugnacious, fiery little bastard'. Coming from a fellow First Grade footballer this was, indeed, high praise.

If there was one way to characterise Rusty's approach to life, it was to watch him play Rugby. Rusty was the kind of player who 'picked a fight at the drop of a handkerchief and battled like buggery for the ball', said his good friend Snow Swift.[1]

On Tuesday, 19 August 1940, the *Sydney Morning Herald* assessed the still-raging Battle of Britain. Although Germany's losses were considerably higher than the RAF's, both in the number of planes and lives lost, the *Herald* warned that the Luftwaffe had clear 'numerical superiority'. Unless this imbalance in air power was quickly redressed with dominion-trained crews and American planes, 'Britain must continue to run grave risks and undergo sore trials'.[2] Both Rusty and Snow were exactly the kind of tough, committed young men the Allies were looking for to boost their ranks in the air.

They had been close friends since Rusty first walked into the Shore boarding house at the age of fourteen; Snow was sitting on his bed, bored, distractedly swinging his long spindly legs. He looked up to see a serious young man, with a shock of thick blond hair, who simply said: 'Where do I put my port?'

(portmanteau/suitcase). Rusty had managed the 450-kilometre train trip from the small rural town where his family lived, as well as the unfamiliar city connections, on his own. If he was tough and resilient when he arrived, boarding school and Rugby would only make him more so.

Since John had last kicked a ball around on the school oval with Rusty and Snow in the 1930s, the pair had made their way up through Rugby's ranks to represent Sydney's prominent Gordon Club in its first year of First Grade competition in 1935. John would have understood the cachet of a Gordon jersey. In 1940, Rusty was working for a bank and Snow as a trainee manager for Frank Packer's growing media empire. On that day in August, they didn't go in. They signed up instead. Rusty's brother, Greg, only two-and-a-half years older, had just joined the army. Predictably, Rusty and Snow picked the RAAF.

The Kierath family's story is a pioneering tale of triumph over adversity, with some foresight and good fortune thrown in.

Rusty's grandfather was, in fact, German.[3] In early 1855 Charles Kierath fled the successive uprisings rolling across the German Confederation as the dramatic disruption of the industrial revolution to traditional trades and crafts collided, head on, with failed harvests and increasing food prices, leaving many Germans jobless, landless, hungry and bitter.[4]

Charles set out to make his fortune in the goldfields of the southern Australian colony of Victoria. In the Wild West 'every man for himself' shanty towns that had sprung up around gold deposits, he set up small shops to service the miners. Early on, he sent home for a German wife, Henrietta, but she and their first son, Karl, died in childbirth within a year of their marriage.

Then, in 1857, Charles was held up, robbed, shot and left for dead by bushrangers on an empty dirt track on his way back from a local race meeting on the outskirts of Beechworth. The

Kieraths' story could have ended abruptly there, on that deserted stretch of dirt track, Charles yet another victim of the desperate, violent men who lived like ferals in the bush and took what they needed by force.

Charles managed to struggle back into town, despite the bullet lodged in his abdomen. He was given little hope by the local doctor and hovered between life and death for eight or nine days. But he did live, sent home for another German wife, Louise, whom he married and with whom he went on to have nine healthy children.

Their second child, Albert William, known as William, was born in 1861. As a young adult, William imagined for himself a more settled and prosperous future so he headed north, across the wide plains and sparse, thinning bush that signals the western limit of decent agricultural land. Drift much further west and the creeks run dry and the expansive reaches of arid land warn observant travellers of even hotter, drier, vaster deserts ahead.

William stopped in a small settlement called Narromine, in the central west of New South Wales. That this district was then only just emerging as promising sheep- and wheat-farming country is evident in an 1881 description of a pioneering family's journey west through Narromine by 'waggonette drawn by four stout horses'. The family aboard was enduring its first long-distance trip through the Australian bush at the height of an especially hot summer, when 'the earth was like iron and the sky like brass'. Stopping at the Narromine Inn, owned by William O'Neill, for the night, the mother, who signed her essay only as F.O.M., describes the lone bush inn as 'a low wooden building pervaded by the smell of stale beer and staler tobacco'.[5] The small parlour, the mother noted, was 'chiefly furnished with oleographs [imitation paintings] and flies', the bush repast on offer consisted of a 'hunk of corned beef, a gigantic cold plum pudding, a loaf of bread and a thin pot of tea'. Luxuries such as milk, butter, cutlery and even chairs were 'conspicuous in their absence'. As unappealing as this description might sound, there is something about the Australian bush that transforms those who take up its challenges and binds them to its bright, raw heat and its stunning red earth. Likewise, William was not deterred.

The Narromine district was, and is, like so much of inland Australia, both familiar and unique. The Macquarie River, with its steep banks and magnificent river gums, waits year after year in the sun, just like other inland river systems. Then, suddenly, flooding rains fill it so fast that it breaches its banks, spreading rich silt across the floodplains to replenish the surrounding soil and to distribute its own seeds, bringing the land back to life. To be fortunate enough to witness the explosion of flora and fauna across Australia's inland after good rains, and to see and feel its vitality, is to be party to one of the most fascinating life cycles on earth. Then, just as quickly, the waters recede and the land and its giant trees again settle down to wait.

Not even scientists know how long these majestic river gums live. Perhaps 400 years, or even 950 years, over which time they grow in spurts, feasting in flood, enduring in drought, to reach up to 40 metres in height. 'This glorious, extraordinary tree . . . is the quintessential Australian—tough, adaptable, enduring and slightly unkempt'.[6] Looking at photographs of Rusty, who grew up swinging on ropes into the river with his friends, gloriously free under their dappled shade, this makes perfect sense.

When I visited Peter Kierath in Narromine in late 2014, the river gums were alive with the raucous energy of hundreds of white-and-pink corellas and white cockatoos. Peter's father was Rusty's eldest brother, so, like me, he had grown up with the Great Escape. Unusual overnight rain had filled the air with that distinct, intoxicating perfume of newly wet leaves, grass and soil; the ions that charge the air when moisture and heat collide seemed buoyant, invisibly lifting the mood of the day. Despite this early morning cool, the sky was clearing, promising a hot day ahead.

❖

William O'Neill was one of the Narromine district's first commercial wheat farmers, arriving in 1878, more than a decade ahead of William Kierath.

William O'Neill had obtained 260 hectares, the land where the southern section of the town stands today. As it turned out, it was a serendipitous purchase. When the inland train line finally came through in 1882, the Macquarie River at Narromine proved to be the last source of permanent water for the steam engines as they headed west. Two reservoirs were established and a railway station. Before the opening of the railway, the inland wool clip had to travel by barge thousands of kilometres down the Darling River, to South Australia. That trip took weeks or months, depending on the river's height. Now, the wool clip, on which so much of Australia's economy relied, could get to Sydney by train for export in a matter of days.

Seizing the opportunity, William O'Neill set about founding the town proper, donating plots of land to every religious denomination for the construction of churches. Today, that initial English-inspired template is still apparent in the wide main street of Victorian buildings and the verdant green lawns of the single strip of irrigated gardens that run down its centre, a notable contrast to the sun-burnished browns and muted olive greens of the Australian bush. At the same time, O'Neill was pushing the local agricultural industry into the future, revolutionising wheat growing using a strange, new tool: the steam plough.[7]

When William Kierath arrived in the district virtually penniless in 1890 he probably recognised that a young and growing settlement would need experienced merchants. Soon, he married William O'Neill's daughter, Ada, and his future direction was set.

The Kierath name was made gradually, built up from humble beginnings. First, a small store under both the Kierath and O'Neill names in that same year,[8] offering basic supplies. Then, increasingly sophisticated and varied goods and the expansion of the Kieraths' trading interests, and the family's role as employers and civic leaders in the town. Over two decades, William and Ada built a fine home and a solid financial base for their nine children. Rusty was child number nine, eighteen years younger than his eldest brother.

Although William was later driven around the district by his sons in a Mercedes or Buick, he was neither flashy nor indulgent. 'The family was very Victorian in its outlook,' Peter Kierath said. William was hardworking and strict, and expected the children to work just as hard, regularly helping in the store.

But if there was one thing he wanted them to have more than anything else, it was a good education, something he had never had himself. He sent them all to Sydney to private boarding schools, the boys to Shore.

Apart from a reliable source of water for the steam train west, Narromine had something else that proved very attractive to a young, modernising Australian nation.

In 1919, the then prime minister, Billy Hughes, had offered the phenomenal prize of £10,000 for the fastest aircraft, piloted by Australians, to fly from London to Australia in fewer than 30 consecutive days.

Although the prize was won when the winning crew first touched down on Australian soil, in Darwin, Narromine had already been surveyed and identified as an ideal site for an airstrip. Its usually clear skies, its stable air and the seemingly endless flat plains to the west combined to offer exceptional visibility for early aviators flying without sophisticated navigation aids and vulnerable to bad weather. The London-to-Australia race-winners, Ross and Keith Smith, decided to fly on to Narromine in their Vickers Vimy (G-EAU), painted with the slogan 'God 'elp Us All', landing to great excitement shortly after their victory.

In the heady interwar years of aviation development, Australia had become an important aviation destination as the world's pilots sought to break distance and speed records, and Narromine played a part.⁹ In 1934, Narromine was selected as a refuelling stop on the Great Empire Air Race from London to Melbourne. The town also boasted one of Australia's first aero clubs, established in September 1929, and soon hosted regular air shows and social events that attracted tens of thousands of visitors.

It's no surprise that Rusty chose the RAAF, said Peter. And, by that time, the RAAF had chosen Narromine too. The airfield was being converted into a training school for the Empire Training Scheme, the program that would prepare Rusty and Snow for the 'war in the air'.

With Greg already gone, keeping Rusty close a little longer would have suited Rusty's mother, Ada.

So large was the brood of Kierath kids that Ada was facing a mother's private anguish for the second time in her life. She had seen Herbert William, her eldest son and Peter's father, off to World War I a couple of decades earlier. Whatever privations Herbert had suffered and what horrors he had confronted, no one knew. These things were not openly discussed but Ada had read and re-read his every letter. She treasured them still and kept them neatly filed away in a leather pouch.

Whether Herbert had offered Greg and Rusty his wise counsel is not known either. 'He didn't talk about either wars . . . [but] the only time I ever saw my father emotional was when we visited a World War I exhibition at the Australian War Memorial,' Peter said.

But when Rusty's orders came through he wasn't heading back home from Sydney to Narromine. There were eleven Empire Training Scheme flying schools dotted across Australia. Rusty and Snow had been selected for the first overseas course in southern Rhodesia.

John, too, was on his way to Africa.

OUT IN AFRICA

No one ever forgot that distinctive mix of odours that clung to every breath of warm air aboard a crowded troop carrier labouring its way through tropical waters. Most pronounced was the pungent sweat of thousands of impatient young men, bored with their confinement and reduced to scrapping in improvised teams over everything from the ship's cork life vests to spoiling fruit. Add to that engine oil, steam and the constant waft of stale cooking oil, overlaid by the salt spray off the ocean.

The officers on the upper deck looked down on the various brawls and mock battles with little interest. Whatever toughening up the new recruits needed, it might as well start now. Being packed tightly together in bunks or rows of hammocks below deck in the humidity and heat was only a hardship if you measured your comforts against those of civilian life.[1] This was war.

John was having a hard time appreciating this ever-urgent war footing as the MV *Durban Castle* headed south.

The modest-sized steamship was one of a series originally destined to ply the peacetime Britain–Africa mail run and the first of a long list to be optimistically named after grandiose-sounding but nonexistent African castles.

John was leaving the war in Europe, as far as he knew it, behind. His ultimate destination was, in fact, then one of the safest places on earth. By September 1940, the Battle of Britain had turned in the Allies' favour but the high cost in lives and planes meant, as far as John was concerned, the constant cry for more aircrew drowned out all else. Meanwhile, the threat was shifting. With the Italians and the Japanese preparing to sign the Tripartite Pact with Nazi Germany, the Axis military alliance was being sharpened to a dangerous point.[2]

The Germans actually had little interest in North Africa; the *Lebensraum* theory of expansion did not suggest they should covet the hot, dry north of the African continent. An accident of imperial history had left the colonial forces of Italy and Britain sitting side by side in Libya and Egypt, divided only by the Western Desert.[3] Mussolini's 215,000 or so Libyan-based Italian troops, and consequently their German allies, were now at war with a meagre 36,000[4] or so British and Allied troops in Egypt who had much to protect. In particular, the Allied forces were tasked with defending Britain's control of the critical Suez Canal, its access to vital oil supplies and its short cut to its colonies in Asia, the Pacific and its antipodean dominions beyond.

In fact, right across North Africa and the Mediterranean enemy forces loomed menacingly.[5] The Allies needed urgent reinforcements in multiple theatres of conflict.

But, when John finally stepped off the *Durban Castle* after almost a month at sea, he was as jubilant as the next man. Liberated from the close confines of the ship, the new arrivals revelled in the fabulous sunshine, the glorious decadence of unrationed food and evening lights after the blackouts of England and the big, bright colours of South Africa. Every ship was met at the port by Durban's 'Lady in White'. With her megaphone and international repertoire of songs, Perla Gibson, a local opera singer, had taken it upon herself to cheer on the troops. As the seas off Durban filled with grey Allied warships of various shapes and sizes, she became a permanent presence at the docks dressed in smooth white satin. A memorial statue fills that place today.

To Perla's welcome, South Africa's white community added both its hospitality and its somewhat premature gratitude to the aircrews defending the empire. Families routinely opened their homes to the new trainees[6] of the RAF-run Empire Training Scheme, most of whom had not yet even sat in a plane, let alone mastered the controls. One group of young British RAF arrivals, still awaiting their first training flight, found themselves blinking in the spotlight at a local cinema. The film had been stopped midway, the house lights turned up. An announcement then came over the PA system, welcoming the brave aircrew to South Africa. There was little else to do but graciously accept the applause.[7]

Anyone who stayed longer would discover that a white, right-wing, anti-British organisation in South Africa was still smarting over the British victory in the Boer War, resulting in isolated attacks on Allied personnel and some open approval of the Nazis.

When Rusty and Snow spilled off their ship, soon afterwards, they'd been at sea even longer. They were among the first batch of Australian RAAF trainees to arrive under the scheme. The Lady in White added 'Waltzing Matilda' to her song list. Rusty and Snow raced around Durban in a rickshaw pulled by a 'native' wearing an alarming-looking headdress featuring various feathers and two large sets of horns. On an evening out,[8] they bumped into John. Rusty was filled with the infectious enthusiasm that adventuring imparts. He was confident and convinced that the fine reputation of Australians had preceded them.[9]

Others' recollections featured drunken Aussie servicemen, weaving their way in unsteady mobs through town, and their various, not necessarily amusing, pranks. In Australia, the press waxed lyrical in describing the 'great achievements' of the RAAF in increasing its strength twelvefold—from its modest 3489 men—in the first sixteen months of the war.[10] If nothing else, the heads of the first overseas trainees were filled with the historic importance of their mission.

'We were entertained by the South Africans in Royal style—our treatment in Durban only added to our swollen heads as "successful" air crew,' said Ted Sly, a fellow RAAF trainee, who later flew as John's no. 2 in the Desert War.

'Since the day we had joined the RAAF, the majority of our time had been spent enjoying a false lifestyle, and we had not yet seen a shot fired in anger.'[11]

John had arrived in Durban to discover a daunting backlog of trainees under the new consolidated empire-wide training program.

Rusty, Snow and Ted faced the opposite challenge. Eager to get going, they found themselves waiting. With so many different drafts descending on southern Africa, particularly from Britain, plus locally recruited white South African and Rhodesian trainees, there were many more students than instructors or planes.

To John, after almost two years overseas, the sound of this mass of Australian accents on the streets of Durban must have felt like coming home. The chance to talk to Rusty and Snow was even better. In a foreign environment, acquaintances from school seemed as close as treasured mates. They spoke the same language, had walked the same streets and knew the same circle of friends, or at least friends of friends. Of course, Rusty and Snow also noticed John. John was three years younger, yet here he was in that distinctive RAF officer's blue, walking with the purpose and assuredness of a seasoned flyer. All the trainees were in awe of anyone who could actually handle a plane.

But at this juncture, Rusty had considerably less reason to regard this chance meeting with John with equivalent significance and warmth. He and Snow had been cooped up with their compatriots for weeks, so another familiar Australian didn't particularly stand out.

If the new recruits were wide-eyed at the sights and sounds of Durban, where the black population seemed to outnumber whites ten to one, three days and three nights aboard a narrow gauge steam train with hardly a settlement in sight was something else again.

Most Empire Training Scheme recruits were quickly dispatched north to southern Rhodesia by train, where the new flight schools had been established to take advantage of the safe, clear skies. The Rhodesian airfields lay well beyond the range of the enemy and were blessed by predictable weather patterns. Over the first part of the journey, two locomotives were needed to haul the train up through the famous 'Valley of a Thousand Hills'.[12] From one side of the train the ships on the Indian Ocean could be seen disappearing in the distance, and on the other the approaching snow-capped peaks (depending on the season) of the towering Drakensberg Mountains. The train ran alongside the Amphitheatre, an astounding natural rock formation within the Drakensberg range that rises 1800 metres from the valley floor, and sits over 3000 metres above sea level.[13]

For the British RAF boys—and those dominion recruits like John who had been in the UK for extended periods—this spectacular scenery was rivalled by the sheer unadulterated joy of ordering a 'full house' in the dining car: a huge breakfast of sausages, eggs, bacon and mushrooms and trimmings, the likes of which they hadn't seen since the pre-war, pre-rationing days.[14] As the train levelled out on the plateau it stopped every now and then at a siding. A single traveller, dressed formally in a suit and carrying a small suitcase, would step down and disappear mysteriously into the scrub as nonchalantly as a businessman walking down a city street. Presumably, these incongruously dressed colonial settlers were returning home to farms somewhere out of sight. Similarly, trestle tables would appear as if out of nowhere by the side of the railway line, laden with sandwiches and cakes served by well-dressed white colonial women, keen to support the war effort.[15]

As the hours and days wore on, the train's windows framed a succession of perfect picture postcards: distant herds of giraffes loping elegantly across the veldt, their distinctive forms silhouetted against the sunsets; elephants gathering around watering holes, scratching their giant heads against the bark of the odd copse of trees. No glimpses of lions, but there were plenty of other strange, unfamiliar animals and birds[16] to help pass the time.

The African population, too, seemed to hang in the background, like extras on a film set. Save for the bare-footed servants padding silently and discreetly around Rhodesia's white colonial masters, and the many faceless manual labourers, this was still a white man's world.

Everyone was heading to Bulawayo ('the place of he who kills'), southern Rhodesia's second-largest settlement, a modest-sized British colonial town named, somewhat alarmingly, after the slaughter that occurred in a battle for control among the descendants of the Zulu tribespeople who had immigrated to the region from the south.[17] In character, said one former resident, it was a bit like a town in British colonial India; full of bureaucrats intent on building a local economy and civilising the natives in their belief that colonial rule was for the natives' own good.

Like the rest of the country, Bulawayo sat about 1200 metres above sea level. Locations for airstrips and the training schools had to be found just above this height to keep aircrew and instructors out of the malarial zones.[18] Of the airfields dotted around Bulawayo and beyond, John was heading for Kumalo.

'Kumalo had a single concrete runway with a cemetery at one end and a sewerage farm at the other, so you were well catered for,' said Derek Wilkins, an RAF trainee of his posting there.[19] He was only half-joking.

In the RAAF alone, over the course of World War II, 27,899 Australians qualified under the Empire Training Scheme. Over the same period, the RAAF recorded 2833 deaths of airmen in training accidents.[20] New trainee pilots were certain to experience their first ceremonial RAF send-off, with the firing of live rounds over the fresh grave, long before they saw any military action.

'Southern Rhodesia in those days was wild frontier country,' Wilkins said.

'The veldt was alive with huge herds of game which we shamelessly buzzed. Crews got lost, sometimes fatally. Survival training was taken seriously. There was the famous myth of the aircrew killed by bushmen giraffe hunters in the desert basin west of Bulawayo.'

Induna, another airfield near Bulawayo that sat atop a rise, had an even more bizarre heritage. The story went that it was named after the rebellious local chieftans who had been caught plotting to overthrow the last local ruler of the Matabele (Ndebele), King Lobengula.

'As a punishment for disloyalty, King Lobengula set himself up a grand feast underneath the sheer 400 feet high cliffs which make up part of the rise,' said John English, a Rhodesian-born RAF trainee who flew at Induna before transferring to Kumalo during John's tenure.[21]

'Then, he had these "indunas", or traitors, pushed off the edge in front of him and they came down "splat" as he enjoyed his feast.'

Lobengula, a great bull elephant of a man purportedly burdened with some 200 wives, later vanished mysteriously around 1893. He is believed to have hidden himself in a cave where he and his second-in-command committed suicide in shame after failing in their uprising against the British colonial forces. Lobengula was contesting an earlier treaty in which he had been convinced to sign over his territory's mineral riches by marking a document he was unable to read with an 'X'.[22] With his demise, all of Rhodesia and its wealth fell under the purview of the British Empire.

What truth lies in such tales is probably debatable but a number of oral histories of the period do tell the same story Wilkins referred to of the aircrew killed by bushmen giraffe hunters and report that Empire Training Scheme recruits and instructors flew armed as a consequence. But the hapless crew of this tale was not killed as a reprisal against the colonial rulers. In fact, they were rescued, fed and housed. It was only when the tribesmen realised that they had fed them giraffe—game reserved only for tribal royalty and so strictly off limits—that panic set in. If they handed them back alive, their terrible crime would be revealed, so they made sure the air crew couldn't talk. Well, at least that's how the story went.[23]

More credible were tales of the high drama of the unpredictable, and unfamiliar, forces of nature in southern Africa. 'I heard an odd sound and suddenly the sky got dark . . . I saw this huge cloud heading towards the camp', said RAF trainee Bill Dundock of being caught out in the bath when the locusts swarms descended.[24] 'By the time I was nearly dry the bath was half full of locusts. I was amazed . . . they were everywhere smothering the trees and bushes.' Then, just as quickly they were gone. The camp was devastated. 'Every leaf had been stripped bare—it looked like England in mid winter.' The swarms of flying ants—and even the crashing, electric storms of Bulawayo's short, sharp wet season—came and went just as suddenly, unleashing just the kind of energy that John had come to love at home.

At Kumalo, John was training pilots on twin-engined Oxfords, preparing them for operational training back in Britain, then live bombing runs. The aim was to train as many aircrew as possible in as short a time period as possible. Faced by the vast numerical superiority of the Luftwaffe in planes and aircrew, the RAF was accepting new operational pilots with just 50 hours of elementary training, and 70 hours of advanced training. The young men going to war in complex, unfamiliar machines were not more experienced than a new worker three weeks or so into a new job.

That Kumalo was considered something of a plum location—close enough to Bulawayo to enjoy access to its polite white society, its cinema, swimming pool, tennis courts, cricket pitches and British gentlemen's club—may have had something to do with the particularly high risks that bomber crews faced on graduation.

As the war progressed, every single time a bomber formation took off to fly over Europe it stood to lose, on average, 5 per cent of its planes and their crews. Over a standard tour of 30 operations, it became statistically impossible, at certain times between 1942 and 1944, for the crew of an RAF bomber to survive. Overall, more than half the RAF's bomber aircrew, six in ten, were not expected to come home.[25]

The reality of that risk meant two things: train hard and study hard; and make the most of every day, and evening. But, for all that Bulawayo offered by way of entertainment and activities, the two were not always compatible.

Trainees were roused by the jarring sound of a stick being run along the corrugated-iron wall of their huts before dawn. The Rhodesian bush was transformed into mock bombing ranges. Over and over again, young pilots practised easing the relatively 'clumsy'[26] Oxfords into exactly the right spot to hit their target with a smoke bomb. That was hard enough. The complex task of navigating over the featureless bush, with barely a settlement as a guide, proved even more difficult, especially when the wind pushed the planes off course. It would not be any easier over darkened European cities, as many bomber pilots later found.

But at night, flying was like being invited into a previously unimaginable secret world. As the heat of the day dissipated, so too did the turbulent chop of the tropical air. Night flying was smooth and calm. With no glare from the sun, and no lights below, the dark African sky was transformed. The soft light of the stars and moon hinted at the true vastness of space and threw out just enough illumination for pilots to pick out the curve of the horizon. In these rare moments of stillness, the night pilots suspended above southern Rhodesia were ensconced in a truly wondrous cocoon, flying along the very edge of the vast, unknown universe.[27]

For instructors, the day was often so long, and the concentration required in the air both so constant and intense—and the administrative load so relentless—that there was little time to do, or even think, of anything else. Apart from regular morning and afternoon flying and lectures, there was something called a twenty-hour turn at the aerodrome for instructors. John scribbled a short note to Mildred, Len and the family. He said little more than that he was 'dog tired', an increasingly familiar term, and had to be up again at 5.30 a.m.

'They [instructors] all wished to fly on ops. [operations] and any man who had been there [into action] was pumped for all the "gen" [information] he could give', an official report on the wartime Rhodesian Air Training Group (RATG) noted in 1945.[28]

> In many ways the instructor has a more arduous duty than the operational pilot, although he does not experience the extreme danger [posed by the enemy] . . .
>
> Consider the instructor. He must be 50 per cent flying instructor and 50 per cent psychologist. He must judge the right approach for each individual pupil, must demonstrate every manoeuvre, must explain each one as it is done, must pounce on every error a pupil makes, must be ready at a split second's notice to take over the controls . . . and must judge when the pupil may safely go solo.
>
> He repeats these processes . . . with different types of youth. When he has sent them all into the air as pilots . . . eventually to meet the enemy, he is left to start all over again with a new batch of groundlings.

John continued to improve his technical skills. He could fly any plane the RAF had to offer. He was also graded 'above average' as a flight instructor and a navigator. He was still not 21, yet he was signing off successive batches of pilots to go to war. The instructor's 'reward', noted the RATG report, was 'that he may occasionally get a letter of thanks from an ex-pupil or see some months later that one of them has been awarded a Distinguished Flying Cross'. Or perhaps, it suggested with more insight, this was the instructor's 'consolation'.

The RAF took the welfare of its personnel very seriously,

particularly its inadequate supply of pilots and instructors. In much the same way as great care is taken in feeding and stabling a valuable racehorse, specialist RAF catering officers worked with medical officers to optimise the airmen's diet, and to match it to local produce and the climate. No airman ever took off without having gulped the first of many mugs of tea and scoffed a bun no matter how early, and there were so many meals and snacks scheduled that they seemed to run into each other.

But, within a few months of arriving at Kumalo, John was more exhausted than even his daunting workload and the hot climate might explain. 'It's hopeless', he wrote of his dream to come home. 'Unless I am posted back, or the war ends.' At the end of April 1940 he collapsed and was taken to Bulawayo Memorial Hospital. He was released just in time to celebrate his 21st birthday on the station, but he was back in hospital two days later.

19

A TALE OF TWO MEN AND TWO MESSES

The new recruits were surprised to be handed tropical-weight khaki shorts and shirts, just when they were expecting to be kitted out like Biggles, in thick, padded flying suits, fur-lined leather helmets and goggles for the open cockpits of the Tiger Moths. They were also given a pair of great big black boots each that reached right up their shins.

'But, we are flying', John English confidently informed the RAF Warrant Officer in Bulawayo, only to be immediately silenced. Ted Sly wasn't quite so lucky when his group assembled for their first parade. He was standing to attention, sweating, the warrant officer strolling slowly along the line, deliberately and theatrically making eye contact with every single young man.

'Hello . . . another shower of shit from Australia,' the WO commented. 'I can still remember it,' Ted said.

Ted's group was briefed on the many RAF rules that now applied, including the many finer points of etiquette that dictated behaviour in the officers' and the non-commissioned officers' mess. That such divisions were dictated by rank seemed ludicrous. It was all the Australians could do not to laugh out loud, Ted said.

The boots and summer uniform, it turned out, were for marching, or square bashing, as it was called, not flying. Without enough instructors, the training pipeline was being deliberately slowed down. Masses of RAAF and RAF trainees were billeted everywhere. Some got straw-stuffed mattresses (palliasses) inside traditional-looking grass-roofed huts; some got corrugated iron sheds. Many got bed bugs. Everyone got drilled for at least six weeks. Some even repeated the theory they'd already studied. No one flew. No one complained.

Meanwhile, the boys were 'adapting themselves' to a life with servants.

Rhodesia had been acquired for Britain in the late 1800s by Cecil Rhodes, the British imperialist extraordinaire whose energy, vision and zeal were unsurpassed. 'I contend that we are the first race in the world, and that the more of the world we inhabit the better it is for the human race,' Rhodes had declared. Many agreed with him at the time. The aspiring Allied air force pilots and their instructors of the 1940s found themselves living among white settlers similarly confident of the superiority of their race.

The local adult men who served the British colonials were referred to as 'native boys' or even 'munts'. They were quartered in huts at the end of the garden and addressed in a kind of rudimentary 'pidgin'.[1] 'We have no work to do—native boys do all that for us', RAAF trainee Len Williams wrote home, clearly uncomfortable to be spending so much time just 'mooning around' while someone else picked up after him.

The Christmas of 1940 came and went and Rusty and Snow and many groups of under-occupied recruits made the arduous but extraordinary overnight train trip to Victoria Falls, and witnessed firsthand the phenomenal power of the Zambezi River. The river runs across the plateau about 1500 metres above sea level before dropping dramatically into a vast, deep ravine, creating a falling curtain of thundering water nearly 2 kilometres wide. This was the kind of natural wonder most people could only hope to read about in a book.

Some trainees were cranky and frustrated over the delays. Others were wide-eyed, lapping up every moment and documenting every detail of the opening chapter of their personal boy's own adventure in Africa.

Then, they finally fanned out for flight training.

Usually, Rusty was a sociable joker. The local council at Narromine still has a record of his audacious prank of 1934. He had led a group of boys in running through the girls' dressing-room before the 'Venetian Carnival' staged at the municipal swimming pool. He and his accomplices were required to publish a public apology in the *Narromine News*. On New Year's Eve, 1940, he and Snow were in bed by 8.30 p.m. at the Guinea Fowl Elementary Training School. He had to be up by 5 a.m. the next day, he told his mother in a letter home.

'Well, at last we have started some real work . . . after a very long time', he said. 'I haven't been out at all since coming here . . . I haven't even patronised the wet canteen once. Wet canteens and flying don't mix.' His instructor, he said, is excellent. He thought his flying was going okay, too.

When Rusty's first package arrived from home, he discovered that he was no longer an individual. From now on, he was part of the group. 'Whenever anyone gets a parcel from home all the blokes gather around and just as you are about to open it, they grab it. All I did was sit on the edge of the bed . . . and watch them rip the string off, open the cake and then hand me a piece', he wrote, in good humour.

'Incidentally, Mum, you should have heard the boys raving about it. "Best cake in show", "By gee your mother can cook", were just a few of the expressions.'

Rusty was just hitting his straps. He had logged 60 hours of flying. Then suddenly and, in his opinion, inexplicably, he was grounded.

'I took the Flight Commander for a flip [short flight] just before my test and he said there was nothing wrong with my flying and that I had nothing to worry about.'

But, on the day of the test in late February 1941, it was 'raining cats and dogs'. Rusty had the controls for only two or three minutes before the instructor brought the plane down. He was expecting to be re-tested the following day. Instead, the chief flight instructor told him cursorily: 'You Australians are too confident and think you know everything.' He was officially out.[2] Snow, smarting on Rusty's behalf, suggested he would leave too. The RAF made it very clear it was not in the business of wasting time and money training pilots to then permit them to transfer out. Snow, too, would be recorded as having failed, something his ego resisted.

'It's possible I will try to join Greg in Egypt or Palestine', Rusty told the family in a sombre letter home.

His brother was by then an Australian Army captain serving with the 20 Anti Tank Regiment, part of the 9th Australian Division, in the Middle East.

'My plans are quite indefinite. All the same I have no intention whatsoever of remaining in the Air Force.'

Many of us like to think we are the masters of our own destiny. When we find ourselves at one of the many, inevitable crossroads in life, whatever direction we choose sets in train the various sequences of events that define us. With the armed forces, there's only one big decision. Once you're in, people you mainly don't know, and who mainly don't know you, make decisions that determine your future, often while sitting at a desk, very far away.

Whether, in the process, those faceless men end up putting you, and not the other bloke, in harm's way in war is determined by what? Fate, God, luck or maybe that notoriously unreliable science of scrutinising the best available intelligence at the time?

Rusty might have never become a pilot. Rusty and John's paths might never again have crossed. Rusty might, in fact, have joined his brother Greg in the Middle East. Greg did cable Rusty to let him know he could help arrange for him to transfer to the army, so they could fight side by side.

But in March 1941, before Greg's cable arrived, Rusty was sent to the group headquarters in the capital, Salisbury (now Harare), for an interview. There was an Australian liaison officer attached to the Empire Training Scheme on the interview panel.

To say there were tensions emerging in this ambitious global training scheme would be an understatement. The RAF was in charge, but the British were relying heavily on large numbers of recruits from the dominions. Disagreements and misunderstandings were simmering, or worse, at every level between the Australians and the Brits, and to a lesser extent between the Australians and the other Allied air forces, over everything from pay and promotions to the definition of roles and administrative procedures.

In particular, the Australian government had been lobbying for a mechanism by which the interests of Australian personnel could be looked after. Various proposals, such as the establishment of a dedicated Australian base or reception centre in Britain, for example, had been rebuffed. The RAF was under intense stress and treated the Empire Training Scheme like a global aircrew production line. Australian RAAF squadrons were on the drawing board but in the meantime Australian aircrew were absorbed as quickly as possible into RAF squadrons with no regard for the operational benefits of cohesion and morale that keeping countrymen together might have offered. The first few thousand Australians were scattered so widely across the RAF that it was hard for any Australian official to keep track of them. In this rush to the front-line, accident rates, too, were mounting.[3]

There were plenty of terse exchanges, officially and otherwise. However, a barely legible footnote in 8 point type in an Australian War Memorial history by John Herington probably says much more than a wordy account of long forgotten cables. 'The illusion that Australians would not conform to normal service discipline died hard among professional [British] soldiers and airmen.'[4]

In particular, the British didn't understand the Australians' resistance to their RAF's two-tiered hierarchy for pilots. On graduating Australian trainees were divided. A small number with the highest marks (and, perhaps, the most compatible pedigrees—school cadets, sporting prowess, private schools and so on) were commissioned as RAAF pilot officers, giving them immediate entree into a separate world reserved for their counterparts in the RAF officers' elite. The rest filled various non-commissioned ranks such as flight sergeant, and were shunted off into their separate facilities and mess. (The South Africans overcame this same issue by simply commissioning all their pilots as officers.)

Herington noted:

> It was natural for groups of airmen who had left Australia together with a common purpose, trained together . . . to retain for each other the warm affection engendered by their common life experience, regardless of the fact that some were now officers and some other ranks.
>
> This camaraderie in off duty hours, regarded as entirely natural by men from the Dominions, was considered undesirable by many United Kingdom commanding officers who attempted to segregate officers and sergeants.

Rusty had 'an excellent hearing' from the interview panel. He was immediately told he was to be posted to undertake the next stage of training. He was staying in southern Rhodesia and was going to train as a fighter pilot at the Cranborne aerodrome, just outside Salisbury.

On 28 April he wrote home with the terrific news that he had passed with flying colours. He had his 'wings', and was now just waiting to be posted to an operational training squadron, then into operations.

He was a sergeant, not a commissioned officer, despite having been interviewed for an officer's role with Snow before his ill-fated test. He and the rest of the sergeants and flight sergeants had exactly the same skills as pilot officers, and faced just the same risks. How ludicrous this division must have seemed to pilots heading for the spartan life of the Western Desert where this line could only be delineated by separate tents. When every man was forced to sleep in a hole dug in the sand alongside a slit trench for air raids, what additional comfort might an officer be afforded? Perhaps a bigger hole?

What Rusty did not yet know was that Greg, his constant companion in childhood and later at boarding school, was already dead. He had been killed in action in Tobruk in mid-April 1941, almost two weeks earlier.

The Italians, reinforced by the first of the Afrika Korps led by the German 'Desert Fox', Field Marshal Erwin Rommel, had launched a major assault on Tobruk and its harbour earlier that month. Greg was among the first wave of casualties.

Tobruk was critical to the Allies' defence of Egypt and the Suez Canal. Without access to the port of Tobruk, the Axis forces had to lug most of their supplies overland from Tripoli across 1500 kilometres of desert, diverting energy and effort away from their strategic goals. Rommel wrongly assumed that the outnumbered, mostly Australian, Allied forces trapped in Tobruk would capitulate. An extraordinary siege ensued. The 9th Australian Division held the port against constant enemy bombardments and in dire conditions over many months. The Germans tried to demean the Australians by dubbing them the 'rats of Tobruk'. The Australians laughed and embraced the label with pride.[5]

> These men from the docksides of Sydney and the sheep stations of the Riverina presented such a picture of downright toughness with their gaunt, dirty faces, huge boots, revolvers stuffed in their pockets, gripping their rifles with huge shapeless hands, shouting and grinning—always grinning—that the mere sight of them must have disheartened enemy troops,

wrote war correspondent Alan Moorehead of the arrival of the Australians, in his famous firsthand account of the Desert War.[6]

Two days later, the news reached Rusty in Rhodesia.

'Please keep your chin up and keep on smiling. Do it for my sake', Rusty pleaded with his mother, in a hastily written note home. 'These blows are coming to mothers all over the world . . . [but] after the finish of this there will be no Germany and the world will be able to live in peace, but until then a good many hard knocks must be balanced with harder knocks.'

Rusty tried to allay her fears that she would lose him too, a subject that became a familiar thread in his letters home. A few weeks later, as his advanced training continued, he described his newly cautious demeanour. 'I go up with the other blokes as the safety pilot—that is how safe I am. If I think a bloke is not doing what he should I just take over and fly the aeroplane myself.

'So now you can see that I take no chances or risks with aeroplanes. My flying at present is very good . . . that, of course, comes from flying very carefully, very correctly and practising over and over what you have been taught.'

By June, Rusty was a flight sergeant with No. 71 Operational Training Unit RAF in Egypt and by August he was cleared for a combat posting to No. 33 Squadron RAF operating over the Western Desert.

He went into battle with the steel hard resolve of a young man who had suffered a deep personal loss and that same characteristic toughness that Moorehead, an Australian journalist working for a British newspaper, had immediately noticed in the Australian troops on the ground.

On and off, throughout 1941, John was in hospital in Bulawayo or convalescing in Durban on sick leave. In between, he continued to instruct or to fulfil a new, risky role. He had been made a test pilot, the first person to take up one of the many different planes assembled in Durban, having arrived in pieces on ships. He was also on call to fly dignitaries in an ever-increasing range of aircraft types.

John was struggling. He lost weight. His opportunity to fight in the war he had seen coming as far back as 1937 floated further out of reach every time his fever spiked, muddling his thoughts and blurring his vision. I have no record of the final diagnosis. He could have picked up malaria in his frequent travels. He may, too, have been suffering from African sleeping sickness. Stinging tsetse flies that carry the voracious parasite that causes the illness were also prevalent in the area.

So much idle time wasn't welcome. South Africa, wrote John, is 'lovely country to look at'. But the more he understood how things worked across the southern African continent, the more uncomfortable he felt. 'Internally it is absolutely rotten . . . the politics is rotten', he wrote.

But, for all his interest in politics and the serious stuff of life, John couldn't help seeing the ridiculous. 'Did you hear about the British planter who came out to Africa?' he wrote to Mildred and Len. He planted pawpaws and waited and waited, but they bore no fruit. Finally he asked for help and another planter pointed out that he had put the male pawpaw trees on one side of the mountain and the female pawpaw trees on the other side. The new arrival was outraged. 'Pray, good sir, you cad!,' he declared. 'Do you think I would come all the way out here just to pimp for pawpaws?'

20
TO WAR IN THE DESERT

Most Australians imagined they had gone to war to defend the Mother Country against Nazi expansionism, yet they now found themselves fighting, on the ground and in the air, in the vast Western Desert that stretched inland from the north coast of Africa, a largely lifeless expanse of sand fringed by the beaches, coastal ports and crystal-clear waters of the Mediterranean Sea.

To wage war in the desert is like engaging the enemy at sea. There is nowhere to hide, no relief from the constant battering of the elements, no source of provisions or fuel; just vulnerable huddles of sun-burnished men dragging their every mouthful of water, their stores and every piece of equipment with them as they alternatively advance, then retreat, across an ocean of uninhabited sand.

On many consecutive afternoons, or even over many successive days, the *khaseem* blew, bringing everyone and everything to a standstill. With barely a rise or fall in the eternally flat desert landscape to impede its progress this 'most hellish wind on earth' gathered speed and sucked up great quantities of sand and dust from the south as it bore down on the northern coastal fringe of the African continent.[1] Everything was suffused in an eerie yellow light. Particles as fine as baking powder snaked in crazy, erratic lines across the few sealed roadways. Windows of cars and trucks were wound up tight against the grit, but it seeped in anyway, rising up through the engine, finding its way through even the tiniest of cracks. It crept up noses and down throats, matted hair and smarted and irritated eyes and skin.[2] Even goggles failed as troops and grounded aircrew groped their way around in the half-light, waiting for it to pass.

In Egypt, during the Odurman Campaign in 1898 to retake the Sudan, one of the officers at the 4th Hussars attached to the 21st Lancers was a young man called Winston Churchill. Already a budding war correspondent, he described the environs of the Upper Nile in his classic 1902 book, *The River War*.[3]

> Level plains of smooth sand—a little rosier than buff, a little paler than salmon—are interrupted only by occasional peaks of rock—black, stark and shapeless. Rainless storms dance tirelessly over the hot crisp surface of the ground. The earth burns with the quenchless thirst of ages and in the steel blue sky scarcely a cloud obstructs the unrelenting triumph of the sun.

But, for Churchill and many others who followed there was one fine hour every day when the colours of the river and the desert were transformed to reveal a rare, unearthly beauty:[4]

> Just before the sun sets towards the western cliffs a delicious flush brightens and enlivens the landscape. It is as though some titanic artist in an hour of inspiration were retouching the picture, painting in dark, purple shadows among the rocks, strengthening the lights on the sand, gilding and beautifying everything and making the scene live. The river . . . turns from muddy brown to silver grey. The sky from a dull blue deepens into violet in the west. Everything under that magic touch becomes vivid and alive.

In 1941, the Desert War, too, inspired hard men in spite of the prevailing challenges on the ground. 'The war in Africa is quite different from the war in Europe. It is absolutely individual,' noted the German commander of Panzer Regiment 5, Lieutenant Joachim Schorm,[5] in his diaries detailing the battle for Tobruk.

> Here there are not masses of men and material. Nobody and nothing can be concealed. Whether in battle between opposing land forces or between those of the air, or between both, it is the same sort of fight, face to face, each side thrusts and counter thrusts. If the struggle were not so brutal, so entirely without rules, one would be inclined to think of the romantic idea of a knight's tourney.

The Allied fighter pilots had also long imagined themselves in such terms.

'The lionisation of the fighter pilot, who appeared to fight an old-fashioned war of chivalric duelling, facilitated the notion that air power was a 'civilised' form of war, the antithesis of the mechanised mass slaughter which characterised the war in the trenches between 1914 and 1918', comments Martin Francis in *The Flyer*.[6]

'In a fighter plane, I believe we have found a way to return to war as it ought to be, war which is individual combat between two people, in which one either kills or is killed', a young Richard Hillary had declared even before joining John's training squadron in Scotland back in 1939. 'It's exciting, it's individual, and it's disinterested.'

When Rusty arrived in Egypt in June 1941, the pendulum was swinging back in the Allies' favour after their success in holding and securing Tobruk.

The seesawing fortunes of the Allied and the Axis forces over the period from 1940 to 1943 have been described in great detail by many historians, observers and participants with varying degrees of eloquence. Every commentator, expert or otherwise, makes the same fundamental point: geography imposed upon both sides, with roughly equal burden, formidable logistics constraints. With the Allied forces based in Egypt to the east, and the Axis forces staging out of Libya to the west, both sides alternatively struck out to conquer only to be forced back into retreat, several times over, at great human cost.

'The ancient law of the desert was, in fact, coming into play', observed Moorehead, referring to the belief that the desert could, in fact, never be claimed.

> One did not occupy the desert any more than one occupied the sea. One simply took up a position (usually nothing more than a pair of coordinates on a map) for a day or a week . . .
>
> The essential governing principle was that desert forces must be mobile: they were seeking not the conquest of territory or positions but combat with the enemy. We were hunting men, not land, as a warship will hunt another warship and care nothing for the sea on which the action is fought.

The trouble was that the farther you got away from your base, the nearer the retreating enemy got to his. Consequently, as you got weaker, the enemy got stronger. That meant any advance, by either side, was anchored in the realities of supply. For every kilometre gained, supply vehicles carrying water, fuel, ammunition and food had to devote more of their precious fuel just to reaching their forward bases. At some point, the law of diminishing returns would prevail and the logistics burden would become untenable. Thus the advance would inevitably falter.[7] The potential solution was to capture ports along the coast, but access by sea, too, proved dangerous and difficult.

The role of the Allied air force in the Desert War was unlike its role in the skies over Europe. It was as unique as the conflict itself. Fighter pilots did engage, one on one, in the knightly duels they called dogfights. But, increasingly the agile single-engine fighters

Mildred Williams with John as a baby in Wellington, NZ, 1919. (Williams family collection)

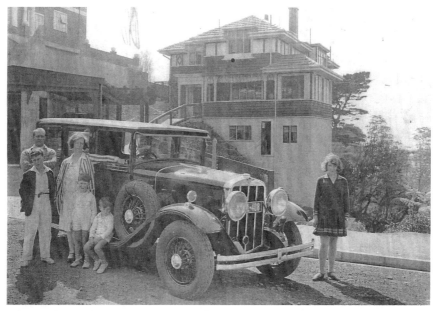

The Williams family at home in Wellington, NZ, late 1920s. From left to right, Llewellyn, John (in front, standing) Mildred, David, Barry and Suzanne. (Williams family collection)

Manly Amateur Swimming Club Juniors, NSW Champions, 1935. John, middle of back row. (Photo courtesy of Manly Library Local Studies Centre)

Surfing at Manly Beach, mid 1930s. (Photo courtesy of Manly Library Local Studies Centre)

John riding his beloved wooden long board at Manly Beach, 1935. (Williams family collection)

Manly Life Saving Club junior surf boat crew, Australian champions, 1935. John at rear. (Photo courtesy of Manly Library Local Studies Centre)

John's German-born surfing mate, Hans Wicke, second from left, who became Australian board riding champion before being interned during World War II. (Photo courtesy of Manly Library Local Studies Centre)

John representing the Sydney Church of England Grammar School (Shore) in the Rugby First XVs.
(Courtesy of the Shore Archives)

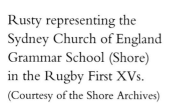

Rusty representing the Sydney Church of England Grammar School (Shore) in the Rugby First XVs.
(Courtesy of the Shore Archives)

Sydney Harbour defences, 1941. (Photo courtesy of Manly Library Local Studies Centre)

Manly beachside defences at Queenscliff, the northern end of Manly Beach, circa 1940. (Photo courtesy of Manly Library Local Studies Centre)

John in England after taking up his short service commission with the Royal Air Force, 1938. (Williams family collection)

John in the Western Desert, 1942.
(Williams family collection)

John shortly after taking over command of the 450 Squadron RAAF, Western Desert, 1942. (Williams family collection)

John on receiving his 'wings' in England in 1938. (Williams family collection)

John with Kittyhawk OK M AK634 that bore his personal moniker 'Mandrake' the Magician in the Western Desert, 1942.

Rusty in RAAF uniform, circa 1940. (Kierath family collection)

Rusty with a Kittyhawk of the 450 Squadron RAAF in the Western Desert, 1941. (Kierath family collection)

Allied air force camp in the Western Desert, 1942 (Kierath family collection)

The scene following a rare downpour in the Western Desert, early 1942.
(Photo taken by Rusty of unknown subject, Kierath family collection)

The 450 Squadron RAAF in the Western Desert, 1942, John front row far left. (Williams family collection)

International Red Cross record of Australian POWs in Stalag Luft III, 1943. John, back row, third from the left, Paul Brickhill, author of *The Great Escape*, front row, third from left. (Williams family collection)

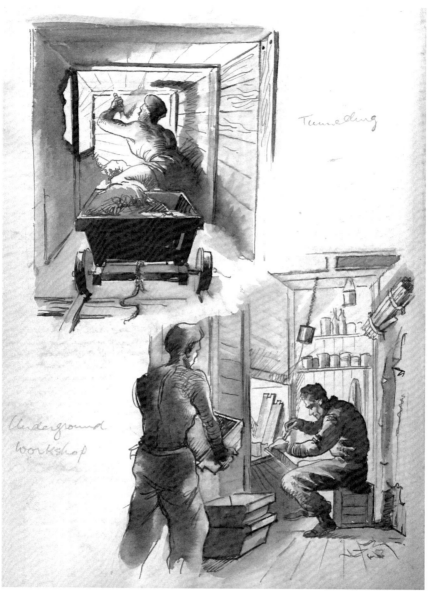

Images from the notebook of Flight Lieutenant Ley Kenyon DFC, the British camp artist at Stalag Luft III who secretly documented the construction and progress of the tunnel. These images show the underground workshop John's carpentry team worked in and the underground 'railway' they devised and built.
(Images courtesy of the RAF Museum, London, © The Kenyon estate)

The mug shots of John and Rusty taken by the Kripo (Nazi era police) in Reichenberg Police Station, in Nazi-occupied Czechoslovakia, shortly after their capture, showing their escape outfits. These are the last photos of the friends. (Original photos held at the National Archives, Kew, England, copies in the Williams and Kierath family collections)

Ley Kenyon secretly sketched a memorial service held for the executed escapees in front of the memorial the POWs had constructed inside Stalag Luft III. (Images courtesy of the RAF Museum, London, © The Kenyon estate)

The author at the memorial that marks the exit of the tunnel 'Harry' today within the grounds of former POW camp, on the 70th anniversary of the escape in 2014. (Williams family collection)

Michal Holy, in the cockpit for Czech Airlines, and in front of the permanent memorial he commissioned and constructed at Most, in the Czech Republic, in recognition of John, Rusty, Leslie Bull and Jerzy Mondschein. (Photos courtesy of Michal Holy)

were called on to support Allied ground forces in very practical ways by strafing enemy supply convoys along the coastal roads, by providing high cover for bombers, by flying reconnaissance missions and offensive patrols and later[8] by operating as innovative 'hybrid' aircraft. Once it was realised that Kittyhawk fighters could carry two 110 kilogram or even two 225 kilogram bombs on racks underneath, the fighter pilots of the Desert War became bombers too. Needless to say, shortages of aircraft and especially of experienced pilots, and the regular losses of equipment and lives, persisted.

Officially, Australian troops and aircrew were sent to the Middle East because of Australia's particular strategic interest in keeping the Suez Canal under British control, and so preserving the Mediterranean route from England to the Pacific.[9] But, although Gallipoli overshadowed all else in the Australian public's memory of the Great War, the Middle East, too, had a special historic significance. Many Australian troops fought and died in the region in that previous conflict, the first arriving in Egypt in December 1914.[10]

It seems just as likely that what the British and others politely referred to as the Australians' 'toughness' was also taken into account when deciding what kind of men the Allies needed in the desert. There were, of course, many much more colourful terms bandied about.

Rusty might have been lulled into a false sense of security in his first months in the desert in mid-1941. Both exhausted sides then seemed to be trying to catch their breath. The lull meant intensive flight training could be undertaken and loud, laughing Australian pilots weaved their way in and out of the narrow streets of Cairo on leave or were dispatched by train to the lovely beachside towns of Palestine.

Rusty told the family not to expect much real news. 'In fact, I should think they [my letters] must be awful to read. This is of course, due to censorship and I cannot tell you very much of what I do, or where I fly. However, I will have a nice lot of things to tell you on a nice sunny day, somewhere in Narromine sometime—before very long I think, the way things are going.'

He did voice his approval of his large shared tent—dug, as they were, into a pit in the sand—and the various luxuries it contained like a couple of empty kerosene cans for storage and an old wooden door serving as a mat for the floor (later to be upgraded to 'a fine carpet of sandbags—minus the sand'). He also relished his squadron's proximity to the 'old Med', and the chance to take a regular evening swim to 'get the dirt and dust out of you'.

He's in a mixed nationality squadron, the No. 33 RAF, flying Hurricanes with plenty of 'good blokes and coves' including Brits, Americans, Canadians, Australians, Rhodesians and South Africans.

More than anything else, Rusty is thrilled when a quiet 'revolution' sweeps through the desert squadrons, opening a new door. The squadron leader of the No. 3 squadron RAAF, the first Australian squadron to go into operations, Peter Jeffrey, has taken on the British establishment. With the backing of the squadron doctor, he is insisting every pilot, regardless of rank, be afforded access to the officers' mess (now renamed the pilots' mess). 'If I am going to fly with a man, I am going to talk to that man', he is often quoted as saying. Or something along those lines. The RAF fell in and issued a similar 'democratising' directive across the desert. The Australians were jubilant. A few RAF officers held out. They continued to gather in one corner of their shared tent, as far away as possible from the NCOs.[11]

Rusty was so pleased that he detailed the various menus at some length. Breakfast of grapefruit and rockmelon (cantaloup), fried eggs, tomatoes, sausages, fried bread and tea or coffee. Lots of fresh vegetables with lunch and dinner. All the cigarettes and beer you wanted at reasonable prices from the bar. Then there are the services on offer for officers: their tailor, their barber and laundry. 'I patronise the whole three.'

'The mess is much more comfortable and the general atmosphere is very much nicer and the food is excellent ... when you think that we are miles from anywhere and altogether very happy.'

Rusty was less than happy, though, when he made his first trip to Cairo, a crowded, energetic and grubby city that felt like one giant bazaar. The RAF's flirtation with egalitarianism did not reach beyond the desert camps' boundaries. Many of Cairo's clubs and facilities, too, only opened their doors to officers; here flight sergeants were still left standing on the steps. Unless they went to the Melody Club; there the band was barricaded behind barbed wire to protect them from brawlers.[12]

That might explain one anecdote in which Rusty, with some mates in tow, swung past a well-patronised up-market Cairo brothel and flung a burning condom filled with paper through the door to set off the fire alarm. There must have been at least some satisfaction in watching the officers run out into the streets in various states of undress.

When the first Axis air raid hit his squadron's camp in August, Rusty was sleeping like a baby.

Suddenly, it was as light as day and the whoosh of planes overhead was followed immediately by the whistle of falling bombs. 'I was under my bed before the bombs hit, and after they exploded I wasted no time getting to a shelter.'

Letters were, of course, not only tailored to the particular requirements of the censors but to the sensibilities of worried families. Rusty's mother, understandably, could not shake her anxiety, especially as her gregarious youngest son was now serving so close to his brother's grave. Official records show Rusty escaped death twice in September 1941; once when he was strafed by enemy fighters as he took off and then when his squadron was 'bounced' in the air (attacked from above) by Messerschmitt Bf

109s, the Luftwaffe's main single-engine fighter, blowing a hole in his wing and wounding him with shrapnel.[13] These incidents are not mentioned in his letters home.

Rusty did, however, explain in passing the loss of the pullover and pyjamas sent out by his mother, blaming 'unfriendly enemy action'. Given the value of aircraft, it was routine for pilots to keep a small personal kit in their planes in case they needed to take off fast, and later land at another airfield out of the enemy's range.

'I had them in my kite [his plane] when they [the Germans] paid us a visit . . . my kite caught alight and I wasn't a bit keen on leaving the dugout [shelter] to take my things out.'

Throughout 1941, the Allies continued to gain ground. But the direction of the wind was slowly changing. Rusty would soon find himself and the rest of the squadron, officers and NCOs alike, on hard rations of tinned bully beef or something known as 'Maconachies'. This ready-to-eat tinned stew was originally devised in the late 1880s for troops fighting in the Boer War, and then sustained the troops in the trenches between 1914 and 1918. In the desert the boys joked that the RAF must have picked up some surplus stock; it tasted like it had been left over from World War I.

From London, Winston Churchill, now the British prime minister, was taking a particularly keen interest in the Allies' progress, or otherwise, in the North African theatre. His commanders in the field could not help but feel burdened by his constant scrutiny; his eyes, and his opinions, followed their every move.

As the young Churchill had observed during his own World War I experiences in the region there is another inevitable moment in the daily cycle of desert life that follows those lovely sunsets: 'Then the sun sinks altogether behind the rocks, the colour fades out of the sky, the flush off the sands, and gradually everything darkens and grows grey—like a man's cheek when he is bleeding to death'.[14]

In Southern Rhodesia, John had been discharged from Bulawayo Hospital only to be readmitted six times by September 1941. He was not yet 22, but the RAF had particular plans for him, so his recovery was important. This was made quite clear in his promotion in August, despite his illness, to flight lieutenant. In October he was admitted to an RAF hospital, probably in Durban but the handwriting on this page of his ageing RAF service record is illegible.[15]

More and more Australian pilots were arriving in the Middle East. 'They didn't have the slightest idea about discipline or drill or anything', said Peter Down, who came out from Britain to command the largely Australian No. 112 Squadron RAF in early 1942,[16] the first squadron John would later join for operations.

'They used to walk around in those Australian hats turned up on one side and in an odd assortment of old Italian uniforms—or anything but their own air force equipment—and those big army desert boots with rubber soles.'

'It was all very basic, you lived in tents, you were covered in sand and with these everlasting sandstorms you were eating and breathing sand,' he laughed.

There were agreements in place to ensure Australian aircrew and ground crew would not merely be absorbed by the RAF but that distinct RAAF squadrons would be formed in the Middle East. In practice, this was proving very difficult. The first Australian squadron, the permanent No. 3 fighter squadron RAAF, had been deployed to the Middle East in 1940, but building additional Australian squadrons was frustrated by various catch-22s. Newly trained Australian ground personnel for the proposed new RAAF fighter squadron, No. 450, had arrived in May 1941 but the squadron could not go into action without experienced pilots. The cables snapping backwards and forwards between Australia and Middle East HQ kept getting stuck on the same issue of the lack of experienced Australian aircrew making it 'militarily unsound to allocate any of the all-too-few fighter aircraft to No. 450 in order to give it operational status'. Instead it was combined, in waiting. The ground crew were deployed to the combat-experienced No. 260 Squadron RAF, to begin training in real operations.[17]

On 14 June 1941, the Australian Air Board had told the British Air Ministry: 'There is no means other than by exchanges with RAF personnel' that the new Australian squadrons could acquire the experience they needed.[18]

John was an RAF officer, but he was also an Australian. He had not been in combat, but his considerable experience in the air and in leadership, and his outstanding skill as a pilot, marked him out for one such exchange. He could be very useful. The RAF was keen to prepare him to be seconded to the RAAF, specifically the fledgling 450 Squadron. By the end of October 1941, John was finally well enough to be discharged from hospital for the last time. He was finally going forward for operational training, then straight into operations.

But there was one last, stupendous adventure on offer in Africa.

With three other pilots, John was flying himself to the Western Desert in an Empire Boat C Class. These flying boats were the ultimate in luxury first-class air travel. They were originally fitted with beds and such spacious cabins as to allow passengers to play quoits or mini golf en route. With so few airports available, flying boats could use any stretch of calm water and so link Britain to even the most remote corners of its empire.

By 1941, many of the flying boats, including several that once belonged to Qantas and Imperial Airways, had been fitted with underwing bomb racks and guns.[19]

The RAF pilots were taking the flying boat from Durban to Cairo, a four-day trip with twelve refuelling stops and—as the zigzagging nature of the route suggested—probably some war business along the way. The trip took John to Mozambique, then inland into the heart of the Congo, landing on Lake Albert. From the Congo they headed back out to the east coast of Africa and hopped up the coast via Tanzania, to Kenya. Then, they turned inland again.

The final stretch was one of the greatest journeys on earth. Lumbering along in the flying boat, like a huge bulging metal pelican cruising well out of harm's way, they located and landed on Lake Victoria, then crossed the vast lake and set course up the Nile. For two days, they hopped their way north, from the southern White Nile to the upper Nile that runs through Sudan and finally into Cairo. On 27 January 1942, just over four years after leaving Sydney, John finally reached the front-line, with more than 1000 hours flying time in at least 20 aircraft types under his belt.

REUNION

Once the British commander of No. 112 got over his surprise at the dishevelled appearance of his Australian pilots and the strange egalitarian arrangements in the mess, he discovered that they were 'marvellous in the air'. Even better, at the first sign of trouble they 'flock around you like birds'.[1]

That his bunch of Australian pilots had decided to don various parts of scavenged Italian uniforms simply marked them, in their opinion, as seasoned men. After the Italian invasion of Egypt of September 1940, the Allies had rapidly pushed back, overrunning Italian positions well inside Libya by early 1941. More immediately fascinating than the Italians' strategic shortcomings, which would precipitate Rommel's entry into the fray, were the riches left behind in the hurriedly evacuated Italian camps. Apart from jaw-dropping volumes of high-quality food like fresh baked bread, bottled cherries, hams and huge wheels of Parmesan cheese, there was 'an abundance of fine clothing of every kind', including the kind of showy finery the fascists favoured, 'like polished jackboots richly spurred and pale blue sashes and belts finished with great sashes and feathered and embroidered hats and caps'.[2] To the Australians and many other servicemen, this opportunity to replenish their wardrobes, both ironic and practical, was marvellous fun.

Down also discovered that the Australian pilots of 112 came with their own relatively luxurious rations. As part of the deal between Churchill and Menzies to deploy Australians in the Western Desert was an assurance on the part of the Brits that the Aussies 'would always be supplied with fresh vegetables'. And so the squadron had its own three-tonne truck dedicated to 'charging the 500 miles [800 km] up and back to Cairo', over and over again, to fill up with vegetables and barrels of beer. So appealing was this arrangement that, on many occasions, when dawn broke, various Allied tanks and other army vehicles could be found parked outside the 112 mess, their drivers and passengers having 'popped over' to partake of refreshments the previous evening and ended up camping overnight.

After completing operational training, John's first combat posting is to Down's No. 112. He selects his own non-regulation attire and settles on an old khaki shirt and shorts and open leather sandals. This flimsy outfit also becomes his flying suit.

John and Rusty are now back in the same neighbourhood, if that's the right term for a series of tent encampments and slit trenches scattered across the same stretch of desert. By early 1942, 450 Squadron RAAF—soon to become famous as 'The Desert Harassers'—had finally drafted enough experienced combat pilots, including Rusty, to, literally, get off the ground. Rusty is now a probationary commissioned officer. Both Rusty and John fall under the same command; Nos. 112 and 250 Squadrons RAF and Nos. 3 and 450 Squadrons RAAF were being brought under the operational umbrella of the new Desert Air Force 239 Wing. The wing trained, fought and socialised together.

John and Rusty were now based within easy reach of their mates, each other and the Mediterranean beaches. The connections from back home lifted everyone's mood.

'[It] makes a big difference when you meet up with someone you know', Rusty told Ada.

'They were close friends', said J.D. 'Jack' Gleeson, part of their same tight-knit group of desert pilots.[3] In a letter written in the late 1980s, Gleeson recalled John and Rusty's friendship as being cemented by the school connection and the common Rugby training days. In fact, two other former schoolmates were also flying with the No. 450 Squadron RAAF.

'Whenever anyone feels like a party and the beer is "on", it's about the easiest thing in this desert to have the time of your life', Rusty told Ada. 'They've got one on a piano accordion and one on the piccolo and plenty of well lubricated voices for drinking songs', he wrote home.

Of the few neutral topics available for letters home that were sure to slide past the censors, sport, food and the weather were right up the top of the list. The joy of swimming was only amplified by the heat and the limited desert ration of about 2 litres of water per man per day, for drinking and washing.[4] Consequently, the same dirty clothes were simply put back on every morning. John allocated some of his water to shaving. Rusty grew a beard but that was soon matted with fine sand and dust.[5] (Beards prompted the Afrika Korps to insult the Australians as 'Barbarians'—it slid like water off a duck's back.) The intense pleasure of a few days' leave to go into Cairo, book into a modest hotel, and run a bath, is only rivalled by a train trip north to the beaches of Gaza, with their modest surf breaks.

The boys discovered the desert camps and Cairo were not just awash with Australians, but with former surf-lifesavers. By 1941 over half the national membership of the Australian surf-lifesaving clubs had signed up. 'The loyalty, efficiency and discipline gained as members of our organisation will help them through . . . no matter how hard the going, they will come up for more', opined *Surf in Australia*, expressing its pride 'in the quantity and quality of the boys enlisting for sterner duties overseas'.[6]

Various donors, including Manly Council, managed to inveigle several surf-lifesaving reels onto troop ships heading for the Middle East. From 1941 on, the Australians were running formal surf-lifesaving carnivals and events in Gaza and swimming competitions in the Mediterranean waters off the north African coast. Ostensibly, there was national pride to be enjoyed in bringing modern lifesaving techniques to Palestine. In reality, it was effective, morale-boosting escapism for the Australians, complete with many of the familiar and fondly regarded rituals of a surf carnival back home. John had his surf-lifesaving 'blue book' with him. It's neither the Bible nor a talisman, but something in between. As sentimental as it might seem, there was something about just touching its cover and leafing through its pages that connected him back to Manly Beach.

'I'm afraid we Sydneysiders have been badly spoiled', wrote the former captain of Manly's rival surf-lifesaving club, Bondi, Carl Jefferson, in early 1942.[7] 'Lazing in the sun at Gaza alongside a surf reel provided by a Sydney council and listening to the Sunday afternoon band program, I have tried to believe for a few moments that I was back on my own beach . . .' Not bad, considering there was a war on—but definitely not as good as back home.

Writing around the military developments of the time risks implying that the tent villages of the Western Desert might have made a decent setting for a wartime comedy, in the tradition of *Dad's Army* or *M.A.S.H.* That's not the case.

Firstly, 1942 brought several very significant challenges. The Japanese had attacked Pearl Harbor, bringing the Americans into the war. Singapore would soon fall and the ongoing advance of the Japanese across the Pacific would raise anxiety among the Australians troops and RAAF air and ground crews, increasingly worried about their own families and keen to be redeployed to fight in the Pacific.

In the Western Desert, Squadron Leader of No. 3 RAAF Nicky Barr had been deeply troubled over one particular clash with the Luftwaffe a couple of months earlier and was worried about what it might mean for the direction of the war.[8]

He had personally gone in to help when he saw a Messerschmitt 109 'shooting the hell out of one of the Tomahawks' and drove the German plane off its tail. He had watched his pilot, Dudley Parker, bail out, so didn't think much more about it. Parker didn't return. Even a few days later Parker hadn't come back. Later, a South African padre came into camp to tell Barr what he had seen; the clash had taken place over South African positions. Four Messerschmitts had dropped down and followed Parker's fall, each taking pot shots until they had cut him out of his parachute and had watched him accelerate into the earth. The South Africans had retrieved and buried Parker's body.

'This came as a great shock to us. We [had] always thought . . . that this type of aerial warfare was basically a gentlemen's war, but from then on we didn't consider it that way.

'[It] really upset me, and it was then I thought "Well, there's nothing, no gallantry about this at all. It's all out war. Kill or be killed."'

On 5 January 1942, a convoy of German reinforcements arrived in Tripoli, setting the stage for Rommel to hit back.

Meanwhile, nearly all the Allied desert pilots were being converted to American Kittyhawks, or P40s. It was a more modern fighter and an improvement on the slower Tomahawk on which it was based, but there were some who still considered it inferior to the German technology the RAF pilots were up against. Squadron Leader Down, of the 112s, had previously been flying out of Britain, where the RAF's highest performance planes were based. He, for one, was furious.

> They were awful things . . . in my view, they weren't operational aircraft compared to the Hurricane or Spitfire. They were slower, they were more lumbering, they only had four guns [other models had six], they didn't have the manoeuvrability, they didn't have the power and they were tricky to land because they had a very narrow undercarriage . . . Actually I sent a note to Middle East HQ saying that in my view this

was not an operational aircraft in any accepted sense and could we have Hurricanes or Spitfires.[9]

Down got a rude note back, warning him 'not to spread alarm and despondency'. At the time, no one disputed that the Kittyhawks had limitations in combat against the Luftwaffe's powerful, fast and agile Messerschmitt 109s and their twin-engine heavy fighter-bombers, the Junkers (JU 88).

But the stage had been set and the Kittyhawk would have to do. 'The Americans might have thought they [the Kittyhawks] were marvellous, but we didn't . . . but I suppose they were better than nothing', Down conceded.

Alamein, The Australian Story[10] puts it like this: 'It is difficult, but essential, to try to recapture the uncertainties of the time. In the opening months of 1942 Allied defeat seemed as likely as victory.'

HOLDING YOUR NERVE

War, the saying[1] goes, consists of long periods of intense boredom, punctuated by short periods of intense fear. But for fighter and bomber pilots on operations, fear, in its many guises, was nearly always lingering just out of sight.

Some pilots described fear as useful, even essential, much like pre-race nerves that trigger just the right amount of adrenalin to spur the keenly competitive athlete onto ever-greater things. Or fear as protective, a brake on that almost imperceptible drift into overconfidence or complacency that cost many a pilot his life.

For the new recruits eager to clamber into their first training plane, fear was easy enough to brush off. 'Me not coming back? Ha. You can't think like that—it's always the other bloke who's not coming back.'[2]

It was, of course, much more complicated than that. As each new pilot edged closer and closer to combat, the more important it became to begin that private search for whatever it is within that enables a man to hold his nerve.

Fear and exhilaration were two sides of the same coin. These were young men who had elbowed their way to the front, clamouring for the privilege, the honour, the thrill, of some of the war's most dangerous roles, yet within them all lurked an insidious doubt. When it actually came to it, would they fall short and be exposed as cowards in a culture that expected only courage of men?[3] Even experienced, proven combat pilots could fall victim to the fear of fear. From the smallest seed of anxiety grew the worry that eventually, one day, on take-off they would discover they could no longer handle their plane with the quick, indifferent precision essential to preserve their own life in the brief, hot flash of a down-or-be-downed, kill-or-be-killed dogfight.

Fear was not openly discussed, and neither grief nor shock shown over the constant parade of death and loss as, one after another, colleagues and friends took off but did not return. Instead, they collectively conspired, knowingly and willingly, to barricade their fears and doubts behind a wall of frenetic activity, jocular backslapping, constant banter and humour, sometimes so black it would wind anyone but themselves.

They added new terms to the ever-increasing dictionary of Desert Air Force slang. The small piles of personal possessions of those lost pilots who had 'gone for a Burton'[4] 'were enthusiastically fallen upon by laughing men, rummaging around for souvenirs to loot. A Burton was a wartime British ale, so lost men were imagined somewhere off set, relaxing, having a well-earned drink.

That the odd lost pilot did in fact return, having walked back across the desert from behind enemy lines, was merely cause for great celebration and more fun. Thus the 'Late Arrivals'[5] club was founded, later to be dubbed the 'The Boomerang Club' by the Australians (No. 450 Squadron RAAF), adding to that long-established 'Caterpillar Club' (those who had bailed out, their lives saved by the silk of their parachute) and the Caterpillar plus Goldfish badge Club (those still alive after parachuting out and landing in water).

Observing Desert Air Force pilots in the field, Alan Moorehead wrote:

> They lived sharp, vivid lives. Their response to everything—women, flying, drinking, working—was immediate, positive

and direct. They ate and slept well. There was little subtlety and still less artistry about what they did and said and thought. They had no time for leisure, no opportunity for introspection. They made friends easily. And never again after the speed and excitement of this war would they lead the lives that they had once been designed to lead. They were no material for peace.[6]

This considered account by one of the keenest and most respected observers of the Desert War is not inaccurate. There were many even less-flattering tales to recount, including the penchant of some battle-hardened Australian pilots for riotous evening mess games, such as an odd version of a favourite English pub game in which the competitors sought to pin a man's ears to the dart board by simultaneously unleashing a volley of darts.[7] But to leave the desert pilots here, apparently so heartless and foolhardy, would merely reinforce a superficial stereotype and provide no insight into what later steeled young men like Rusty and John to 'push on'.

'The newspaper picture of the laughing aviator, carelessly risking his life, is not really a flattering likeness. It is no compliment to a man to say he is too insensitive to know when he is in danger,' argued[8] the Oxford historian and author, Lord David Cecil, in 1942.

'The airmen preserve a rigid appearance of imperturbability and good spirits; but one soon begins to realise they are living in a state of tension.'

More than 70 years later, it is easy enough to play the amateur psychologist. Looking back in 1993, Bobby Gibbes, one of Australia's most famous Desert War aces and, coincidently, also a Manly boy, said:[9]

I think you have to be frightened. If you are not frightened you're going to get yourself knocked down . . . I was always very nervous but I think I hid that pretty well from my fellow pilots. Courage and cowardice are pretty well one thing . . . a pilot shows courage by doing things rather than being seen by his friends for what he really is, probably half a coward underneath. I think you used to bulldust quite a bit and carry on [with] a certain amount of bravado.[10]

Gibbes took over the command of No. 3 when Barr was injured in mid-1942. John worked closely with both men as a fellow flight, then squadron, commander within the Desert Air Force's 239 Wing.

Barr said: 'My own form of fear was very deep and internal. I aimed to never show it, but I am not certain I succeeded . . . I always had a feeling that I could handle it, but until you actually experience the situation you don't know.'

The mechanised warfare of World War II offered so many terrifying, terrible, gruesome ways to be injured, maimed or killed—in any of the services and in any of the civilian areas of conflict—that aircrew faced no special horror, except, perhaps, the unique fear of bailing out of a burning plane to discover their parachutes had been burnt off. What they did uniquely face were proportionally much higher casualty rates. Only 2 per cent of Australians who served in World War II crewed on bombers, but they made up 20 per cent of Australian combat deaths. At times, fighter pilots faced even steeper 'attrition rates'.[11]

In World War I, cowardice was seen simply as a failure of will. Many forces executed their own men as deserters or cowards, believing that they were just not putting in sufficient effort to be brave. By World War II, there was some inkling that the accumulation of operational stress might be the result of real, finite human limitations, not flaws in the character of individuals. Still, those pilots who did baulk, right at the beginning or even after serving full tours, were sent home disgraced. They were labelled LMF, or having a lack of moral fibre.

Psychological studies since, based on detailed RAF records of World War II flyers, have concluded that even pilots 'with an average or better capacity for sustained effort' could be expected to undertake fifteen to twenty sorties 'without great effort', but thereafter would face the gradual onset of mental fatigue, then evident 'flying stress' and, without adequate rest and respite from the constant threat of a front-line posting, an ever increasing risk of neurosis.[12] In World War II, 200 hours of operational flying was initially calculated by the Air Ministry as a reasonable limit that would give pilots a fifty-fifty chance of survival. From 1943, a first tour was limited to 30 sorties, and a second tour to 20 for bombers.[13] In the Desert War, fighter-bomber pilots flew many more sorties without a break. Aircraft also were routinely on stand-by if they were not in the air. That meant the men sitting for hours in their cockpits, alert and ready to scramble, in conditions so hot that even brushing the metal of the aircraft blistered their skin.[14]

Psychology has also since devised the 'snake puzzle': that is, the recognition that there is rarely a simple correlation between the degree of peril or risk and the extent of fear experienced by an individual or a group. Fighter pilots demonstrated this perfectly.[15] Although life expectancies for bomber crews were, in general, longer than for fighter pilots, 'bomber crews consistently demonstrated higher levels of fear than fighter pilots. Fighter pilots, in sole control of highly manoeuvrable aircraft, could maintain the myth of being in control of their own fate.'

Roald Dahl, who was a World War II RAF fighter pilot before becoming a well-known author, put it less scientifically: 'Fear creeps closer and closer . . . like a cat stalking a sparrow'. It does not, however, pounce, but simply whispers in a pilot's ear. At first the whisper is heard only at night, then at times during the day, then 'you hear it all day and all night and all of the time'.[16]

How individual pilots armoured themselves against fear ranged from total denial, the firm belief that ill fate would befall 'the other bloke', to a grim acceptance of the inevitability of death and a consequent 'wonderful liberation' from further anxiety.[17] Most pilots accepted that even in a single-engine one-man plane there was always an extra passenger along for the ride.

Some pilots, Hillary included, made a big show of eschewing protective clothing, accepting whatever fate had in store for him. (Hillary was tragically wrong in believing he would be killed instantly, and spared the agony of serious injury, if he did go down. He had chosen not to even pull down his protective goggles, resulting in his eyes being badly burnt.)

When John began flying the Western Desert in early 1942, he was mentally fresh and sharp, and desperate to get into the action. In the pile of letters I have collected over the years from his fellow pilots, they all make the same observation. He was known for two constants: his good spirits, and his shorts and sandals. He never wore protective clothing when going into action.

FLIPPING THE BIRD

Rusty wasn't one to pass up the opportunity for a practical joke, even if it was at the expense of a minor British royal.

In the first half of 1942 there was little else to laugh about. Both sides had been reinforcing their land and air forces for months. Rommel was pushing back very hard against the Allies' significant territorial gains of December, 1941. He intended to finally drive the Allies out of Libya and Egypt and wrest control of the Suez Canal, a feat that would be disastrous for the wider Allied war effort.

In late January 1942 Rommel's new campaign began in earnest. And, it rained. The fleeting joy of rain in the desert soon dissolved into the resulting quagmire.[1] The Allied retreat was a slow, painstaking slog through mud. Planes were grounded. Trucks and vehicles were bogged. No one had ever seen anything like it. Hail pinged off the desert; front-line troops claimed to have seen flakes of snow.[2] Energy and will, too, seemed to drain away into the vast expanse of shallow groundwater, only to then slowly evaporate when the sun reappeared, leaving everyone spent.

By 6 February, the Allies had been forced back to a new defensive position, the Gazala line. They were still well inside the Libyan border and beyond the strategically, and psychologically, critical port of Tobruk. It was an ignominious retreat, nonetheless. The British sought to explain away their failures by mythologising the wily German 'Desert Fox', a master of mobile warfare. Hitler was delighted with the apparent British acknowledgment of his then favourite general.[3] In the Pacific, the Japanese were advancing aggressively. Singapore had fallen, Darwin was bombed.

Then in the Western Desert, both sides paused.

The Duke of Gloucester, Prince Henry, was to make a whistlestop tour of British and Allied forces in the Middle East in April, to boost morale. Rusty, now close to the end of his first operational tour, was selected to lead a fighter formation to escort the duke in.

'I won't comment on our view of the relative value of a visit by HRH compared to other contributions the squadron might have made to the war effort . . . [but] this was generally regarded as a stooge operation', wrote squadron mate[4] Jack Gleeson.

As simple as Rusty's instructions were to intercept the royal transport plane at 500 feet (150 metres), Rusty, somehow, failed to make the planned rendezvous. The royal plane lumbered in on its own. Then, not far behind a perfect fighter formation appeared, flew in low and fast, peeled off dramatically, then finally came in to land.

'The British were not amused at this cavalier treatment of a Royal personage. We did not see it quite the same way,' said Jack.[5] The squadron was even more pleased with Rusty's irregular 'air show' after Prince Henry walked up and down their lines without saying a word. 'Nothing to do with the foul up—of which he was blissfully unaware—we were told this was just his style.'

In May 1942 Rusty's first tour was up. It had been a long, hard slog, despite the levity of his letters and his reputation for letting off steam. Behind it all, he was just as committed as the next man. Now, he was going back to Southern Rhodesia, this time as a flight instructor. His role in the fledgling No. 450 Squadron RAAF, the first of Australia's Empire Training Scheme squadrons, had been vital. Once it had finally been cleared for operations in February 1942, Rusty had been transferred in. That he brought with him much needed operational experience from his stint with the RAF was one thing, but not the only thing that the founding squadron leader of 450 Squadron, Gordon Steege, noticed.

Living, flying and fighting in the desert meant Rusty had arrived at 450 Squadron with a good understanding and acceptance of the harsh realities of squadron life. Many of the new Australian arrivals did not. They were sullen and restless. They railed against water rationing, the sand, the sandstorms and the basic living conditions. Morale was at risk; there was tension in the ranks. It was Rusty who talked them around. He rallied them against a common enemy, he 'got them in line': something Steege would later say he had always been very grateful for.[6]

24
A BIG FLAP

John called it a 'big flap'.

Steeped, as he was, in the air force culture of understatement, this said a lot. There were two good reasons to play things down. First, the RAF's and RAAF's long-standing aversion to 'shooting a line'—that is, to unnecessarily exaggerating or dramatising events, usually to draw attention to oneself. Or, second, as was more likely, unfolding developments were so overwhelmingly alarming that the best way to cope was to look around for some neutral-sounding terms.

In June 1942, John's secondment from the RAF to the RAAF had come through. He was transferred to the No. 450 Squadron RAAF as a flight commander, to lead the 'B' section, marking him as the heir apparent to eventually take over the squadron's command. Like the Rats of Tobruk, the squadron apparently owed its name to the Nazi propaganda broadcaster Lord Haw-Haw, who had dismissed 450 Squadron as 'Australian mercenaries whose harassing tactics were easily beaten off by the Luftwaffe'. And, like the rats of the 9th Australian Division who had held Tobruk, 450 Squadron laughed, called themselves the 'Desert Harassers',[1] and strived to live up to the name.

John would still be flying and planning with the RAF under the 239 Wing structure, but this was his first Australian posting.

From a practical point of view, it wasn't a big change: he was flying with the same group of pilots. But it was a sentimental shift for a young man who had, for so many years now, yearned to go home. Not just for John, but for the entire family. In Sydney, war anxiety was rising with developments in the Pacific—in June, Japanese submarines had entered Sydney Harbour—and there was some quiet pride in knowing that John was now serving under the Australian flag. And there was something reassuring about the Australians' self-image: 'Mates who contained their fear, but freely shared their courage and strength'.[2]

Rommel was already on the move. From the air, his forces could be seen on the horizon 'steadily metamorphosing through the morning haze', until row after row of tanks, army trucks and vehicles came into view, as they advanced on the Allied positions along the Gazala line, about 180 kilometres inside the Libyan border. 'The tanks which led the way formed the chilling shape of a large spear . . . as they charged relentlessly through the dusty, stark landscape', Barr, the commander of No. 3 Squadron RAAF, reported.[3]

'I am sure you agree', the early morning cable to all squadrons from air command snapped on 12 June, 'that (the) visit of Rommel and (his) toughs to our area is a personal insult. Good luck in your reply to his damned cheek'.[4]

The demand on the Kittyhawks was relentless. They were providing high cover for heavier bombers, strafing Rommel's forces with their machine guns, carrying and dropping bombs themselves and taking on Axis planes in aerial combat. Allied planes were even reported in mid-air clashes, still carrying their bombs.[5]

So much was happening in these shrill days of late May and June 1942, so many jubilant 'scores' and tragic losses were logged and diarised that a sandstorm of information obscures and confuses, emulating the chaos on the ground and in the air.

By 17 June, the German fighter planes had been moved forward close to the Gazala line. The Allied defence line ran from the cliffs of Gazala on the coastal road far into the desert. Troops camped on constant alert inside a string of mined and wired boxes, mini fortresses stocked with water and ammunition, intended to hold any advance back, should the Germans break through the tank brigades out front.[6]

John took off with the bombers and fighters of 239 Wing. To avoid detection, the formations flew so high that they pushed their Kittyhawks to the very limit of their technical capabilities. They swung wide out to sea to avoid detection, then back to cross the coast, surprising the Luftwaffe in their new position and destroying or damaging fifteen planes on the ground in a low-level swoop. It wasn't nearly enough. The German land forces just kept coming.

The pilots of 450 Squadron were ordered to move their planes back immediately to Sidi Aziez. The ground crews evacuated. By 4 a.m., the 21st Panzer division was settling down on the landing ground 450 Squadron had only just left. When dawn broke, John was still awake, leading the first pair of reconnaissance planes back over their lost ground. Then, a Messerschmitt 109 came into view.

'For ten minutes we weaved and circled and dived. The German pilot gave me several bursts but missed. Then my turn came and I got in three short bursts and the Messerschmitt hit the ground and exploded,' John told Australian Associated Press, in a story published back home.[7]

This dispassionate, vague description is unsurprising. Many pilots reported being unable to remember exactly how dogfights unfolded, even immediately after the event. From the moment of engagement, their minds and pulses raced. Fear evaporated with conscious thought. Whatever action was taken, however violently the aircraft was manoeuvred or its weapons unleashed, combat was usually recalled in a handful of bright, dislocated images. Many engagements, in fact, lasted only a couple of long minutes.

'Perhaps a picture of two Me-109s [Messerschmitts] belting down on your tail from out of the sun and already within firing range.[8] Perhaps another picture of your cannon shells striking at the belly of a Me and the aircraft spraying debris around. But, for the life of you, you can't remember what you did,' said one pilot. Some pilots returned to base feeling exhilarated, eager to take off again.[9] Others were so sapped that they could barely function.[10]

The common evidence of the intense mental effort was a shirt soaked through with perspiration and a jagged insomnia that beat back sleep.[11]

The week rolled on in a blur. The adrenalin rush of constant sorties and quick relocations further back behind the moving lines meant sleep was disrupted, fleeting or impossible. John was momentarily elated by all this 'bloody good fun'.[12] Fighter pilots chose to see the enemy as machines of twisting metal, not as human targets. They sought to live in an abstract world, far above the human agony on the ground. When German planes strafed the squadron, John rushed around putting out fires.[13] Numbed by the urgency of the situation, he didn't even notice he was bleeding. A bullet had grazed his shin sufficiently deeply to scar.

Throughout this chaotic period of retreat on the ground, the Desert Air Force kept up the offensive in the skies. 'The ground crews and the fighters kept going until the Nazi tanks were within ten miles [16 km] of their fields, an unprecedented thing', Moorehead observed.[14]

'They worked in a frenzy of energy, day and night. Under shaded lights the mechanics worked all night . . . they packed their tents onto trucks and kept everything ready for instant departure and while waiting for the arrival of the enemy tanks, they still kept "bombing up" the machines, rethreading the belts of fighter ammunition, filling the tanks and getting pilots into the air.'

Once they got word the Germans would be upon them within the hour, 'pilots and crew threw their bedding into their machines and took off, they dropped their last bombs and hastened to airfields further back. The ground crews jumped onto their trucks and took off before their camps were overrun. These men, half dead with the lack of sleep, delayed Rommel for several days.'[15]

'It was an extraordinary withdrawal . . . we had continued throughout to provide constant air cover and support for the fleeing columns of the army below us. I am sure what we were able to do went far in preventing that quite disastrous retreat from deteriorating into a full rout,' said the commander of No. 112 Squadron RAF, Billy Drake, who often flew with John and 450 Squadron.[16]

The Allies' own casualties were mounting. The Kittyhawks were operating in roles they had not been designed for. There were new skills needed, and new risks. Flying low, strafing, planes were vulnerable to the devastating 'ack-ack' that brought many of them down. Aircrews also discovered that if their own armour-piercing bullets bounced off the roadway they could shoot themselves down—and some did.[17] Sometimes they fired in error. 'Kites go off to attack anything in that area, strafe our own Indian lorries by mistake. Big panic—tanks approaching . . . new "gen" [information] every minute,' read one pilot's rushed notes.[18] The next day, 'same again . . . sleep in trench now'.

'Only those who had experienced war knows what it means to live for days, weeks, months . . . even years, with the fear of violent death gnawing at your guts', wrote Ted Sly, who flew as John's no. 2 during much of this period.[19]

> We watched those numerous tiny dots appear [on the horizon] and grow and grow in seconds to become a mass of spitting, twisting, death. We saw our comrades die before our very eyes, and watched them plummet earthwards, balls of molten fire and mangled bodies. We watched in vain for that small parachute to blossom forth from the doomed machine before it struck the ground . . . we counted the giant black pillars of smoke rising from crimson bases of fire and blood. They were funeral pyres of friend and foe alike . . .

Sly, and many other pilots of the era, clearly recalled the smell of cordite in their nostrils, the thud of machine-gun bullets and cannon fire tearing at the metal of their aircraft and even the 'pain of the vicious lead' hitting your body. Warm blood oozing, a pilot 'might wonder if he is already dead'.[20]

More than anything else, Sly was ashamed that those who survived thanked God it wasn't them and 'rejoiced in their continued existence', even while watching their friends die. They worried not so much about the lost, but whether they would be next.

On 26 June 1942, 450 Squadron flew eight bomber escorts throughout a terrible day, several straight into German Messerschmitt patrols.[21] At 8.30 p.m. the order came for all serviceable aircraft to be flown out by experienced night pilots. A flare path would be lit further back behind the lines to guide them in. All ground personnel—it took hundreds of men to keep twenty or so planes and their pilots constantly in the air—were to abandon the tents and evacuate. The roads were so clogged their progress was frighteningly slow. For the fleeing pilots there was a different peril. The flares at the nominated new airstrip had not been lit and several planes were damaged landing in the dark.

The following morning three trucks and a handful of 450 Squadron pilots headed back to try to salvage some of the tents and other equipment. The British army had beaten them to it. Fires were burning. The army was destroying anything useful. The Germans were very close. The pilots were ordered to leave immediately. The following day, they remained packed up and on '30 minutes notice' to move further back again.[22]

Rommel's push against the Gazala line had begun on 26 May. By 30 June, eleven pilots of 450 Squadron were dead, one was missing in action, seventeen planes had been destroyed and another life and aircraft had been lost in an accident on take-off. This, out of a total of about twenty pilots and planes in a squadron at any one time. The 450 Squadron bore the heaviest losses of any single squadron of the combined nationality Desert Air Force. The 239 Wing had lost 30 pilots.[23] To everyone's shock and dismay, this time Tobruk had fallen. The Allied ground troops had their backs against the wall along a new defensive line at El Alamein, well inside Egypt and within striking distance of the prime targets of Alexandria and Cairo.

The first battle of El Alamein was about to unfold. The squadron kept flying, clocking up 500 sorties and losing two more planes in July from its new base near Alexandria. But Rommel's advance was finally stalled. Unlike every other previous defensive line that ran into the endless desert, always enabling the enemy to go around, the El Alamein line had a critical, topographical feature. The vast and impassable Qattara Depression, 64 kilometres inland, meant the Allies could not be outflanked and significantly narrowed the stretch of land the Allies had to hold. A breathing space had been won.

Much later, Drake told this story to illustrate the impact of such extreme, prolonged stress. He had been without sleep for three days and three nights.

'I was prevented from shooting a man who I thought was a coward. I was too tired. I had pulled my gun. Thankfully, the medical officer knocked it out of my hand,'[24] he still recalled vividly many decades after the event.

25

WHILE WE STILL HAVE BREATH IN OUR BODIES

They called them 'mothers' meetings', those huddles of flight commanders in the desert discussing what to do next. Billy Drake didn't think about it at the time, but the older he got the more he came to appreciate that military history was being made. Never before in the history of combat, he thought, had men so young gone unaccompanied into battle. There was no senior officer, no wise, battle-hardened strategist standing shoulder to shoulder with them on the front-line, no king to lead the charge, no flag-bearers to ride out first. Nor did they have a reliable doctrine to rely on, particularly flying the Kittyhawks in their new multi-purpose fighter-bomber role. Given the great leaps in technological development since World War I, this was an entirely new air war. They were working it out on the run.

The average World War II squadron leader, and even wing commander, was in his early or mid twenties and such was the stress that even young men needed to be relieved from operational duties every six to nine months.[1] The theory at the time was simply that only a fit, agile young man could 'throw the aircraft around violently and with total abandon', and so survive a dogfight.[2]

John was 23 when he took over command of 450 Squadron, shortly before the second battle of El Alamein. The outgoing squadron leader, Alan Ferguson, was the same age; he and John had been in the same year at school at Shore. John was assigned a personal aircraft. On the nose is a cartoon image of his personal mascot, Mandrake the Magician, holding a bomb, presumably implying that he could confound the enemy with his fast, hypnotic style in the air.

John was an 'aggressive pilot'. He was a 'strong but unassuming personality'. He was 'well liked'. He was 'a smiling, good-natured and first class fighter pilot'. He was scruffy and particularly 'non-regulation' in his sandals and shorts.[3] But he was also a serious and highly disciplined young man.

'He had a good sense of humour and would, jokingly, from time to time, threaten to post me to Chad or beyond . . . usually as a result of some of my one line jokes I was infamous for', wrote fellow 450 Squadron pilot, Hector Fullerton.[4]

On 4 August 1942, Winston Churchill arrived in the desert. Egypt had become Britain's top priority and he wanted a final decisive victory over Rommel. He changed commanders, bringing in Lieutenant-General B.L. Montgomery to lead the Eighth Army. Ironically the chaos of the retreat had reaped rich strategic rewards; the cooperation between ground units and the air squadrons had never been so efficient or effective. The Desert Air Force had become a large force and 'notably efficient in maintaining and repairing aircraft in primitive conditions and skilled in mobile warfare'.[5] And the ancient law of the desert was coming back into play. Rommel was stretched. He was far from his bases. By contrast, as the Eighth Army retreated, the air force 'became better able to operate for longer periods from secure bases' inside Egypt. Air power was becoming one of the 'crucial determinants' of the Allies' fighting ability.[6]

The Allies now also had many more boots on the ground, more tanks, more armoury and more planes. The Nazis didn't know it, but the Allies also had ULTRA. The British had cracked the Enigma codes used by the Germans and were filtering out limited information—just enough to assist their forces, but not enough to reveal their hand.⁷ The balance had finally tipped in the Allies' favour.

The declassified air force and intelligence files of the era make fascinating, if voluminous, reading. Wading though this paper avalanche of bureaucratic efficiency is alternately sad, funny, poignant, surprising (and, of course, often tedious and irrelevant). The dates show that, against this dramatic backdrop, the regular flow of administrative and bureaucratic messages persisted. The dishevelled desert pilots were reminded to please wear their uniforms on leave trips into Alexandria. They were instructed to please use rubbish bins, not just throw rubbish out of their tents. They were informed of the day's password—'cigarettes' being one of the least imaginative, and probably least secure—on the list. They received notice of the various Red Cross comforts coming their way, like bars of soap that they had insufficient water to use. They also received warning of various Nazi booby-trapped items, should they overrun an Axis camp; there were fake tins of Harris Wiltshire sausages, thermos flasks and dinner carriers all packed with explosives.⁸

In the bulging correspondence file of No. 450 Squadron⁹ RAAF one personal message from a Lieutenant Digby of the 11th Hussars stands out.

> Day after day we see you going over us and we long to be able to tell you how much it cheers us to see you and how anxiously we count your numbers when you come back. Of all the air attacks against ground troops nothing is so utterly soul destroying and terrifying than machine gunning day after day.
>
> So, I hardly need to say that although yours may seem a thankless task, there are thousands here who are thanking you every minute of the day.¹⁰

It was a rare and welcome personal communication between ground troops and the air force and good for morale. So too was the camaraderie of a shared trauma. Set against the deprivations and operational stress, the desert became a place of great comradeship and deep and abiding friendships.[11]

There were also cables praising the extraordinary efforts and skills of the often-overlooked grounds crews in keeping the planes airworthy and constantly up in the air, the pilots' lives in their hands. There was a strong feeling of a well-oiled team; many, many faceless young men were doing extraordinary jobs watching each other's backs.

While both sides continued to pick at each other's positions, something very big was being planned. With Montgomery in charge, the Allies were rallying the troops. Right across the desert, visiting dignitaries and officials were delivering rousing messages to every camp. 'Good luck in your usual brilliant work; this defensive land fight for Egypt will be followed by an offensive . . . the battle is on',[12] the air commander promised in September.

On 19 and 20 October, all squadron and wing commanders were grounded, including John. In the preceding days, they had been active in delivering 'softening up' blows. They had since been briefed. They knew what was planned. The risk of them being shot down and forced to talk under duress was now considered too high to keep them flying.[13]

It is impossible to truly appreciate the level of anxiety and anticipation when you know how the battle turned out. But, when Montgomery's message was read out, every one of the 200,000 men lining up to face Rommel's forces yet again understood that they were not only fighting for their lives but to influence the course of history. Montgomery promised that victory would be the turning point in the war that would bring them home to their families. You are fighting 'one of the decisive battles of history', he told them. 'Let every officer and man enter the battle with a stout heart and the determination to do his duty, so long as he still has breath in his body. AND LET NO MAN SURRENDER SO

LONG AS HE IS UNINJURED AND CAN FIGHT [capitals in original].'[14]

Hitler's famous order was simpler. 'Victory or death', he snapped at Rommel. The Desert Fox was now out of favour, having been prevented from sweeping right through Egypt in mid-1942 by the Allies' stand at El Alamein. Hitler was adamant; there would be no Axis retreat.[15]

The full moon rose, spilling soft light across the desert. At 9.40 p.m. hours on 23 October 1942, more than 1000 British heavy guns unleashed the greatest barrage since World War I on the narrow front between the Qattara Depression and the Mediterranean Sea at El Alamein. The ground shook for many kilometres around. From a distance, the constant flashes looked like sheet lightning. Words, no matter how carefully crafted, cannot do this scene justice. Twenty minutes later the assaulting Allied infantry finally moved forward—after months of hardship and loss in retreat. Rommel was on sick leave, soon to be rapidly recalled. He had, however, laid half a million anti-tank mines, his so-called 'Devil's Garden', which hampered, but did not stop, Montgomery's push forward.[16]

At dawn on 24 October, John led the 450 Squadron fighters on their first armed reconnaissance mission over the 21st Panzer division. This time, the Desert Air Force was not improvising on the run. With secure, well-supplied bases in Egypt to return to, they were able to provide aggressive air support to ground troops. Rommel, on the other hand, was far from his supply lines. He was seriously hampered by fuel shortages that limited the mobility of his usually formidable tanks, and locked them in a slogging match they could not win. Allied air and ground attacks progressively destroyed over half his tanks. In the air, too, the Axis planes were outnumbered. John's logbook details every truck, petrol dump, tank and aircraft destroyed. Hundreds of pilots were similarly jotting down the many seemingly small details that added up to victory.

No one expected the battle to be quick, and it wasn't. After a week of constant operations, John took off at 1.40 p.m. on

31 October in a formation of four on a long-range strafing mission, deep behind enemy lines. One of the planes turned back with engine trouble. The three remaining planes followed the coast road. John set a petrol dump alight. His no. 2, a role charged with watching the leader's back, hit a truck. The third pilot, Sergeant Max Jenkins, hit three trucks. There were no enemy aircraft in sight.

Then everything went wrong. The no. 2 pilot, who was relatively inexperienced, became separated from both John and Jenkins, flying at about 200 feet (60 metres). Suddenly, he was coming straight at them, Jenkins later reported. He opened fire in a panic, executing a full-deflection shot,[17] one of the most technically difficult in the book. His screaming lead collides with metal. He has shot down his squadron leader.[18]

26
DOWN BUT NOT OUT

John had rehearsed this moment in his mind, over and over again. All those years of forced landings in training when he had cut the engine and forced his student to think and act fast, to immediately work out how and where to land safely. All those times he had had to cope with real technical failures in training and in operations, turning his plane around and nursing it back to base. All those times when 'the other bloke' hadn't come back, and was last reported bailing out, or easing his injured kite down onto the sand. He knew instinctively how to glide the Kittyhawk in safely; that wasn't the issue. He was on a long-range mission. He knew exactly how far he was behind enemy lines.

He hit fairly hard anyway, but clambered out, winded but unhurt. Jenkins and his no. 2 briefly continued to buzz impotently overhead. The ground was too rough to attempt a rescue and so soon they wheeled away. Rescues had been made before but not often. To bring two men back in the tight single seat of a fighter was very difficult.[1]

Then, nothing. John was alone, save for the familiar, vibrating warmth of the late autumn desert day.

It was over 60 kilometres back to the El Alamein line, and between John and safety lay Rommel's ground forces—eight divisions, two of tanks—and a vast expanse of minefields. All the

Allied pilots knew this stretch of ground like the back of their hand. The desert might look blank and empty at first glance but it soon became a familiar and detailed carpet; every ancient camel trail, rocky outpost, dried-up salt lake, ridge and even the smallest mound served as a reference point.[2] The nearest road, now crawling with Axis vehicles, was about 3 kilometres away. Beyond was the small railway station at El Daba, now deserted, and the former RAF Landing Ground 105. The Luftwaffe was in residence. All of this had been the Allies' less than six months earlier. Only in July, John had successfully engaged and shot down a Junkers Ju 88 'fast bomber' nearby. In a tragic irony, this area would very soon again be under Allied control after Rommel, facing annihilation, ordered a general retreat.[3] Rommel's defiance of Hitler, saving the lives of thousands of Axis troops, was the turning point in his break with the Nazi leader that would end up costing him his own life.

The Australian war correspondent Keith Slessor wandered the same stretch of road only a week or two later in November to report on the hasty Axis retreat; even the road crews had simply dropped their hats, picks and shovels where they stood when they ran. 'Nothing escaped the fury of our air squadrons . . . around the airfields of El Daba, Sidi Barrani and Gambut the gaunt remains of Junkers and Messerschmitts lie rusting like bones of pre-historic monsters'.[4]

John didn't know it yet—and wouldn't know for some time—but for his part in the Battle of El Alamein and all that preceded it, he had already been awarded a DFC (Distinguished Flying Cross) for 'courage, determination and devotion to duty'.

As night approached the temperature began to fall. We rarely associate deserts with the cold. By day, the sun still shone warm and strong but winter was approaching. At night, the cold crept. It felt freezing; sometimes it actually was. John was in his trademark shorts and sandals.

In any other circumstance, he might have felt a rush of poetic calm. Many combatants have, in many successive wars.

But, solitude was no longer such a familiar state, despite

John's natural inclination to withdraw into music or books; something that now seemed like a distant memory. Those pilots who would seek out their own company and wander off alone under those desert stars worried their colleagues. Social isolation, just like laughing too much or too loudly, was feared as a sign of operational stress.[5] Every evening for months now the outliers had been gathered up into the collective embrace of the mess, its cacophony intended to drown out all else.

Or, perhaps John was actually relieved? He had flown 112 sorties since April, sometimes landing and taking off four times in a single day. Once Montgomery's Lightfoot assault had been launched, he had been constantly moving, leading twelve operations in a handful of days. Long after the war was over John's contemporary in No. 3 Squadron, Bobby Gibbes, wrote of the 'trauma and fear' of the desert campaign and his own experience in being shot down by a German plane earlier in 1942.

> I parachuted from the flaming torch which my aircraft had become and made a heavy landing in a high wind. I lay on the ground surveying the bend in my left leg and I was in agonising pain. I was wondering if I was in enemy territory or on our side of the lines and was ashamed at feeling gladness, knowing that I would not now be killed in a aerial combat, at least for some time.[6]

(Gibbes was back in time for the decisive battle of El Alamein.)

So what did John do? Did he set off to walk back anyway? Did he yell, scream, even cry, or just silently turn his options over and over in his mind? Did anyone even have the energy or inclination to worry about his fate?

But, then this, and all that followed, might never have happened 'but for the fateful finger' of the unnamed pilot, wrote John's friend and fellow 450 Squadron pilot Al Markle in a private letter.[7] The pilot's name was, of course, well known, but in many accounts it has been thoughtfully omitted. It was an accident and no one sought to attribute any blame. The pilot had returned absolutely distraught to base and had been posted out of the squadron immediately, as was the practice with friendly fire incidents. Tragically, he was shot down and killed two months later. By 9 November 1942 the terrible numbers had been provisionally tallied up. The 'desert was full of dead men'.[8] The headlines described 'avenues of death', 'ruin in the desert'.[9] This decisive, historic battle had cost the lives of 2350 Allied servicemen; 8950 had been wounded and 2260 were posted as missing, including John. The 9th Australian Division, about one-tenth of the Eighth Army's strength, suffered disproportionate losses: 520 dead, 1948 wounded and 218 missing, half of whom were found dead. British investigators put the German losses at 1149 killed, 3886 wounded, 8050 captured. The Italians lost 971 dead, 933 wounded, and 15,552 captured. Mopping up would net 30,000 or so Axis prisoners.[10]

Every mother feared the telegram. Popular culture is filled with images of long-suffering World War II mothers. She weeps, rages, sobs, even runs down the street, apron flapping, neighbours' arms outstretched to catch her, just to delay the moment when the telegram is placed in her hands.

Mildred wasn't like that. She believed in keeping up appearances, in strength of character. In public she was stoic, guarded, polite. When the first telegram arrived on 7 November 1942 she did not react emotionally, my uncle David said. It was not the worst news. John was missing.

'He is not necessarily killed or wounded and in view of this it may be of some assistance to you in your anxiety to know what action is being taken to trace missing members of the Air Force', a following letter said, enclosing the standard pamphlets that families pored over, looking for any hint of how their precious son might now be found.

27
THE FACE OF THE ENEMY

So, this was the enemy.

Three young, smooth-faced, clean-shaven German guards were charged with securing each Allied air force officer in transit. They were not, of course, friendly, but they were not unfriendly either. They spoke a few words of English. John spoke schoolboy German. The standard ration for the prisoner was a single slice of black bread as a meal. The guards had more and better food. They shared.[1]

John had not been treated particularly harshly. He had not been pushed into a windowless, stuffy cattle truck. He was moved across Germany on a regular passenger train. The only difference was that the windows of the compartment had been nailed shut, leaving only a small gap for air at the top. Outside, passengers milled around in the corridor, some of them visibly annoyed that a prisoner and his young escorts were taking up the seats.[2]

By all accounts, the German forces in the Western Desert were careful with Allied POWs. Every Allied prisoner who escaped in the desert, and there were dozens every day, came back with the same story. 'The Germans behaved extraordinarily well. They gave us food and water at once. There was no third degree—nothing like that at all,'[3] one prisoner reported. The Allied wounded, too, were given exactly the same high standard of medical care as the

Axis troops. Perhaps they were genuinely guided by the limits of the Geneva Convention, at least at this stage of the war. Perhaps they were banking on quid pro quo: if they treated Allied prisoners well, their own should be afforded similar respect. Or maybe it was part of a larger ploy: if Allied personnel were confident of good treatment, they might find themselves keener to capitulate than fighting to the death.[4] Whatever the reason, the mid-air killing of Dudley Parker, apparently for sport, seemed an aberration, a crime committed by a rogue element operating well beyond the limits of acceptable behaviour, even in war.

For most prisoners captured by the German forces in the desert, the next handover was to the Italians. Then, if they were especially unlucky, a stint in 'The Palms' of Benghazi, in Libya; a filthy, scorching dustbowl of a camp, perhaps ironically named given its complete lack of vegetation and its vile, overflowing open latrines.[5] But all air force prisoners fell under the personal control of the commander-in-chief of the Luftwaffe, Hermann Göring, a former World War I fighter pilot and ace. John was going straight to Germany. Given the alternative, this did not fill him with dread.

The first air war in World War I, with its quaint, flimsy biplanes made of fabric and wood, had been marked by a 'special chivalry' in which 'the star airmen of the opposing armies regarded each other with a curious mixture of personal esteem and deadly hostility'.[6] Consequently, there was a pervasive belief that Göring regarded Allied pilots and aircrew with at least professional, if not personal, respect.

This belief had only been reinforced when one of the RAF's most famous Spitfire aces, Douglas Bader, was shot down in 1941 over German-occupied France. Bader, a double amputee who had been badly injured in a crash a decade earlier, lost one of his artificial legs when he bailed out. The RAF and the Luftwaffe made an extraordinary arrangement to get a spare leg out to him. In an operation under the heading 'Circus 81', the official cable notes: 'the leg for Wing Commander Bader became airborne at 1051 and was last seen floating down gracefully [attached to a parachute]'. A message was broadcast to the enemy and acknowledged. The RAF Blenheim bomber then went back to work, wheeling away to rejoin its formation and unleash its bombs.[7]

And then there was the Allied airmen's famous arrogance. They did see themselves, literally and figuratively, as above the fray.

The fact that Göring was one of the most senior Nazis, and the founder of the Gestapo, afforded him his own personal empire within the Third Reich; his Luftwaffe held sway over their own large network of POW camps, and guarded them jealously as their own territory.[8] Whatever regard Göring had for the accomplishments of the Allied airmen, it rippled through the Luftwaffe, shaping the attitudes of even the most junior of ranks.

John was on his way to Dulag Luft, the Intelligence Assessment Centre near Frankfurt and the centrepiece of the Stalag Luft prison network, where the interrogators stepped in. The holding room was breathtakingly stark and alarmingly quiet after the train ride. 'I had a sense of absolute emptiness, there were not even any bugs to tame, no floor boards with nails to count', said Australian navigator Cal Younger,[9] also captured in 1942 and sent on to Stalag Luft III. Another arrival in late 1942, British pilot Alex Cassis recalled these cells as solitary confinement.[10] That there were other air force officers in the compound could only be ascertained if they were heard shouting or banging on the walls.

Consequently, the interrogation interviews, complete with cigarettes and even the offer of refreshments in attractively furnished, comfortable rooms, often came as a relief. Which was, of course, straight from the psy-war handbook. The Luftwaffe also used highly educated, knowledgeable young men with superb English skills, many of whom had studied at Oxford and Cambridge,[11] as their apparently convivial interviewers. They had a disarming array of facts at their disposal pertaining to each prisoner's squadron. They reassured the airmen by offering them fake International Red Cross forms to fill in. All of this was intended to trap the unwary into revealing more than the required name, rank and serial number. But, by the end of 1942, the relentless Allied bombing of Europe was foremost in the Germans' minds. The Desert Fox was discredited and out of favour. Whatever strategic plans John had been party to, they had already unfolded.

Inside Dulag Luft, notes were efficiently taken. Personal possessions were logged for return at the end of the hostilities. A single paperback book was thrown into each cell; some got *A Midsummer Night's Dream*, others detective novels. There was no reason to suspect the Red Cross documents were fraudulent. The POWs' cards were made up and filed away: a photo and some pertinent personal information. That such cards would later be retrieved and sorted into two piles, nominating who would live and who would die, was frankly unimaginable.

Today, the notion that war has rules, or even mutually respected codes, morals or mores, seems foreign and, sadly, almost naive. In an era of YouTube terrorism no horror is too appalling to visit upon another human being—combatant or civilian, man or woman, adult or child, culprit or innocent—just as long as it elicits abhorrence, revulsion, shock and disgust, worldwide. But military personnel on both sides in World War II did, at least in Europe in 1942, expect reasonable treatment within the bounds of the Geneva Convention. The code 'relative to the treatment of prisoners of war' was signed in 1929 by 47 nations, including all the future belligerents of World War II, except the Soviet Union. It set out 97 articles that were supposed to govern every aspect of imprisonment from capture to release.[12] Germany had, in fact, ratified the Convention in 1934 when Hitler was well on his way to absolute control.[13] He and his senior men were, at least, familiar with its requirements and, in their own military culture, honour had, historically, played an important role.

At Dulag Luft, the Germans were practical. They waited for the rows of stark, lonely cells to fill up sufficiently to make up a full train carriage before 'purging' a group out to a prison camp. Some men were stuck in isolation for so long they wondered if they were going mad. Others were processed in a day or two. The trip to Stalag Luft III near Poznan was, again, not uncomfortable; the locked carriage was second-class with padded seats. Basic meals were served. The prisoners' main worry was that the train was travelling so slowly, stopping frequently to give way to priority traffic, that they might end up stuck overnight in a railway siding, a prime target for Allied bombers. There were reasonable fears, too, of German public rage; the Allies' revised policy of area bombing—targeting populated areas with incendiary bombs—was extracting an ever-mounting civilian toll.[14]

Today, it is difficult to imagine that the POWs might have felt humiliated, ashamed and impotent as they were herded toward their designated camp. (The Japanese held Allied POWs in absolute contempt as cowards because their own code of honour required them to fight to the death.) It would be years, if not decades, before POWs, and escapees in particular, would become popular 'post war cultural icons',[15] those fascinating individuals we have since adopted as symbols of courage and resistance in the face of tyranny and of the will to overcome and survive, against all odds.

Churchill had described the lot of the POW as 'a melancholy state'.

> You are in the power of your enemy. You owe your life to his humanity, and your daily bread to his compassion. You must obey his orders, go where he tells you, stay where you are bid, await his pleasure, possess your soul in patience. Meanwhile the war is going on, great events are in progress, fine opportunities for action and adventure are slipping by. Also the days are very long . . . .[16]

Few accounts of the era overlook that famous first line supposedly uttered by arresting German officers: 'For you, the war is over'. Most of the half-a-million or so Allied POWs heard these words, or something like them, between 1939 and 1945. As a POW, John's war, as he had known it, was over but another was about to begin:

> Waged against boredom, despair, hunger, brutality, disease and, ultimately, death, this was a battle fought with no weapons other than one's own wits and character. Moreover, it was conducted against a fully armed captor who also had at his disposal barbed wire, search lights, dogs, solitary confinement cells, cunning and brutal interrogation techniques, secret state police and the right to exploit prisoners (excluding officers) for their labour.[17]

For air force officers, especially, captivity was just another phase of their active service. Statistically, airmen were much more likely to be killed than captured, but sufficient numbers survived coming down over enemy territory to keenly focus the minds of their superiors on giving them the best chance of getting back. They were invaluable to the war machine so, unlike regular soldiers, they were briefed in advance by intelligence officers of the fledgling intelligence service, MI9, and equipped with sophisticated escape kits. These included everything from miniature compasses and maps on silk handkerchiefs to money, chocolate and Benzedrine. If they were not seriously injured, airmen were expected to try to reach neutral or friendly territory. If they were imprisoned their first priority must be 'to escape at the EARLIEST OPPORTUNITY'[18] and many repeated attempts were made to do so.

The Canadian military historian Jonathan Vance described pilots and aircrew as 'almost the ideal' escapers.[19] They were highly motivated, well educated and aggressive, and were accustomed to operating either alone or in small groups. They had the drive, the self-reliance and the ability to cooperate that clandestine escape efforts demanded. Between them they also had a potentially formidable arsenal of skills. Above all else, they were natural risk-takers.

When the train pulled in at the station in Sagan, the prisoners were marched to Stalag Luft III. It was a bleak-looking place; a large flat denuded wasteland cut out of the straggly Silesian forest. There was not a single tree to soften the rows of wooden huts or a blade of grass left to carpet the sandy soil. In late 1942, officers were confined to the east compound, then only six huts, a cooking block, a bathhouse and a toilet block, but a massive camp expansion program was already underway. In time the Sagan region would accommodate hundreds of thousands of POWs.

'Ha,' laughed RAF pilot, Thomas Nelson, recalling the camp's rather favourable reputation as something of a holiday camp', relative to other POW destinations of the time. 'Yes, it was built on Göring's orders to house "his English flying friends". As he was a pilot in World War I, he thought he'd build them a nice camp—with slightly better conditions!

'It was just a larger cage—that's all really.'[20]

John's group were hustled into a big administration room where they were looked over by a tough, swaggering German sergeant-major type. He strutted around before announcing, flamboyantly: 'Good morning gentlemens. Welcome to Stalag Luft III. You will find the beer is piss poor, but the gen [inside information] is shit hot.' Or something along those lines. This particular German officer proved incorruptible, efficient and amusing, an unhelpful adversary for escapers, but one to like and respect. His reference to gen merely alerted them to the Germans' (valid) suspicions that the prisoners had home-made radios secreted away somewhere inside the camp, bringing them the BBC news. They just couldn't find them.

Then the cage gates swung open and they were in. They were all *Kriegsgefangene* or 'kriegies' now.

It seemed strange to the new arrivals that men were pouring out of the huts to meet them, searching hopefully through the new faces.

'When we walked in there were several hundred prisoners waiting to see if there was anyone they knew in the new intake', recalled Younger.[21]

'They were anxious to know about friends from their squadrons and also, of course, they wanted news. What had Churchill said, how many U-boats had we sunk, and how many of our ships had gone down and how were the Russians doing? We could hardly get through the throng.'

John was a long way from the Western Desert and a very long way from home. No one's eyes lit up with recognition when they looked his way.[22]

28
IN THE BAG

Never walk into a room talking. If there was any Williams family advice for life, this was it. My father was an unassuming, gentle man who made up for his limited emotional vocabulary with a repertoire of often-corny jokes. He wasn't one to have talks with the children or to seek to impose his opinions or will, so, when he did offer us a few serious words of advice, we listened.

Of course, as a child, I thought this merely meant that I shouldn't charge on into the house, rush into the living room and interrupt the adults. As I always had something to report, I took this as a suggestion to at least wait for a pause in the conversation before regaling my parents with my latest idea or news— more an issue of good manners than anything else.

But I've since come to appreciate my dad's keen skills of quiet observation; he painted watercolours in his spare time and, like John, listened with great attention to classical music (and he also insisted on wearing shorts and sandals in virtually any weather). He would often remind us to look around, usually prompted by his own sense of joy and gratitude for life, at the sun glinting off the waves, or the changing colours and textures of the landscape as the evening light faded. He was a quiet role model for the wisdom of looking, listening and learning. He encouraged us to seek first to understand the lay of the land, socially, professionally and even politically, before rushing to judge. It has proved sound and enduring advice, and has helped me navigate my way through many difficult situations, especially as a foreign correspondent working in unfamiliar cultures, a long way from home.

One of the most dominant images of John in the many books written about the Great Escape is of him standing, arms crossed, at the back of the room, listening, while the big personalities of the escape committee talk. He did contribute briefly, but only if he had something important to say.

I imagine, then, that he didn't walk into his bunk room talking on that first day. He probably approached POW life in much the same way as he had approached each new subculture he had come across along his bumpy life path; he too was one to look, listen and learn. Hans had told me with some pride that they both understood how to read the ocean. Surfers recognise that many undercurrents and rips are concealed by a calm-looking surface and that often the roughest whitewash is, in fact, the safest place to swim.

The atmosphere inside Stalag Luft III was not unlike that of a rowdy, third-rate British boys' boarding school.

This was, at least partly, because the RAF and its men dominated—and many of the young English POWs had, indeed, only recently left boys' boarding schools before they signed up. And, at least partly, because the men were all cramped up together in bunk rooms, in true boarding-school style. This meant many of the POWs were well schooled, so to speak, in the kinds of pranks and petty challenges to authority that would be sure to annoy their German captors, and bored enough to be continuously inventing new takes on the same old theme.

Despite the presence of POWs from the United States, the dominions of Australia, New Zealand, Canada and South Africa, as well as Poles, Czechs, Dutch, Flemish, Greeks, Lithuanians and Scandinavians, the RAF ran the Stalag Luft camps internally. A senior British officer, or SBO, his adjunct and various other senior ranks organised the Allied POWs for the compulsory German *appell*s, or rollcalls, liaised in their interests with the Camp Kommandant and other senior German officers, while juggling the various subterfuges, plots and escape plans that were obscured behind all the activity and noise.

On the face of it, it must have seemed like fairly ineffective and immature stuff. News had just filtered through of another assassination attempt on Hitler, for example, before the POWs gathered for *appell*. When the SBO presented his men to the senior German officer, he used his British salute. When the German replied with 'Heil Hitler' the parade ground erupted in guffaws of laughter.[1] The POWs routinely pretended not to speak German, although many had German skills ranging from fluent to useful for eavesdropping. They also feigned their inability to understand their captors' English. One former POW recalled prisoners clapping and cheering repeatedly when German military successes were announced, until the German officer finally slunk off shaking his head, having lost confidence in his command of the English language. Prisoners also regularly sought to confuse multiple daily head-counts, mainly by exploiting the chance to 'bed hop' in sick bay to add or subtract from the totals, but sometimes turning up with a mop or two that had been dressed in a cap, scarf and coat, supported on the arms of his 'mates'.

And no opportunity, it seems, was overlooked to take an indignant complaint to the very reasonable and personable Kommandant Colonel von Lindeiner, a 61-year-old schoolmasterly figure who was, in fact, well respected by his staff and the POWs alike as an 'officer of the old school'.[2]

Rather than simply ignore propaganda organs like the official English language camp newspaper—unimaginatively entitled *The Camp*—the SBO typed up a lengthy and legalistic objection in June 1943.[3] He argued that the use of propaganda was an instrument of war 'for use by and against non-combatants' and 'has nothing to do with fighting men'. 'We can only assume the Germans think by this method to undermine our loyalty and our sense of duty . . . [but] even the most optimistic of German officers will hardly look upon us as a beaten nation.' Consequently, he officiously informed the Kommandant, 'we resent the attempt to introduce it as an insult to our honour'.

Even a serious transgression like the theft of official documents and other handy escape items like torches from a visiting senior officer's car didn't seem to overly ruffle the Luftwaffe.

'We rushed over to the [visiting officer's] Mercedes. It had its hood down and just a chauffeur standing guard. Before he could say boo, we had everything out of the pockets and the boot open,' said RAF navigator Eric Foinette,[4] who also arrived at Stalag Luft III in 1942.

'When the officer came back he was so happy we were impressed by his car that he gave us a demonstration of its accelerating power.'

Meanwhile, the POWs had made off with his special pass allowing him to visit the Silesia region and had their forging team get to work on copying; a clandestine group everyone optimistically called Dean & Dawson, after well-known British travel agents. Once the officer discovered his pass was missing, he was unable to leave Silesia. Remarkably, its return was negotiated by Colonel von Lindeiner and the document was handed back marked 'inspected by officers of the RAF and signed Winston Churchill'. The German officer, Foinette said, took it in good humour.

The RAF had its own psy-war plans, of course, and well-established intelligence-gathering procedures, including the dispatch of coded POW letters to communicate with Britain, not just to provide information but to request all kinds of items that might prove useful for escape and could, with some careful planning, be smuggled in via the mail room. Bridge scores were used as codes, and new arrivals often came in with useful observations of conditions in Germany—and potential bombing targets—on the ground.[5]

Escape talk, escape planning and escape efforts were a constant. The Germans knew it, and tolerated it in good enough humour, probably because most of those who made it over or under the wire or through the gates were soon hauled back into the camp. Although, three POWs did succeed in making a 'home run' in 1943, having dug a tunnel out of Stalag Luft III using a wooden vaulting horse to disguise its entrance.[6]

Officers were not required to work, so theoretically, apart from the dull routine of *appell*s, they could laze around all day in their bunks reading and smoking. That was a recipe for rapid psychological decline. POWs were incarcerated indefinitely; they had lost control of both the present and the future. But they understood that life needed structure and forward momentum. In its absence, they created it themselves.

As amusing at it might seem now, POWs at Stalag Luft III took to running personal diaries. Then, they pooled their talents and organised an extraordinary calendar of events and regular activities to fill them. They began classes in virtually every subject you could think of. 'In the early days our classroom was the sand outside the hut, which we used as a blackboard writing and drawing with a stick for a piece of chalk. We had no textbooks—we relied on memory.' Eventually, with aid from the Red Cross, Stalag Luft III achieved university status and offered degrees. 'It was the proud boast that it was impossible to mention a subject to be studied and not be able to find someone in the camp who could teach it', said RAF pilot William Greenaway.[7]

Every sport imaginable was on offer too; one winter year the Canadians even managed to build a huge shallow wooden frame for an ice hockey rink, filled it with water and waited for it to freeze over.

Stalag Luft III racing carnivals were held. The 'huskier' prisoners piggybacked the slight ones. Bets were made, odds were calculated (the mathematicians were needed to do some fast mental arithmetic) and some POWs won big with 'camp currency'.[8] While physical activity depended somewhat on the food available at the time, the camp's famous theatre was less exposed to the fluctuating energy levels of young men fed on various kriegie specials like 'Reich glop' and 'Reich soup'.

'My philosophy was that you had to keep busy. Whether you were going to lectures, playing football, giving lectures, digging tunnels, performing on the stage, or whatever you were doing', said British RAF pilot Leonard Hall, 'you had to look at your diary and say, "Sorry, I can't do that on Friday, I have a prior arrangement".[9] If you were in that situation you were all right, because the morale in the camp was very good.'

MI9 lectures had warned the airmen in advance that morale was 'NOT maintained by Concerts and Gramophone records. Real morale comes from the maintenance of a determination to escape. Watch and plan—don't be content to abandon yourself to the situation. That way lies depression—the destruction of initiative and a feeling of dull hopelessness.'[10] Keep up an 'offensive spirit' and stay fit: to that end—and just to get out of their huts— the POWs ran and walked endless circuits around the perimeter of the camp.

Stalag Luft III was, of course, designed and built to be escape-proof, drawing on the lessons learned in earlier POW camps that had proved insufficiently fortified. In between its two 2.5 metre-high barbed-wire fences lay a deadly no-man's-land, a 1.5 metre-wide gap called the Lion's Walk, which was overlooked by a string of sentry towers manned by well-armed guards with orders to shoot. The entire perimeter was fitted with rotating floodlights. Even inside the camp, a warning line drawn between 10 and 20 metres back from the first fence marked out a potential kill zone. Any prisoner who crossed this line could be shot, unless he immediately stopped still and raised his hands in surrender.[11]

This was the lay of the land. It wasn't the worst place to be in the middle of a war. Even a stint in the cooler—solitary confinement—could be welcomed as a chance to get away for a break with a good book. As the Red Cross noted after a visit to Stalag Luft III in 1943, 'the camp gives an excellent impression from every point of view. This is due to the co-operation between the German Camp authorities and Camp Leaders being so good. We believe that the authorities do all that lies in their power to make the lot of the prisoners for whom they are responsible more tolerable.'[12] John was photographed with the other Australians in a school photo-type group.

Scientists studying the animal kingdom have long observed that some animals never adapt to confinement. Even if they are kept in very large enclosures within which all their needs are met, they continue to wear a path around the perimeter fence looking for a way out.[13]

29
BIG X

RAF Squadron Leader Roger Bushell was confident, autocratic, even arrogant. He was not someone John would normally warm to, and I am not sure that he ever did. Bushell had been transferred back into the Luftwaffe's relatively benign custody at Stalag Luft III from the menacing clutches of the Gestapo shortly before John's arrival.

The Spitfire pilot, barrister and glamorous ski champion had started flying with the pre-war millionaires' club of the No. 601 Squadron Auxiliary Air Force. He was just the kind of over-privileged socialite John had recoiled from in his early days in Britain. Having been shot down over the coast of France on his first day of aerial combat in 1940, Bushell knew more about escaping than just about any POW. He had been contacted by MI9 by coded letter soon after capture and had assumed the role of intelligence officer for the so-called 'X' Organisation, MI9's clandestine escape infrastructure, then in its infancy.[1] After twice having succeeded in making it out of the bag, he relished his reputation as an incorrigible escaper. The consequences of his most recent escape had stoked his rage and, consequently, his determination not only to break out again but to create the maximum possible chaos in the process. Bushell had been re-arrested after months on the run when the Czech family who had hidden him in Prague had been exposed by a neighbour. The family had been executed by the Gestapo.

Whatever John thought of Bushell's personality, he was just the kind of man to galvanise the haphazard and largely ineffective escape efforts inside Stalag Luft III. As abrasive as Bushell could be, he was also considered—variously—magnetic, persuasive, ambitious and decisive. He was a formidable figure.[2]

'He cursed all Germans indiscriminately but inside was a clear, cool-headed hatred and it found sublimation in outwitting them', noted Australian journalist and fellow POW Paul Brickhill, who later wrote the first account of the breakout, *The Great Escape*.[3]

The prisoners in the east compound already knew they were being moved to a new north compound once the huts had been built by Soviet POW labourers, scheduled for early 1943. There was no point in digging now. Instead, there was intelligence to gather. Many POWs took up the Kommandant's offer of odd jobs at the new site, diligently noting the locations, dimensions, construction methods and numbers of the new huts and pacing out potential tunnels as they moved between chores.

With Bushell now in charge as 'Big X', supported by the SBO, Group Captain Herbert Massey, a new approach was being formulated. From an initial meeting to shoot ideas—'some wild, some good'[4]—emerged an unprecedented plan for a camp-wide effort to break out 200 men. It would take about 600 men to build three separate underground tunnels, codenamed Tom, Dick and Harry. With three projects constantly on the go, if one or even two tunnels were discovered, the Germans would be caught off guard. They would assume the POWs would have to go back to the beginning again.

'They'll realise how much thought, labour and skill have gone into making it [the tunnel] . . . they'll think we have put everything we have into that one project. If they find two, we hope they reach the conclusion that we've exhausted our efforts,' Bushell is quoted as saying in *The Longest Tunnel*,[5] based on the recollections of former POWs.

John was standing at the back of the room, listening. Bushell paused to make sure his next point sank in.

'Everything hinges upon security. Our security measures must be faultless. From now on I never want to hear the word 'tunnel' mentioned in the camp, and I'll trust you to pass that directive on to every kriegie in every barrack block. I don't care if the person is dead certain that no ferret [intelligence officer] can hear him. The word is expunged from his vocabulary.'

When Bushell described the planned trajectories for Tom, Dick and Harry from three different huts in the north compound to concealed spots in the woods, outside the wire, the gathered crowd groaned. It was a total of hundreds of metres of deep tunnelling in sandy soil.

'Groan, gentlemen, groan', Bushell said, smiling. 'But, remember the Escape Committee are trying to outthink the Germans . . . and Hut 104 [requiring the longest tunnel] is the very last place the Germans would expect a tunnel to originate . . .'

Bushell looked up. 'You got a question, Willy?' he asked, referring to John by his long-standing nickname. John, 'a redoubtable Australian fighter pilot', had 'languidly raised his arm' according to this particular account.

'Tunnel, my friend. You just said a dirty word,' laughed John. The audience roared. Bushell grimaced.

'Dead right. And you can see how easy it is to slip up. Let that be the last time we ever hear that word.'

They planned and waited. Meanwhile, by stopping all other escape efforts, they hoped to lull the Germans into a false sense of security. Exactly how John had come to join Bushell's escape team at this early stage is not clear; there were hundreds of willing men in the camp.

John had, in the past, told Mildred and Len, 'I don't think it's a good thing to shoot a line about oneself. Let someone else do it and it is a lot more convincing.'[6] Perhaps he struck up conversations around the camp about his experiences working with wood during his surfing days, expecting someone to suggest his name as a potential carpenter. Perhaps his senior rank helped. Or he might have come to the attention of the others when he arrived; the Allies' rout of Rommel at El Alamein was very big news and every POW was always keen to hear from a player in any battle that was turning the tide of the war. In any event, John became the escape effort's chief supply officer in waiting. He was to be responsible for sourcing the huge variety of materials they would need.

As the winter of 1942–43 set in and the snow piled up around the drab huts 'what Bushell could do was to muster his team and finesse his plans so that the X Organisation could leap into action as soon as the move took place'.[7]

In his recent book, *The Real Great Escape*, British historian Guy Walters questions the wisdom of Bushell's leadership and his culpability for the manner in which events later unfolded. But of this particular winter, Walters says: 'The men that Bushell drew together . . . must be considered to constitute one of the most talented escape organisations that has ever existed.'

30
SECOND TIME UNLUCKY

Australia. It's just something that one dreams about, Rusty lamented. 'And then in the morning you wake up and you ask yourself, "Well, where is this Australia?"'

He promised Ada that the day would come. He would come home. 'Until it does the only thing is to make the best of what you have', he wrote, just before the Christmas of 1942.

After being spelled from the desert war, Rusty was back in Southern Rhodesia training as a flight instructor. The familiarity was heart-warming; short of getting back to Australia, it felt a bit like coming home. Then the work began in earnest—the hardest work he had ever done, he said. Up at 5 a.m. and either flying or studying until falling into bed exhausted at about 7 p.m., then back up early to start the cycle all over again. The Allies still needed more and more pilots and crew, especially bombers. They were pounding Germany relentlessly and life expectancy for bomber crews had fallen to six weeks.[1]

In April of 1943, Rusty was called up for a second operational tour. It was unusual for a pilot to be asked to go back into operations after surviving a first tour. Everyone knew the statistics; the likelihood of surviving a second tour was considerably lower than for the first. But he was going back to North Africa, not to Europe. The Battle of Alamein was long over and the Axis forces in the Western Desert were in steady retreat. He was buoyed at the prospect of returning to 450 Squadron, another tight-knit surrogate family. The squadron had been moving continuously west since Rommel's defeat and were now in Tunisia. The squadron was nipping at the heels of the Germans and the Italians as they fell back.

The battle-scarred wasteland Rusty encountered on his way through Egypt and Libya by car made him shrink back into his seat. He felt like a tiny insignificant speck on the earth, surrounded by so much twisted and scorched metal strewn across the empty sands. The now-quiet coast road was a narrow ribbon of safety. From the window it was the same scene for hour after hour: an endless parade of warning signs indicating uncleared minefields beyond.

Then, finally, Tunisa. Arriving, he was confronted with an unexpected and disarming burst of beauty. 'After coming from the desert sands . . . the prettiest fields I have ever seen are in Tunisia. They are blazes of red poppies, white, mauve and yellow flowers—it is something one will always remember. And there are terrific olive groves which run for miles.'

The cheerfulness and the keenness of 450 Squadron was just the same, he said, or 'probably a little more'. Morale, too, was 'stupendous'. 'As far as the air force is concerned we have complete air supremacy. So much so that whenever we run into the Hun or the 'Ities', they turn and go for their life.' On the ground the Eighth Army is mopping up and has, he thought, just one 'final burst' to go, then 'the Hun will be completely kicked out of North Africa'.

By the time she received his letter, he told Ada, 'this show will be over'. He was right. The Axis forces abandoned Tunisia three weeks later, on 13 May, and the North Africa campaign was finally won.

But only a couple of days later, before his letter was even

on its way, Rusty found himself stepping out onto the wing of his Kittyhawk, looking down as the heavy metal machine fell with leaden certainty towards the familiar waters of the southern Mediterranean Sea. His plane was peppered with flak, his engine disabled. He was, for the first time, bailing out. That morning, 23 April, he had taken off on the first operational flight of his second tour. He was part of a sweep by the Desert Air Force's 239 Wing across Tunisia's Cap Bon Peninsula, a strategically important landmark within reach of southern Italy. His plane was hit by anti-aircraft fire; its engine seized. He knew instantly he would have to jump.

'I stepped over the side, pulled the rip cord and had a very pleasant journey down to the water. I spent about two hours in the water during which time I drank a flask of brandy,' he told Ada, the flask a fortuitous gift from the mother of his old friend Snow Swift.

'Then a boat load of Germans came and picked me up. I didn't get a scratch . . . but I was really cold. That was put right in a German hospital and I'm none the worse for my experience.'

Now Rusty, too, was in Germany 'as the guest of the Government'. He wrote his first letter as a prisoner in early May 1943 from Dulag Luft, where he was in transit. 'I am quite alright and apart from being a P.O.W am quite happy', he said.

When the next purge went out to Stalag Luft III, Rusty was on the train. From letters home, we know John and Rusty found each other immediately. I imagine John spilling out with the other POWs to scan the new arrivals. This time, he has an old friend in the crowd. He's smiling from ear to ear. Rusty grins back.

31

THE SWIMMING POOL

A swimming pool! Splendid! Two of the bigger blokes hefted a disabled British pilot into the water. 'Thank you very much, chaps, wonderful show', he called and swam off.

'These were memorable times,' said Australian pilot Geoff Cornish of the swimming pool at the new north compound. All the buildings and the prisoners' huts were constructed with double walls of wood, and coal or coke fires burned throughout much of the year, so a fire reservoir was essential. This large, deep brick-lined pool made a popular swimming hole in that heady spring and summer of 1943, the first such recreation facility most POWs had seen for a long time. Swimming was, of course, *verboten* (forbidden), but the Germans didn't mind, Cornish said. If the prisoners were in the pool the guards could be sure they weren't working on anything else.[1]

John wrote home requesting some swimming trunks; he had his surf-lifesaving 'Blue Book' in his small pile of possessions in his bunk. Splendid, indeed. The pool went a long way to 'lightening the psychological load', Cornish said. So too did the fresh, clean smell of freshly sawn pine boards that drifted across the new compound day and night.

In Sydney and Narromine, Mildred and Ada finally had something to be pleased about too. John had arranged a swap as soon as possible, and he and Rusty were now in the same bunk room. They were on the same cooking detail; they were in the same sports teams. They were together, watching each other's backs. All they had to do now was wait out the war.

But the sense of momentum in the camp and the mental relief it brought were actually more closely linked to the POWs' new secret lives. Their days were split in two: their busy schedules above ground and their clandestine roles, mostly below ground. Morale, says the first camp history compiled in late 1945 from records kept by the POWs, 'was closely bound up with the escape attempts',[2] and this was the largest, most sophisticated and most intricately planned escape effort yet.

In the spring of 1943, the transfer of 850 prisoners to the new north compound had finally gone ahead. The ratio of prisoners to guards was low; the Germans had allocated between 500 to 600 guards and other personnel to manage and secure the POWs[3] at Stalag Luft III. The gradient of the challenge was extreme.

'We were young men, and by and large wanted to do something that had purpose to it. Otherwise, it was pointless waiting for the end of the war. Escaping was a real objective . . . [and] of course, it was such fun,' recalled British RAF officer and POW Walter Morison.[4]

To others it was at least worth a try, no matter how slim the chance of success, if only to get a breath of fresh air to 'get over the monotony of just walking around the camp'. This was a goal many 'were anxious to achieve, even for a day or so'.[5]

Then there was a core group of POWs for whom the psychological need to work towards escaping was so deep that it was almost a 'mania', said Jimmy James. It was all they could think about, day and night.[6]

Since the end of World War II, the story of the Great Escape has been scrutinised in ever-greater detail by documentary makers, historians and commentators, many of whom claim to have uncovered a truer, newer or more comprehensive version of events. The prisoners themselves kept careful records and drawings that were concealed underground or in the camp's walls and later retrieved to form the basis of the camp history. This has proved an invaluable resource. There are also scores of lengthy oral histories recorded with former POWs, as well as large piles of declassified files, bulging with communications, intelligence reports, post-war investigations and personal statements.

From this blizzard of detail emerges one common theme. Memory is fickle and unreliable. The same events are recalled differently by many people or not remembered at all. Memory never works like a recorder that can replay exactly what has occurred.[7] It is mediated by what happens next and what other people say. It is more 'akin to putting puzzle pieces together than retrieving a video recording'. We reassemble different bits of the same picture to make up our own personal memories, steered by what is most important to us, and seen from our individual points of view.

One of the first discrepancies I came across in my own research was the difference in the accounts of the order in which John and Rusty's group emerged from the tunnel. Some members of that party even seemed to have difficulty remembering exactly who had been with them during that long, nervous night on the train. This is unsurprising, given the extreme levels of stress. John and Rusty's story can only be told within the constraints of these fallible human memories, with the added handicap of the passing of time.[8]

At home we have a lovely old, worn fabric-bound book called *Spotlight on Stalag Luft III* by Scangriff that was passed on to me by my uncle David. Scangriff was the name used by the editorial team of the underground paper at the camp, an amalgamation of Scandal Press and *Angriff* (the attack), the name of the Nazi newspaper of the time. A small number of copies were published privately in 1947 by that same editorial team, when memories were relatively fresh and long before the escape had been translated, or reinvented, for the screen by Hollywood. It is a slight, simple and poignant series of recollections dedicated to the escapees and then sent to their families. To me this seems like a good gauge of the mood of the time.

Scangriff lets Paul Brickhill, a member of that editorial team, sketch out the big picture. He had carried the manuscript of his first bestseller on the escape, *Escape from Danger,* out of the camp on the terrible 'long march' of the then half-starved Stalag Luft III POWs ahead of the liberation of Silesia by the Soviets in 1945. *The Great Escape*, *The Dambusters* and other famous Brickhill books followed.

'Yes, I was in that camp, but now I find it hard to believe all the fantastic things that happened', he begins. 'You see it was no simple tunnel . . .' It was, as we know, three tunnels: the work of 500 or 600 men for fifteen months.

> 'We carried out the whole show in a pretty barren compound . . . swarming with German security guards night and day, snooping with probes and torches.
>
> As well as the tunnels we had to organise factories for mass forgery, map and compass making, for producing iron rations, tailoring, carpentry and metal work shops. We had to use a couple of hundred sentries to conceal our operations.

The cast of this drama was large, talented and diverse. The hundreds of kriegies who signed up had to be vetted first. Two members of the original planners had to vouch for each new participant. Then the kriegies had to be put to work. There were the hands-on team and the security men. Working out how to keep the operation secret was just as important as all the engineering and ingenuity that went into tunnelling deep underground through hazardously sandy soil. The first line of defence was the rotating duty pilot, who parked himself at the camp's front gate on a chair officiously recording everyone and everything that came in and out in his logbook. His team of runners, part of the POWs' intelligence network known as 'stooges', slouched around casually in case they had to tail a new arrival. The duty pilot used a shovel set, an old Red Cross parcel box, an incinerator and a coal bucket in various configurations to signal the alert level. A shovel in the bucket on top of the incinerator might be the signal for high danger, due to the proximity of ferrets.[9] The 'ferrets' were specially assigned German intelligence officers, the most tenacious and dangerous of whom the POWs nicknamed 'Rubberneck' as he always seemed to be peering into everything and anything.

Above ground, the POWs had to give the impression of business as usual, while covering the absence of the underground workers and diverting guards from the areas of activity.

Not every prisoner relished the thrill of such subterfuge. Bushell had famously regaled the prisoners with his view that, having already beaten poor odds to survive being downed in the air war, they were all 'living on borrowed time'. Consequently, what did they have to lose by seizing the day? Others, still traumatised or injured, were not so keen to continue to tempt fate. Although tensions sometimes emerged between the edgy, enthusiastic 'cloak and dagger boys' and the 'Tally-Ho' stayers, they were never sufficiently serious to expose or hinder the escape organisation.[10]

At first, three teams worked three shifts a day of about two-and-a-half or three hours each.[11] The new wooden huts were elevated, to prevent tunnelling, so the shafts had to be dug by hand using improvised tools through the foundation piles in the cases of Tom and Harry, and through the drain of a shower room for Dick. Each needed a perfectly disguised seal too, exactly replicating the original floor. For Harry this meant exactly re-creating the tiled hearth of the stove in room 104 on a wooden framed 'lid' that could be moved backwards and forwards to open and close the tunnel, even while the stove was burning. The problem of the heat was solved by using wooden brackets that fitted around the stove to move it quickly.

To call the tunnelling painstaking does not do the men's efforts justice. Imagine a 100 metre-long sprint track, set on sandy soil. Then imagine sinking a 10 metre-deep shaft by hand, bracing it with accurately pre-cut wood panelling against collapses, then hollowing out three chambers below: one for storing excavated sand, one for equipment and a workshop and one to house an improvised ventilation system to keep the diggers alive. Now imagine doing all this secretly working only with a small knife or a sharpened spoon. By the end of May 1943, all three of the tunnel shafts had been sunk in just two months. Other prisoners were transforming whatever garments were available into 'civilian clothes', the forgers were mocking up very persuasive fake documents and a nutritionist was even experimenting with the optimum means of concentrating kriegie food into high-kilojoule escape rations.

At first, John was busy stripping the wooden bunks of bed boards. The order had come directly from Bushell. Why John had been picked for this job isn't clear. It might be because he was considered good-natured and amusing, so he would have had a reasonable chance of talking any reluctant 'donors' around, or that his senior rank would ensure both cooperation and discretion. Not everyone was happy to endure an increasingly saggy bunk. But, said one POW, it was no use saying 'you can't have two of my bed boards. They had to go and the beds got progressively less and less smooth.'[12]

Ostensibly, Rusty was a cheerful, cooperative and helpful POW. He had been quickly recruited to help run the camp's sports activities. There were long lists pinned up all over the camp, filled with hundreds of names of POWs nominating themselves for a mind-boggling array of sporting contests.

Rusty wrote home in detail about the various matches, hut versus hut, block versus block, the 'fighters versus the bombers', one nationality against another. In cricket, Scangriff noted, 'the Aussies really got down to the game and defeated all challengers, although finely matched fixtures such as Australia v. The Rest were grand games'.[13]

But the lists and the scheduled games did not necessarily match up. Many of them were, in fact, for volunteers wanting to work on the escape effort and so qualify for the ballot for the 200 available places on the escape list. About two-thirds of the camp applied.[14] 'Rugger', for example, was originally for men wanting to dig. Then, as there was insufficient room for sport on the grand scale that the lists suggested, the names were quickly resorted into a special education file 'listing' applicants, and then participants, in study courses to avoid arousing suspicion. 'History' became those willing to disperse sand and the 'German' classes denoted those who were to make useful contacts such as corruptible German guards, ironically because they already spoke the language well. A complex card system was developed that helped the education office keep track of all available skills and how they were being deployed.[15] The 'Cricket' list, it seems, was, in fact, for playing cricket.

The tunnel they called Tom was initially prioritised because it was closest to the perimeter fence. Then a ferret 'accidentally dug his probe-iron spike into the edge of Tom's trap door and that was the end of Tom', reported Brickhill for Scangriff.

'After that blow we found that Dick was unsuitable because the Germans suddenly cut down the wood where it was to come up and built another compound there.'

It was all down to Harry, the longest and most difficult tunnel of them all.

32
ANOTHER GERMAN FRIEND

Much of the appeal of war stories lies in the heroic struggle of the good against the evil, just so long as the good are on our side. Real life is never so clear-cut. The Allied POWs worried about potential 'stool pigeons' among their own who might see some personal advantage in trading information with the 'ferrets'. But the Germans seemed to be paying insufficient attention to the possibility that information, and goods, might flow in the other direction.

If there was one thing the prisoners had a lot of, it was cigarettes. They also had useful amounts of chocolate. Both came in with the Red Cross parcels that supplemented the meagre kriegie rations that, on their own, provided less energy than an adult needed to lie around all day—what the POWs called 'bed bashing'. By their own calculation, without the extra Red Cross food, they would have been down to about 6700 kilojoules a day, only enough for a child,[1] and only enough to lie around listlessly.

Such luxuries were also useful for palling up with the goons, the regular German guards, whose own lives were affected by wartime shortages. Certain small and useful items and seemingly innocuous, but important, snippets of information could be obtained this way. Once a guard had been bribed, he was forced to continue cooperating or risk being exposed to his own superiors.

One German intelligence officer and translator in the camp, Corporal Eberhard 'Nicky' Hesse, was deeply offended by such transactions. He would have been equally upset to hear the term 'tame goon' thrown around to describe those Germans persuaded, by various means, to assist the escape efforts.[2]

As 1943 wore on, Hesse engaged in many lengthy and earnest conversations with a small circle of POWs, including John,[3] according to a statement he later provided to British investigators. His closest contact was Sydney Dowse, a British Spitfire pilot and tunnel digger from within the inner circle of the X Organisation, but he listed John with the other POWs he became acquainted with and came to trust.

Hesse, then 25, was no fonder of the Nazis than any of the Allied POWs were. He was a well-educated lawyer, he spoke good English, had travelled in Europe and had been brought up by his parents 'to be cosmopolitan'. He said he was 'hampered at first by the un-cosmopolitan' attitude of those Allied POWs who spoke only English and who had, until the war, barely ventured beyond their own village or town. 'We German anti-Nazis could not see any sign that the Allies could differentiate between Nazis and their German enemies'—that is, Germans who were seeking to oppose the Nazis from within.

Hesse had moved to Switzerland briefly after the war broke out but risked being interned as a deserter. When he returned to Germany he managed to find a quiet, out-of-the-way post in German-occupied Poland, before being called up for compulsory military service and posted to the Soviet Union. When he fell ill he was sent back to Germany and posted to Stalag Luft III.

'I held back from cooperating with the POWs because I believed that although my help would be accepted they would despise me for doing it', he said.

'It took long debates with English officers . . . to convince me that this was not true. They believed, as I did, that the only normal thing for people with the same political ideas to do would be to cooperate and this way my fears were removed.'

This was an extraordinary breakthrough for the escape effort. Hesse gathered around him a small group of like-minded Germans, including one of the mail censors, who provided invaluable help in sourcing and copying documents and in providing information on trains, for example. Hesse's personal link to John may also answer one question we have always had: how was it that John had managed to go on walks outside the camp to pick up intelligence before the escape, a detail that appears in virtually every account of the great escape and was mentioned to me personally by Jimmy James? Perhaps Hesse's network assisted him in getting permission.

The layers of subterfuge and misinformation were, of course, murky and complex. But, like much of politics and even war, it is often the personal that makes the difference. When a kriegie was ordered to repay Hesse for his help with coffee and cigarettes, the whole thing almost came unstuck. 'I refused. This showed me how misunderstood my motives were, it showed my political ideas had been misunderstood,' he said.[4] Hesse didn't have much to hold dear in Nazi Germany but he did have his pride and his honour. His help was only available for free.

As the escape plan progressed, Hesse was arrested by his own men eleven times, but nothing compromising was ever discovered. He merely went back to work. Later he would express his appreciation for the 'extremely generous hospitality' he and the POWs' German friends received in the various huts. 'I am indebted to the officers of Stalag Luft III for the impressive and harmonious hours [I spent with them]', he told British investigators. He was particularly thankful to Sydney Dowse, who kept his promise to get him out of Germany at the end of the war.

To me, these two scenes are worth dwelling on. Today, Stalag Luft III is little more than ruins, the outline of the huts only barely discernible in the forest. But the fire reservoir is intact, if empty. It's easy to picture it full, and to imagine the pleasure of diving in on a hot day. So, too, the energy and the intensity of the clandestine conversations between Hesse's group and the POWs. Something very special was unfolding.

33

COOKING AND CARPENTRY

Rusty was baking a cake. It was not a complicated recipe, he told Ada. First take some stale biscuits, of the 'Sao' type, and some old bread, and grate them finely into something resembling flour. Add some milk powder, margarine, raisins and water 'and stir the whole lot like hell'. Then 'pour into a homemade baking dish, place in the oven and hope for the best'. Should your rations allow, you might also like to make some icing. This can be achieved using condensed milk, cocoa and margarine, he advised. It's hard not to smile, reading Rusty's letters home.

The psychological aspect of food is perhaps the most interesting: the compelling effect on morale, noted Lieutenant David Lubbock in Scangriff's 1947 retrospective.[1] 'It is said that people will go to any lengths for food, but one had to experience real shortages to realise the full meaning of those words.'

The food in Stalag Luft III was, above all, monotonous. 'It used to amuse me how people, for variation, would try to find a new way of cooking this or that, when practically all our parcelled food was pre-cooked and only needed heating.'

One of the most plentiful packaged items provided by the Red Cross was Klim powdered milk, the brand name impossible to forget given it spelled 'milk' backwards. The ubiquitous Klim tins were also unforgettable as they gave the POWs a steady supply of metal cylinders and solder. These were refashioned, among many other things, into the critical ventilation flues that drew fresh air into the tunnels and took stale air out, using a crude bellows made from old air force kit-bags, hockey sticks and wooden valve boxes.

There was, too, a highly efficient and complicated food bartering system called Foodacco in the camp. At least 50 different categories of food, tobacco and common goods like sewing equipment and basic clothes were assigned a set number of points. All prisoners got much the same rations but Red Cross parcels from different parts of the world varied, as did preferences and appetites. Whatever wasn't wanted could be brought into the Foodacco shop to be traded and the points earned either saved or spent on other stock. A camp book was kept with a day-by-day calculation of each POW's account. Rare items, like tins of salmon, might warrant the carnival of a public auction. There was even a reserves department: booking a certain item before it came in cost 10 per cent more points. Loans were available, at no interest. And, for those unfortunate enough to get a Red Cross parcel containing goods damaged in transit, Foodacco would replace them out of their small profits.[2]

Foodacco was fascinating, not just because of how efficiently it worked but in how it reflected business in the outside world. At first, it was a private initiative but some POWs were profiting by shrewdly trading up, leaving some others with less than their share, so it was 'nationalised' and the points system standardised.[3] But, like any market, it was always subject to fluctuations. If a rumour went through the camp that POWs were going onto half parcels, meaning instead of one Red Cross parcel they would only get half, everyone would rush the shop.

'A kind of panic wave went through the camp, the same as one finds at the Stock Exchange when war is declared', wrote Lubbock, as the shop was swamped by people trying to convert their points for food to stockpile. Then, rationing briefly came in until supply was resolved.

That incarcerated men, with no idea of when they might be freed, could run such as sophisticated and largely fair scheme to meet their most fundamental of needs for food goes some way to understanding and appreciating the level of organisation and cooperation that was running in tandem, underground. Even today, the X Organisation itself is still often regarded as a masterpiece of project management that 'ticked all the boxes' in terms of cost, quality control, time management, risk, integration, communications and the maximisation of human resources.[4]

In August 1943 John finally heard that he had been awarded a DFC. Rusty was thrilled for him. He passed on the good news to Ada but also their disappointment that there was no beer to be had for a celebration, not even a 'good feed' of bacon and eggs.

John received a different promotion of sorts the following month. He quietly took over as the head of the carpentry section for the X Organisation.[5] With the discovery of 'Tom' in October 1943, already 85 metres long and the result of much planning, sweat and toil, the emotional temperature in the camp rose considerably. The Germans decided to blow Tom up, taking off part of the roof of the hut in the process. Dick too remained firmly closed up, given that there was no longer any tree cover to shield the escapees on their way out.

By chance, one of the German-speaking POWs on intelligence-gathering detail overhead the head of security in the camp, Sergeant-Major Hermann Glemnitz, telling a ferret that there shouldn't be any more trouble in the north compound 'because the prisoners must have used every scrap of available wood to shore up the tunnel'.[6] That meant any further wood that went missing would be noticed. They would have to move fast.

Immediately, Bushell sent John out on 'the biggest bed board levy yet'. Whatever was missing would be assumed to have been used in Tom. Bushell led by example, giving up all his remaining bed boards and persuading his roommate, Bob Tuck, to do the same. The string net that replaced them, however, was less sturdy than was required for such a big man. That night Bushell fell straight through, crashing down into Tuck, and taking them both through to the floor—a scene that suited Hollywood well when it came to lightening the mood of the film version of the escape.

John's effort reaped an extra 2000 or so bed boards in two days, which he hid down the shaft of the now suspended tunnel, Dick. With no detailed records breaking down the roles of all the other individuals, we can assume Rusty was working closely with John, given their friendship and their plans to escape together. And it was also Rusty's sporting past that gave him the skills to join the carpentry team. He was always managing to fix the camp's cricket bats, recalled Group Captain Harry 'Wings' Day, the most senior POW to escape, in a private letter to the Kierath family after the war.

'He was also very neat and clever with his hands—and with very primitive carpentry tools and under difficult circumstances—he used to make all kinds of useful things for anyone who asked him.'

That same month, the X committee met. For the first time, John was included.[7] It is easy to forget John was still only 24 years old and had willingly carried great responsibilities over many years. Nowadays, we think of young men of his age as barely out of adolescence. Over the past decade, neuro-imaging has ushered in big changes in the way science understands the development of the human brain.[8] While adolescence used to mark the beginning of adulthood, we now know that our brains are still developing well into our twenties. This makes me think of John as a fourteen-year-old, entering himself to swim against the older boys at school. At 24, was he still that same young adolescent, chasing the approval of the older men?

The X committee meeting decided all work would pause for the winter, in the hope of consolidating the impression that Tom had, indeed, been a spectacular find, leaving the POWs spent, demoralised and unwilling to try again. Just as Bushell had initially imagined when the three-tunnel plan had first been conceived, they were hoping the Germans would now let their guard down. It would be a cold, dull winter at Stalag Luft III with the snow deep on the ground outside, and the tension thick within.

Leslie 'Johnny' Bull rushed into his room with a big smile on his face and the news that Harry was to reopen and that Bushell wanted a 'blitz'.[9] It was 4 January 1944. Johnny Bull was usually a serious, almost grimly determined man and he took to tunnelling with all the energy this suggested. He was married and had a young son in London he had never met. He was, as John, Rusty and Jerzy would discover as they slogged their way over the mountains into Czechoslovakia, absolutely driven. He just wanted to get home.

With the blitz in progress, John was now responsible for the trap of Harry[10] and the underground cavern where the carpentry team produced everything from the pre-fabricated tunnel supports to the wooden rails that the underground trolley or 'train' system ran on and the trolleys themselves, as well as sourcing the ever-scarcer supplies of wood. Their saws were contrived from the springs inside a gramophone player. Glue was actually tree sap.

Sydney Dowse, one of the most senior diggers, described his shifts lying in the confined tunnel like this. In a space barely wide enough for a man to rotate his shoulders, he lay on his stomach, propped up on his elbows. He carefully scraped at the earth in front of him with a knife, then pushed the loosened sand back as best he could to the man lying behind him, who would bag it up in small sacks. He would, in turn, pass the bag back again to either another man, or put it onto the trolley on wooden rails that would be pulled by rope back to the tunnel's mouth. As the tunnel progressed, there were two intermediate 'stations'—bigger caverns allowing some more movement—built in between each tight, narrow section.[11]

Was it hot and claustrophobic? Not overwhelmingly so, Dowse said. The improvised ventilation system of Klim tins worked remarkably, in fact surprisingly, well.

The wooden supports came down the tunnel the same way. They had been precisely pre-cut to clip together into a box frame to hold up each new section of the tunnel. Even then, digging the roof often proved impossible without a collapse, and often enough the front digger found himself half buried in sand, the man behind scrabbling at his feet to pull him clear.

The way Dowse told it, you were either claustrophobic or you were not, there were no shades of grey. He was not claustrophobic, he said, so even a sand collapse didn't unduly spook him. 'Some people did have claustrophobia . . . they would come rushing back [to the outside]. They would be genuinely scared and they would be honest enough to say so. They would be taken off [the digging team].'

Guy Walters puts it more graphically. 'The whole process of tunnelling was more than a bit nasty. Many of the kriegies regarded the tunnellers as a breed apart, who were able to put up with the prospect of being buried alive, intense claustrophobia, heat, stuffy air and the smell of the fat lamps and their co-workers' bodies.'[12]

The sweat was bad enough, Walters writes, but what caused a real stench was urine and faeces. 'If you were caught short, you dug a little hole and did your best,' he quotes POW, Ken Rees, as saying. It was no joke when a digger had a stomach problem. 'At the end of the shift men would find themselves covered in sweat, sand and excrement, a combination that would cake their long johns.' Consequently, most of the men dug naked.

In a snowbound winter, dispersing the sand was a new challenge. The innovative 'penguins'—those men who had carried tubes fashioned out of long johns filled with sand and concealed inside the legs of their trousers—could no longer use this same technique to spread the sand around the campsite. It would be immediately visible on the snow. Instead, it was spirited out to the camp theatre and dropped in the voids under the seats.

The blitz was working. The tunnel had reached the 60 metre mark by mid-February.

In 2011, a British television crew documented the attempts of a group of RAF pilots, including veterans of Iraq and Afghanistan, to re-create a tunnel using only the same equipment. Advised by several former POWs and backed by a team of technical experts, they did manage to replicate some aspects of the escape, such as the forging of documents using stamps cut out of shoe heels, the fabrication of compasses using gramophone records moulded into cases and even a wooden trolley on rails. They failed to build a new tunnel alongside Harry. The sand just kept on collapsing in on them.

'As you scrape away the sand you've got to get rid of it in a very, very confined area—just 2 ft 9 in [0.8 m] square. You have to manoeuvre in the bed boards to shore up the tunnel. And you can't even nudge the sand in the gap you've just carved or it will collapse,' said executive producer Simon Rakes.[13]

As the pace of the tunnelling quickened, so did the tempo of daily life in the camp. In retrospect, there were a number of potentially ominous signs.

As early as 1943 Heinrich Himmler, the second-most powerful Nazi and head of the SS (Schutzstaffel) made it clear he was willing to interfere with the Luftwaffe's control of its own POW camps, jeopardising the protections enshrined in the Geneva Convention.[14] An internal SS security report of August 1943 said in part: 'The attitude of British prisoners to the Reich is absolutely hostile. They make fun of Germany, German institutions, and leaders on all possible occasions.' It went on to outline some now-familiar undergraduate humour, like giving their names to their captors as Churchill or Roosevelt.

> Their attitude is self possessed and, indeed, often borders on arrogance. Their bearing and their whole behaviour are doubtless intended as effective propaganda. The manner in which the British behave . . . leaves no doubt of their confidence in victory. They take every opportunity to show that Germany will lose the war. This assurance of victory and self possession does not fail to impress the [German] people.

In February 1944, Camp Kommandant von Lindeiner, well aware of the chilly wind now blowing through the Nazi hierarchy as their fortunes on the battlefield waned, called together the senior officers from each compound. Italy's Fascists had wavered throughout 1943, forcing the Germans to rescue Mussolini, draining the Nazis' energy and resources. By early 1944, the Soviet offensive was gathering pace and its troops had entered Poland while the Allies had landed in southern Italy.[15] Von Lindeiner warned the POWs' representatives that they were at increasing risk of serious consequences if they persisted with their escape efforts. On 4 March, the so-called 'Bullet Order' was issued by the Gestapo, stating that all recaptured prisoners—except the British and the Americans—would be made to disappear: they would be sent to Mauthausen concentration camp in Austria where they would be shot. British and American prisoners would be held in police custody, enabling the Gestapo to decide their fate on a 'case by case' basis.[16] This goes some way to explaining the decisions made in late March.

The tunnelling just kept on going at an ever-increasing pace. It seems the men were, perhaps, blinkered to the risk. Instead, they saw their window of opportunity closing. Rather than pausing to reconsider, they charged ahead. Their momentum was such that they could no longer stop the behemoth the escape effort had become. They were intent on only one thing: they had to get through before the window slammed shut.

And there was also some good fortune coming their way. The chief ferret, Rubberneck, was going on leave for a couple of weeks at the beginning of March, so the intense pressure would briefly be off. By way of a departing gesture, Rubberneck appeared at *appell* to announce the immediate transfer of nineteen POWs to a new camp about 8 kilometres away—a shock development. Some of the most senior members of the X Organisation were on the list, including the chief engineer, the tunnel king, Wally Floody, a Canadian Spitfire pilot. Bushell's feigned lack of interest in escaping—a cover he maintained by taking part in plays and learning languages—had apparently worked. He was not singled out.[17]

'The tunnel advanced inexorably, almost frantically—in nine days 112 feet were dug and shored [up], the record was 14 feet in one day', wrote Jimmy James in his post-war autobiography.[18]

'Momentum didn't slacken, indeed it had to be speeded up if "Harry" was to be finished before the chief ferret came back from leave.' Over two months about 80 tonnes of sand had been excavated and redistributed, the tunnel was 110 metres long (other accounts say 106 metres) and a 7.5 metre-long exit shaft was within metres of the surface, 'outside the wire'.

How exhausting was this period? Sydney Dowse, again, does not recall being overly tired. 'We were pretty fit, we didn't carry much fat, we were young, strong and athletic, even food doesn't matter all that much when it comes to endurance', he said.[19] What was so special about Harry compared to the hundreds of other tunnels that had been dug out of Stalag Luft III and countless other POW camps? 'Its exit—it had one!'

34

A TICKET IN THE LOTTERY

They could hardly believe it. Harry was finished. They were stunned. The atmosphere in the camp was electric; the air was so heavy with anticipation that it felt like a massive thunderstorm was about to break.

When Rubberneck got back from leave he immediately homed in on Hut 104, where Harry was located. But, after a four-hour search that turned the hut inside out, the ferrets had not found the hatch. This was no cause for celebration. He had suspected the correct hut, despite its unlikely location far from the perimeter. Bushell decided it would be time to go very soon, despite the exceptionally cold weather. In fact, on the next moonless night.

There are many inconsistent accounts of how the order of escapees was determined. The RAF camp history based on the POWs' own records says the first 30 places were reserved for the X committee. Their order of departure was drawn from a hat. The next 20 were selected from the 40 'most prominent workers', including John and Rusty. Before his death, Jimmy James told me John was first on this list as no. 31 and Rusty was no. 32. Other POW memoirs suggest they may have been numbers 32 and 33, or even 32 and 35. It doesn't matter. Then came the 50 'most important' workers, although the distinction between this and the earlier group is not clear.[1] The final 100 places were allocated by a general ballot in which all 600 men could participate. At this point a few men withdrew for different, personal reasons. Cornish, for example, decided it was more important to stay in the camp to help as he was a trainee doctor.[2] A handful of others discovered the extent of their claustrophobia only during a test run underground, so stepped aside.

Jimmy James said he was absolutely 'delighted' to be no. 39 and in John's group to catch a train. There was little expectation that many of the 'hard arsers' would make it on foot. But Wings Day had reassured Bushell that there 'would be a flap all over Germany . . . we would have done something useful'.[3]

Did anyone have doubts at this late stage? 'Nobody thought seriously, if indeed they thought at all, of the possible, or probable, consequences of a mass escape on this scale', Jimmy later wrote. How many of the men, he asked, had told themselves 'I am not going to be shot down?' In war, he said, 'it is always the other fellow who is going to buy it'.[4]

John's last letter home from Stalag Luft III did not survive the flood that damaged my uncle David's home. Rusty's letter did last. He was in a good mood, despite having little to report to Ada beyond his dishwashing duty, the method of making a kriegie mop and some exceptionally good theatre performances by the camp's budding Noel Cowards. He was even able to joke about the German music and war communiqués blaring out all day long via a series of loudspeakers newly deployed across the camp. 'I fear I shall be doing the goosestep, or . . . going crazy in the near future'. He signed off, as usual, with love to all 'and lots for yourself'.

The story has almost come full circle. As much as I'd like to, I can't loop back on the past again to avoid the inevitable conclusion.

There was a last kriegie supper to eat. It was deliberately as nourishing as the rations allowed. There were each POW's escape documents, clothes and backstory to finalise. There was the moon's cycle to check. Then, once the lock-up guards had made their final rounds at 10 p.m. on the night of 24 March 1944, it was time to go. At 10.15 p.m., a chill gust of wind rushed down the tunnel. They were through at the other end. To say they were jubilant, excited, exhilarated, nervous, anxious and unsure would all be true and much more. John and Rusty were sufficiently high up in the list to have been already out or to have been lying waiting underground when the air-raid siren went off around midnight and the makeshift electric lights went off. I am not sure which it was. If it was the latter, I just hope that Sydney Dowse was right about claustrophobia.

35

SHUFFLING THE CARDS

This is where the truth and the Hollywood story diverge. On the big screen in 1963, the world came face to face with Steve McQueen playing the 'bed board' guy, a fictional American POW, Captain Hilts. Among other things, Hilts is seen making his rounds of the huts, conducting a bed board levy. The film characters are, of course, only loosely based on any of the participants and most are composite characters that deliberately mix up the roles, personalities and foibles of the real men. Hilts not only rides his motorbike in a spectacular fashion to jump a barbed-wire coil along something that looks like the Swiss border, but survives to be thrown back in the cooler. He is last seen back in the camp, pensively bouncing his baseball over and over again against the cooler wall.[1]

It's early morning when the phone rings with instructions to heat the ovens. There are bodies coming in.[2]

The ugly concrete crematorium is set on a slight rise overlooking the cemetery just outside the town of Brux (now Most), at least 160 kilometres west of the Reichenberg police station via the quiet mountain backroads. Two days earlier, Ivo Tonder had glimpsed an ashen-faced John and his group being taken back into the Reichenberg cells. Tonder had since been told the men had been shipped back to Stalag Luft III.[3] At 4 a.m. that same morning of 29 March 1944, a Russian prisoner had reported seeing them being ushered out.[4] It was five days since they had crawled out of the tunnel into the forest, anxious, excited, free men.

At about 8 a.m. five Gestapo officials arrive at the crematorium in a truck with bodies piled in the back. They are accompanied by two more senior Gestapo men in a car, one with four stars on his lapel, denoting the rank of Sturmbannführer, the equivalent of a major. All spoke with formal 'high German' accents, so presumably none was a local recruit.[5]

Under Nazi occupation, local Czech officials do not ask questions. But these bodies are well-muscled young men, military types, which a civilian crematorium is not accustomed to receiving. (POWs were required to be buried in coffins with appropriate military ceremonies.[6])

The Gestapo men supervised the process themselves, said the crematorium's chief, Anton Sawerthal, in his evidence to the post-war British investigation.

The urns are removed by the Gestapo the same day, at about 7 p.m at night.

'One of the Gestapo officials told me that the dead men had been shot, but I did not see their wounds personally. They were cremated in their clothes without coffins.'[7]

When Sawerthal enters the details in his personal cremation book, he carefully writes out: 'Williams, John 6925; Bull, Leslie 6926; Mondschein, Jerzy 692; Kierath, Reginald 6923'. Their death certificates and their cremation orders had been typed out and signed in advance the previous day, citing 'shot while trying to escape'. Other documents produced by the Gestapo claim: 'Wills existed': allegedly the men had told their captors that they wished to be cremated.

I am well aware that I have a tendency to side, instinctively, with the underdog. Some might say I over-empathise. Recently, this was apparent to me when I was swimming backstroke in the early morning at Manly pool, looking up at a perfectly empty, clear-blue patch of Australia's big sky. A flock of huge, majestic black cockatoos, flying up very high, swept languidly into view. Trailing the group was a solitary bird, not quite keeping up. As the flock crossed through my line of sight the loner lagged, finally peeling off to fend for itself, a single black silhouette against the blue. I worry about birds like that, literally and figuratively. I don't think this is the same as syrupy sentimentalism but I do realise that I am not able to tell this story from a dispassionate perspective, nor do I want to.

In some ways I feel embarrassed to be so emotionally entangled in a tale that I have only ever experienced second-hand. Just to type out that brief account of the scene at the Most crematorium filled me with a dull, reverberating sense of unresolved loss even though the tragedy of John's life and death has never been mine. That is probably because I believe that empathy is precious. It defines us as human beings. It elevates us above the base instincts of survival. After the war, John's friend and former no. 2, Ted Sly, remained profoundly affected by what war could strip away, as did many returned servicemen. He understood what it was to become a 'frenzied creature, more animal than man', under fire. That, in itself, is reason enough not to harden our hearts.

The way Geoff Cornish described his feelings was so uniquely Australian that John would have laughed. Having given up his escape slot to another POW, it was many many years before Cornish finally steeled himself to return to Poland to visit the graves of 'the fifty'.[8] He likened the experience to that of a surfer who has trained hard and well to ride a steep two metre wave, only to find himself confronted with a towering 12 metre swell.

'For a few minutes I couldn't recall much, I was literally overwhelmed', he said of his visit.

'When I walked up to the line of graves stones of the guys

they shot the first one I came to was Charles Hall, the man who took my place.

'I just stood there and that is when the scenes came flooding back to me and the realisation that he had no life at all after 1944.'

For as long as I can remember, I have had a deep and enduring sympathy for my grandparents, my dad, his siblings and, more recently, for the Kieraths, the Bulls and the Mondscheins, and everyone affected by these premeditated, unexpected murders. And, of course, for our four young men. I know Peter Kierath feels the same way, although we have not openly discussed it. But, on several occasions over the past few years, we have found ourselves both smiling and wiping away tears.

In World War II, more than 55 million people lost their lives, many in such terrible circumstances that a clean shot to the head or heart might seem relatively humane. The sheer magnitude of the suffering and loss that washed around the globe seems to diminish the significance of individual deaths. It should not. We say 'one death is a tragedy, one million deaths is a statistic' for a reason. We can only really understand what war means if we look carefully, up close.

John and Rusty are no more important than any other victim of this, or any other, war. They are not unimportant either. There is no hierarchy of loss. I admire the many, many people all over the world who have been empowered by the internet to explore their family histories and to build personal websites and to publish memoirs. These are precious and valuable offerings to that fundamental human need to preserve the past. And, if we are willing to engage with the powerful and often disturbing emotions that violence and grief engenders in our own family stories, we come one step closer to understanding the recent history on which we now all stand.

When news of the mass breakout from Stalag Luft III reached Hitler it was immediately clear that, regardless of any of the usual rules or processes, the fate of every single recaptured escapee was in the Führer's hands.

It was the Sunday after the escape; a 'tense, angry and excited'[9] Hitler was ensconced in his mountain retreat at Berchtesgaden near the Austrian border. Many of the escapees had been caught within 24 hours near the camp. Others were still being hunted further afield and only three would never be caught, travelling vast distances across Europe to achieve that holy grail of a 'home run'.

Hitler had summonsed his three most senior lieutenants: the Luftwaffe chief, Göring; Himmler; and Field Marshal Wilhelm Keitel, the German defence chief.

'No one will ever know the precise course of the acrimonious conversation among the Nazi leaders, but the evidence from several of our German informants gave us a pretty fair version of the truth,' reported Lieutenant Colonel A.P. Scotland, the formidable chief officer of MI19's War Crimes Investigation Unit. The unit, better known as the 'London Cage', interrogated thousands of German prisoners immediately after the war, itself employing questionable methods.

The Führer watched his three men trying to blame each other then called a halt to the discussion. 'All the prisoners are to be shot on recapture!' he insisted

Scotland's[10] account says that Göring protested loudly but not out of squeamishness for the task at hand or any apparent concern that the intended victims were his 'English flying friends'.

'If we shoot them all it will look like murder, besides which I shall never be able to send my fliers over England again for fear of reprisals. If you must kill some, shoot half.'

Göring's standing had, however, been seriously undermined by such a stunning and humiliating breakout from his escape-proof camp. Himmler argued dismissively that the escape was merely confirmation of the Luftwaffe's incompetence in exercising its security obligations. Himmler then suggested 50 men. Hitler conceded.[11]

By the end of the day the Sagan Order, under Himmler's name, was being transmitted to the Berlin headquarters of the Gestapo, men who 'more than any other in Hitler's Germany stained their nation's character' with their ruthless murder squads.[12]

The order read in part:

> I am disappointed and indignant about the inefficient security measures. As a deterrent, the Führer has ordered that more than half of the escaped officers to be shot . . . After interrogation the officers are to be returned to their original camp and to be shot en route. The shootings will be explained by the fact that the recaptured officers were shot whilst trying to escape or because they offered resistance, so that nothing can be proved later.[13]

The selection of the names of the Allied officers to be executed finally fell to the Police General Arthur Nebe. Nebe, Scotland reported, became 'excited and uncontrolled', because he seemed to be aware of the 'monstrosity of the deed he was about to carry out'.

And so, the prisoners' cards were gathered together in Nebe's office and shuffled and reshuffled.

'On receipt of a telegram reporting his recapture, the prisoner's card and his record sheet were placed before him', according to declassified British documents.[14] 'After a few minutes consideration, Nebe decided who was to die and who was to live. The decision was influenced by the prisoner's age and status. Middle-aged and with a family, and he lived. Not too young, unmarried, and he died, as did nearly all the men of foreign origin and an unduly high percentage of men from the Dominions.'[15]

❖

Perversely, the momentary triumph of evil can mark a turning point. By briefly galvanising and uniting us around a profound belief in what we are not, the summary executions of the 50 of the recaptured 'great escapers' sparked shock, outrage and one of the biggest war crimes investigations of the post-war period.

On 23 June 1944 in the British House of Commons, Foreign Secretary Anthony Eden condemned the murders as 'an odious crime against the laws and conventions of war'. The British government recorded its 'solemn protest against these cold-blooded acts of butchery'. They would never cease in their efforts to collect the evidence to identify all those responsible. 'When the war is over they will be brought to exemplary justice.'[16]

The post-war investigation coincided with the post-war idealism that spawned decolonisation, the international declaration of human rights and a whole raft of new international institutions, treaties and agreements as a yearning for a common good washed around the globe. The investigation was infused with a heady mix of institutional righteousness, genuine grief, personal rage and the need to make good on the bold promise to leave no stone unturned. Except, as it turned out, in Czechoslovakia.

36
THE BEREAVED MOTHER'S BADGE

Grief can cut so deeply that it feels like the world has stopped turning. Everyone else still insists on rushing around, sticking to their petty daily routines, as though nothing has changed. They tread, insensitively it might seem, around the grief-struck. They don't seem to notice that the newly bereaved are no longer even sure how to draw their next breath.

In the remote highland villages of West Papua, tribal women cut off a finger at the second joint when a dearly loved family member dies.[1] The ceremony serves two purposes. First, the intense physical pain usefully overwhelms the emotional grief, just when it is at its sharpest. Secondly, for the rest of their lives everyone around them can see they have suffered a significant loss and can treat them accordingly.

What could Mildred and Ada do? There was a war on. Many mothers lost sons. More than 10,000 air force personnel were killed between 1939 and 1945 and more than 78,000 killed, wounded or missing from all the Australian services.[2] The role of the mother was to suffer in silence, to remain stoic, no matter what. They had other children, husbands, responsibilities to worry about. Mothers did not wail or cry in public, or even in front of the family. Life went on. They followed that well-worn path of habit and duty as best they could in the hope that familiarity would prevent them from stumbling. There were few rituals they could turn to to mark their loss and, in doing so, ask others to please tiptoe carefully around their fragile feelings.

Only the youngest Williams sibling, my father, Owen, his older sister, Suzie, and her young son, Stephen, were home when the telegram finally arrived. Mildred didn't seem to be able to take in the news.

When the story hit the newspapers, the death of so many Allied POWs, allegedly shot 'while trying to escape', was sensational and shocking (the true extent of the Nazi horror was yet to be revealed). There had been a brief moment of false hope for the family when only three RAAF officers had been listed among the dead. Nevertheless, Mildred saw Rusty's name and her heart sank. She had followed Rusty's humorous take on life through John's letters. She knew he was a close and valued friend.

The other two Australians were Warrant Officer Albert Hake, a talented Australian pilot who had crafted the escape compasses, and Squadron Leader James Catanach, who had made it all the way across Germany and was only just short of the Danish border when he was recaptured with New Zealand Flight Lieutenant Arnold Christensen. Catanach, it would later be revealed, had challenged his executioners and the illegality of the manner of his death. His last word was simply, 'Why?'[3]

The only other New Zealander among the escapees, Flying Officer Johnny Pohe, was presumably picked up relatively close to Stalag Luft III. He was a 'hard arser' without a train ticket and had severe frostbite when he was re-arrested. An Australian air force memo initially approved the release of only the three Australian names to the newspapers, with an assurance for the next of kin of other RAAF officers 'that there is no need for anxiety'.[4]

But, John's name, on the RAF list with another executed Australian-born RAF escapee, Flight Lieutenant Thomas Leigh, was not far behind—just one day, in fact. Mildred had posted that last letter only the previous week. The realisation that John had already been long dead was a sickening blow. Her golden boy's life had been extinguished for no better reason than to assuage the anger of a petulant, prideful, cruel man. By the time the telegram reached the family, it was almost eight weeks since John, Rusty, and probably Jerzy and Leslie, had been pushed out of a car into a lonely forest in Czechoslovakia by their Gestapo guards and perfunctorily shot,[5] first in the back, then the head.

Mildred didn't know what to do with herself. Len, my grandfather, was in northern Queensland. He was an RAAF squadron leader himself, but his rank was a technicality. As an engineer and architect, he was building airstrips to bolster Australia's defences against the Japanese. David, the second son, was in the Australian Army, fighting the Japanese in Borneo, and Barry, the third son, was in the Australian Navy. Only my dad was too young to enlist. In the early days, John had implored his parents to keep 'the kids' out of the war. They hadn't.

Mildred just kept on writing. She carefully scrutinised the many letters of regret and sympathy that arrived from various official quarters, including those from senior British officers and politicians still reeling from the manner in which the men had been killed. She wrote back and thanked them properly and politely, but was also careful to point out any errors such as the omission of John's DFC or his Mention in Despatches or an incorrect use of his rank. She wrote directly to Australia's Secretary of Air, for example, telling him she was 'very disappointed to note that in the list of names my son was not credited with his DFC, whilst others were'. No one was too senior to hear from Mildred.

She received a list of John's personal effects so meagre that it is difficult to look at it without feeling her sadness. What came back home was just one packet of 'snapshots', a poetry book and John's beloved Blue Book, his surf-lifesaving handbook. Typed out on a single piece of paper, the list is pathetically small and short, dwarfed by empty space on the aged sepia page.[6]

But, more than anything else, Mildred wanted one precious thing.

She wrote to anyone and everyone she could think of asking for help in applying for the Australian armed forces' Bereaved Mother's Badge that was issued to Australian mothers who had lost a son on active duty. John was serving with the RAAF, but was on secondment from the RAF. In Mildred's mind John was always an Australian, despite having been born in New Zealand. The correspondence went backwards and forwards unhappily until a faceless bureaucrat at the Department of Air typed up the following reply: 'As the late S/L Williams was a member of the Royal Air Force, it is advised that this headquarters has not the power under existing regulations to issue Mrs Williams with the badge in question'.[7] That was it. Her country would not acknowledge her loss.[8]

Peter Kierath and his older brother John were young children when the news of Rusty's death reached Narromine. They vaguely remember muffled tears as the telegram addressed to Ada, then widowed, was handed around the extended family. After that, there was silence. They lived in an era of the stiff upper lip. Grief was beaten back by simply refusing to acknowledge it. Surely, if you ignored it pointedly—and for long enough—it would eventually give up and wander off?

Many decades later, Peter moved into the original family home, a lovely rural Australian homestead with those characteristic deep verandahs that hold back the heat and a carefully irrigated and tended garden that feels like a green oasis on the red earth plains. It was then that he found Ada's leather folder with every one of Rusty's letters and all his photos lovingly catalogued. Greg's letters had been just as carefully preserved, too.

Hans felt dreadful. He had no one he could talk to. He had been living behind barbed wire for almost four years when he heard the news on a makeshift radio the German POWs had fabricated inside the Tatura internment camp in rural Victoria. Images of the camp, with its guard tower, searchlights and low wooden huts, are not dissimilar to those of Stalag Luft III. 'He was my friend . . . but in the camp, who cares?' He couldn't discuss John's death with anyone, he told me, recalling his feelings, still vivid many decades later. About half the German internees were against Hitler, he said, but no one dared show their hand. He kept silent and went on waiting for the war to end.

Could it possibly have turned out any other way? Of course, but the wisdom of hindsight was not a luxury available to these young men, especially cut off, as they were, from the perspective that reliable information, or even maturity, might have offered them. There are so many 'what ifs' along even the most ordinary of life paths that there is no point in raking through the coals looking for someone or something to blame.

Jimmy James believed his first name, Bertram, might have kept him off the death list as he could have been mistaken for a Brit of German heritage, given that the name was used both in English and German. But, when I looked at the list of 'the fifty', it was clear the dominions and other non-British nationalities were the most harshly treated, perhaps because of the fear Göring voiced of British reprisals. Fewer than half of those executed were British born. All the escapees from the Australian, New Zealand and South African air forces were executed, as were all but one of the eight Canadians. The list of those spared was dominated by RAF officers; the one Australian citizen whose card was sorted into the smaller pile of 23 survivors was Paul Royle, who, like John, had enlisted with the RAF. But John had been listed by the Germans as an RAAF officer, right back at Dulag Luft.

After the war, many ex-servicemen wondered why they had survived. Ted Sly, John's friend from 450 Squadron, turned this over and over but came up⁹ with no better answer than 'the luck of the draw'.

Jimmy said much the same thing. From the pile of prisoners' cards he was picked with only three other escapees to be sent to Sachsenhausen concentration camp, the site of appalling Nazi medical experiments and routine mass murders that cost tens of thousands of lives, including those of many German political prisoners who opposed the Nazis. And, still, he lived.

For those other surviving escapees who were returned to Stalag Luft III, conditions would become increasingly harsh as the Germans faltered on the battlefield and supplies, both within and outside, the camp became increasingly scarce. They determinedly constructed a handsome memorial to 'the fifty' by hand nonetheless. With the Soviet Red Army massing and steadily advancing, the Nazis decided to evacuate the POW camps in the east, including those in Silesia, in the depths of the brutal winter of 1944–45. Hundreds of Allied prisoners died as they were herded towards northern Germany in below-zero temperatures with little water, food and shelter. Many were abandoned by the roadside once they had collapsed from malnutrition or exhaustion, leaving them at the mercy of local populations, themselves suffering intense deprivation after years of war.[10]

It was our second lengthy phone call—Jimmy at home in Shropshire, me in Sydney—when he paused audibly for a moment to think: 'It's a matter of luck in wartime. You had to be very lucky to survive flying fighter planes, you had to be very lucky to survive being shot down. If the bullet has your name on it—then it gets you.'

IN MEMORIAM

To everyone else, 24 March 2012 was just another date on the calendar. For the relatives of our 'Most four' it was a remarkable and unexpected day.

The spring weather was brilliant. It was as unseasonally warm and sunny as it had been unseasonally cold on the day of the escape, exactly 68 years earlier. A Czech air force fly-past split the air above us. On the ground, a ceremonial honour guard carried wreath after wreath on behalf of the gathered families and dignitaries and laid them, formally, at the newly unveiled memorial to John, Rusty, Leslie and Jerzy.

The polished granite stone sits in the garden of the same cemetery where that ugly crematorium still stands, just outside the town of Most, near the Czech–German border.

We were so surprised to receive an invitation to attend the unveiling of the memorial in the Czech Republic that we almost didn't accept. The usual list of ordinary excuses like finances, work, great distance, children at home jumped immediately to mind. Unlike the Brits who had grown up on annual screenings of the Hollywood film on television over the Christmas season and endless memorial services, events, anniversary media coverage and books, the Australian families had been largely overlooked. For a short while they were kept informed. The British authorities made sure all parents were sent a beautiful reproduction of a drawing secreted out of Stalag Luft III by the POWs showing the memorial they had built to honour 'the fifty'. Each family was allotted a senior representative to attend the first big memorial service on their behalf at the famous St Martin in the Fields church in London in June 1944; a welcome, but symbolic gesture.

But, without the benefit of instant, digital communication, Australia remained a distant land. When the Hollywood movie opened, Peter Kierath was working and studying in Canada. He went to the cinema and was surprised and moved to see a list of the names of 'the fifty' up on an honour board outside. Of course, no one in the audience could have known the movie was, to him, much more than a fine adventure story.

Sixty-eight years later, the families met for the first time. Jerzy Mondschein's daughter, Małgorzata—who introduced herself as Margaret—was forced to spend much of her life denying her father's existence. In post-war Poland any association with the West, and especially with Western military forces such as the Polish RAF squadron that Jerzy had served with, was extremely dangerous. Once Poland had been 'liberated' from Nazi rule and swept up into the Soviet bloc, those Poles who had fought with the West faced lengthy jail sentences or even execution, she said. This after enduring a war that had cost more lives in Poland, in percentage terms, than in any other nation. Some 5.6 million Polish civilians were killed in World War II alone, including about 3 million Jews: about 16 per cent of the entire population. Yet, after Hitler, the shadow of Stalin fell over their lives.

Margaret still remembers Jerzy's letters home. '"Eat up and stay well", he used to tell me, "so you will be strong and healthy when I get home."' No one had ever honoured him, she said, overwhelmed. For the memorial's unveiling, her son flew into the local airstrip. At the end of the Cold War, he had followed in his grandfather's footsteps to qualify as a pilot.

Leslie Paus, who was named after her uncle Leslie Bull, had a different story. Her aunt, the widow of the famous tunneller, had eventually moved from Britain to New Zealand to avoid the endless 'great escape fuss'. Leslie's cousin, the son the tunneller had never met, had since died. Leslie, too, recently passed away.

And the Australians? They had never had a memorial to visit either. As a New Zealand-born RAF officer, John's name had not even been added to his local war memorial back home at Manly Beach. After the war, the men's ashes had been moved from within the POW-built memorial at Stalag Luft III to an Allied war cemetery in Poznan, Poland. It too then fell behind the Cold War iron curtain, so was out of reach.

The construction of the Most memorial was the culmination of Michal Holy's determined campaign to remember the four men. But, again, why? After all these years, and in a country that also suffered so terribly under Nazi occupation, and then, like Poland, under Communist rule, why would a stranger and his friends devote their time, energy and resources to a project so remote from their own life experience?

Part of the answer, I think, lies in geopolitics. At the end of the Cold War, the histories of the Eastern bloc nations like Poland and the Czech Republic could be retold, without fear of recriminations. Western nations that fought during World War II against their Nazi occupiers could, for the first time, be recognised.

In the early 1990s in the Czech town of Ostrava, to the south-east of Most, Brigadier General Zdenek Skarvada, a former pilot of 310th Czechoslovak Fighter RAF Squadron, and Czech Colonel Jan Pavlíček, set out to right a historic wrong. Within the grounds of the local primary school they constructed a memorial to two of the great escapers who had been executed nearby: British Squadron leader Thomas Kirby Green and Canadian Flight Officer Gordon Kidder. When the Ostrava memorial was unveiled in 1992, the locals had no way of contacting the families of the men—so they waited. Almost twenty years later, with the help of the internet, the families did finally come.

After visiting Stalag Luft III on his earlier research mission,

Michal had come to the conclusion that there was a part of history missing in Most too. That is the obvious reason for his effort, and that of his many supporters. But Michal is a modest person. He doesn't talk much about himself. It was some time before I heard a little more of his personal story, and his efforts began to make more sense. As a boy growing up in Communist Czechoslovakia during the tension of the Cold War, he had always been fascinated by planes and had dreamed of learning to fly. Locally, there was a gliding club that he had been desperate to join. But he would never be a member. The Communists believed in collective punishment and Michal had an uncle who had escaped to live in the West, in Canada. That alone meant the opportunities of all members of the extended family still living in Czechoslovakia would be limited, indefinitely.

Eventually, his family too decided to try to leave. They sought and received a holiday visa to Austria. At the age of fourteen, with his parents and brother, he walked out of his home and his life with only his holiday clothes, knowing he would not be able to return. After a year in a refugee camp in Austria his family was granted entry to Canada. It was there he got the education he had hoped for and learned to fly.

When Communism fell, Michal was keen to return to the new Czech Republic. I can't help thinking that difficult life experiences change us in one of two ways. They can make us more resilient but less sympathetic to the trials of others. Or they can make us more empathetic and quietly determined to make a small difference in our lives.

I realise now that my grandparents never knew exactly what happened to John, Rusty, Jerzy and Leslie. I am glad. All the books, and the Hollywood movie, sketched a painful-enough overview. They didn't need to go looking for any more heartache. They also wrongly believed that those responsible for his death had been brought to justice during the high-profile post-war war crimes trials. Again, I am glad they did.

My own belated attempt to follow in John's footsteps is mostly down to Michal.

The Nazis were obsessive record-keepers. Michal, in his own reading, first stumbled across a crucial piece of the four men's paperwork in an old manila folder among the public records in Prague. This was the original German order for their cremation in Most on 29 March 1944, claiming they had been shot 'trying to escape' and signed by the SS the night *before* they were killed. Even more strangely, and incongruously, the Nazi documents claimed no 'third party' was involved in the deaths. This crude, false paper trail was deliberately set up to deflect any inquiries from the International Committee of the Red Cross. 'There was something about this story that I had to follow,' Michal said.

We have done three trips together since 2012, both with various Williams family members and Peter Kierath, to trace the men's footsteps. On our third visit to Stalag Luft III in 2014, for the commemoration of the 70th anniversary, we met other relatives of those incarcerated in Reichenberg, in particular the family of Ivo Tonder, the last man to see John and the group alive.

Ivo, a Czech, was separated from the others and sent to Prague for interrogation. He did not expect to survive. He was sentenced to death as a traitor, but the chaos leading up to the Nazis' collapse and the end of the German occupation of Czechoslovakia intervened. His relief, however, was short-lived. Once the Communists took power in 1948, those who had fought the Nazis from the 'wrong direction', the capitalist West, were stripped of their status as honourable 'freedom fighters' and recast as potential imperialist spies. Many were jailed, persecuted or worse.[1]

Tonder and his wife, Jirina, were both jailed. Petra, his daughter, was then a baby. She and her brother were billeted out separately. A year or so later, the couple managed to escape to Britain and the CIA then managed to spirit the children out to London to reunite them with their parents. It was the kind of childhood trauma that no amount of time can erase.²

The family of John Stower knew even less than we did. No witness had ever been found to his death at an unknown location, at the hands of an unknown executioner. It was a humbling experience to stand with them all in front of that first stone memorial the POWs had built in 1944 inside Stalag Luft III.

Michal's first document led me and my sister, Megan, to the National Archives in London, where most of the declassified war records are held. The files on the killing of 'the fifty' are voluminous and well thumbed, as are the records detailing virtually every aspect of the escape and of life inside Stalag Luft III—except for a thin file marked 'Secret Czechoslovakia File 12'.³ It is within this small collection of documents that the crematorium manager's evidence can be found—both the original in Czech and an official English translation. The first British inquiries in Czechoslovakia in 1945 yielded this reply from the post-war Prague administration shortly after the Nazi surrender: 'Whether they [the escapees held at Reichenberg] were interrogated, or who could have interrogated them, we are unable to ascertain as all of the officials of both the Criminal Police [Kripo] and the Gestapo, who come into consideration, have fled'.

In 1946, a fifteen-man investigation team led by Wing Commander Wilfred Bowes of the RAF Investigation Branch did pursue the killers of 'the fifty' relentlessly, across Europe, including those of the five executed escapees who had been held at Reichenberg. But apart from assuming that the men were shot on the orders of the then Reichenberg Gestapo chief, Bernhard Baatz, and possibly by two Gestapo officers named Robert Weyland and Robert Weissman, no firsthand accounts of the deaths were ever obtained and no one was ever taken into custody. By contrast, the wider investigation into the murders of the other escapees, the so-called 'Reckoning', led to the trial of eighteen German officials in Hamburg in 1947, fourteen of whom were sentenced to death (one sentence later being commuted to life). A second trial in 1948 dealt with several more men.

In 1948 when the Communists took full control of Czechoslovakia, the British embassy sent a cable to the air ministry that said: 'conditions have changed dramatically since Wing Commander Bowes visited the country in 1946. It is therefore impossible to make the enquiries among members of the Gestapo who are still lucky enough to be in circulation.' Effectively, any further inquiries would prove fruitless.

Bowes and his investigators did retrieve the last photos of all the men taken by the Germans. It probably seems entirely inappropriate to find any reason at all to smile. But to see them in their 'escape clothes' is remarkable. They had done a great job in disguising themselves as grubby foreign labourers, using only their old uniforms. It really was, as John's Canadian friend Al Markle wrote, 'shameful, after such a bloody good breakout show!'

As a foreign correspondent, I heard many truly sad tales. That the media gravitates towards the dramatic and the disastrous is not surprising: there is something in human nature that tempts us to live vicariously, to test our own emotions against other people's tragedies. As a journalist, I learned that listening is important. If there is one thing that can ease the burden of loss it is the belief that it matters. No loss should be allowed to slip past, unnoticed or undocumented.

This is consistent with an increasing body of academic work that is scrutinising memory and war. 'When threatened with destruction, we resist oblivion by marking our existence—writing fiction, creating art, producing memoirs, or composing poetry.' Just as importantly, 'everyone gets tallied in official statistics and records'.[4] Family members often learn to value archives by clinging to these documents as personal memory devices. 'In the midst of battle, even as we are reduced to our basest human instincts to destroy, we still search for ways to document and remember'. John and Rusty's story is just one of millions of life stories that have been pieced together by historians, writers, relatives, descendants and friends, not just since World War II, but since records began.

In Australia, to go beyond the main cities is to truly embrace the great open road. Many towns post warning signs on their outskirts letting motorists know how far it is to the next petrol station. It is often a very long way. But even the smallest settlement, without a shop or a petrol pump, has a well-tended war memorial with a proud list of names.

Memorials are, according to the renowned psychoanalyst Vamik Volkan, 'hot' or 'cold'. They are either invested with the intense, highly charged feelings of a recent, grievous event or they hold the memories or recognition of loss, inviting individual contemplation and the development of long-term perspective. When they do their job properly, they help groups move through the grieving process to complete their mourning and 'eventually cool off'.[5]

Without a memorial or a grave, the grief of what psychologists call a 'complicated loss', like the murder of a young person, is difficult to resolve. There is nowhere for the bereaved to safely put down their feelings so that they can eventually find a way to get on with the rest of their lives. Unresolved grief can become a burden that is always carried with you. It can be passed, as it has been in many conflicts, from one generation to the next.

With Michal's generosity we now have John and Rusty's story and, in Most, we have a fine granite memorial bearing their names. A perfect stranger has finally given four extended families somewhere to safely lay their loss down.

SURFING AT MANLY

Many remarkable things have happened since Michal set this story in train. I have met Hans twice and have talked to him at length about the past. I was nervous, given the dramatic family split. He might have been nervous too. He had always wondered if things would have turned out differently if he hadn't recommended the air force to John.

Hans, or Harry as he has now long been called, was never able to return to surfing or to his once-idyllic life on Manly Beach. After the war, he applied to rejoin the Manly Life Saving Club. He was, unceremoniously, turned down. 'There were still a lot of bad feelings after the war, so it was not possible to go back—I understand people suffered, but why be so petty about something like that?' he said. In his own mind, he was an Australian. He had been a child when he had left Germany and hadn't been back since. (Many years later, the club reinstated Harry as a life member.)

While interned, Hans had been able to study aeronautical engineering. There were many highly qualified Germans in the camp with him, and he considered this opportunity for a higher education a great privilege. But, just as BMW in post-war Germany was forced to switch from making aeroplanes to cars, Hans was released on the condition that he never again worked in the aircraft industry. Hans married, had a family and forged a new manufacturing career, but he never spoke publicly about being interned outside his tight family circle. This was a secret so painful that he had always thought he would take it to his grave.

When we met at his unit in a retirement village in Queensland, overlooking the ocean, he decided it was finally time to open up. He was 97 years old. In retrospect, he said, it was 'probably the best thing that ever happened to me'. So many of his generation did not live long enough to enjoy their adult lives. Like John, he would have enlisted in the air force. 'Ten to one I would have been captured by the Japs and put to work digging on the railway and wouldn't be alive now.'

There is no way to fashion a happy ending for Mildred out of this tale.

Her life was never the same. My dad, now living with a mother dazed by loss, was profoundly affected too, as was the entire family. Mildred internalised her grief, as was expected. The loss seeped through the family home nonetheless, settling like a dank, invisible fog. Family life for my father was now defined by John's death. Even his proudest teenage moment was John's: the day he stood beside his mother in his school uniform and then stepped up onto the podium at Government House in Sydney to receive his brother's DFC, posthumously.

In declining health, Mildred took to attending seances. Like many bereaved mothers of the era, she imagined she had found her son. It was a longing that is easy to understand. Unsurprisingly, Mildred saw John back riding the Manly waves. Even in my own reading of John's letters, a generation on, and many decades later, there is one image that always stands out.

John is in northern Scotland training new pilots, as yet personally untouched by the war. It is January 1940. It's freezing outside. He is exhausted after clocking up 120 hours on dual-control aircraft and landing over and over again, blind in the snow. He has commandeered a scratchy gramophone.

He wrote:

> We went night flying in the snow the other night. There was a bright moon and the northern lights turned themselves on for a while. It was like a fairy landscape, everything seemed white and it was nearly as bright as daylight. The aeroplanes throw up great plumes of snow as they take off and the moon glinting on the fuselage looked like great shiny silver fish leaping in the spraying surf . . . it was an unforgettable scene.
>
> At the moment I am sitting before my fire in my room and listening to Tchaikovsky's 5th and feeling very content.

It would be tempting to leave John there, happy, in his warm room. But there's a more realistic ending that Mildred hung onto and that offered her a modicum of reassurance.

She never failed to mention the importance of John's friendship with Rusty and their good fortune in sharing a bunk room at Stalag Luft III. No matter what happened, she said, 'I feel sure John died trying to escape with Rusty Kierath.'[1]

POSTSCRIPT—THE LOST LETTER, FOUND

A month after the unveiling of the Most memorial in the Czech Republic in 2012, a letter was posted from the north coast of New South Wales, addressed to me. On the back of the envelope, the sender had written in capital letters, 'AT LAST, RETURNED TO SENDER, KIND REGARDS'.

Inside was a delicate single sheet of paper covered with my grandmother's handwriting, inside an old yellowing envelope. It was the last letter she had written to John.

How it had been lost is a circuitous tale. First, it arrived in wartime Germany long after the shootings of 'the fifty'. But, as John Williams is a common name, it meandered its way from one RAF office to next before finally being sent back to Australia, via the RAF office of India.

Then, when my uncle's house was flooded, it was with some of the boxes of badly damaged papers that were cleared out by a contractor and taken to the tip. The contractor later found it caught in the back of his truck and, seeing the address 'Stalag Luft III', held onto it, thinking it might be important.

He had never got around to finding out where it had come from until he saw news of the new memorial in the Czech Republic and tracked me down.

Now it is back in our family files.

NOTES

1   The Lost Letter

1. Weather description in *Sydney Morning Herald*, 15 May 1944
2. Manly Library Local Studies centre, photo Queenscliffe Beach, 1943
3. 'Sydney Harbour', *Australia's War*, <http://www.2australia.gov.au/underattack/sydharbour.html>, accessed 29 June 2014
4. 'Information in letters, censorship warning', *Sydney Morning Herald*, 28 November 1941, p. 6
5. Weather description in *Sydney Morning Herald*, 15 May 1944

2   The Other Side of the Wire

1. Martin Francis, *The Flyer: British culture and the Royal Airforce 1939–1945*, Oxford: Oxford University Press, 2011, pp. 106–7
2. Guy Walters, *The Real Great Escape*, London: Bantam Books, 2013, p. 205
3. Walters, *The Real Great Escape*, p. 216
4. As RAF Flight Lieutenant Bernard 'Pop' Green told it: Bernard Green, 'Now it can be told', published as Appendix 1 in Laurence Green, *Great War to Great Escape*, Herts, England: Fighting High Publishing, 2012
5. Green, 'Now it can be told'
6. B.A. James, *Moonless Night: The Second World War escape epic*, London: Pen and Sword Books, 2002, pp. 100, 101.
7. Interviews with James, June and October 2006, plus James, *Moonless Night*, pp. 100, 101
8. James, *Moonless Night*, pp. 100, 101
9. Flockhart, C.B. (1945), *Camp History of Stalag Luft III (Sagan)*, Air Force personnel reports, April 1942–January 1945, bound, typescript book, original, RAF Museum Archives, RAF Museum, Hendon, p. 9

3 How to Tell a True War Story

1. Tim O'Brien, 'How to Tell a True War Story' in Paula Geyh, et al., eds, *Post Modern American Fiction: A Norton Anthology*, New York: W.W. Norton, 1998, pp. 179-180
2. O'Brien, 'How to Tell a True War Story', pp. 174–83
3. O'Brien, 'How to Tell a True War Story' p. 179

4 Great Expectations—the Making of a Young Man

1. <http://artreview.com.au/contents/1267034087-sydney-sandstone>, accessed 10 June 2014; 'Mr. Edwin Williams', *The Cyclopedia of N.S.W. (illustrated): an historical and commercial review, descriptive and biographical, facts, figures and illustrations; an epitome of progress*, Sydney: McCarron, Stewart & Co., 1907, pp. 430–1
2. 'Mr. Edwin Williams', *The Cyclopedia of N.S.W*, pp. 430–1
3. Michael King, *The Penguin History of New Zealand*, Auckland, New Zealand: Penguin, 2003, p. 172
4. Mark Derby, 'Conscription, conscientious objection and pacifism—Conscription', *Te Ara—the Encyclopedia of New Zealand*, <www.TeAra.govt.nz/en/conscription-conscientious-objection-and-pacifism/page-1>, 2014, accessed 11 June 2014
5. King, *Penguin History of New Zealand*, p. 302
6. King, *Penguin History of New Zealand*, p. 303
7. 'Wellesley College: Governor-General's advice', *The Evening Post*, 15 December 1928, <http://paperspast.natlib.govt.nz/cgi-bin/paperspast?a=d&cl=search&d=EP19281215.2.145&srpos=31&e=-10-1928--12-1928--10--31----0Wellesley+College-->, 2014, accessed 11 June 2014
8. 'The British Empire through time', *Bitesize*, <www.bbc.co.uk/bitesize/ks3/history/uk_through_time/british_empire_through_time/revision/5/>, 2014, accessed 11 June 2014
9. *Evening Post*, Wellington, vol. CXII, issue 147, 18 December 1926, p. 17
10. 'Wellesley College', *The Evening Post*, 18 December 1926, <http://paperspast.natlib.govt.nz/cgi-bin/paperspast?a=d&cl=search&d=EP19261218.2.142.3&srpos=2&e=17-12-1926-29-12-1926--10--1----0Wellesley+College-->, accessed 12 June 2014
11. 'Exceptional security for the new A. & N.Z. Bank's funds', *Sydney Morning Herald*, 1 November 1930, p. 8

5 The Next Leg

1. Norman Davies, *Europe: A history*, Oxford: Oxford University Press, 1996, p. 998
2. Davies, *Europe*, p. 998
3. Davies, *Europe*, pp 428–9
4. Anthony Beevor, *The Second World War*, London: Weidenfeld & Nicholson, 2012, p. 18
5. It is not, of course, possible to adequately pot such a complex historical legacy up into a few, dense paragraphs. (My favourite reference book on European history, an extraordinary achievement summing up centuries of power plays, is 1365 pages long. Likewise, any decent book on World War II runs to a similar length)
6. James, *Moonless Night*, p. 101
7. Interviews with B.A. 'Jimmy' James, June and October 2006
8. Interviews with James, plus several published versions of this story including Alan Burgess, *The Longest Tunnel*, New York: Pocket Books, 1990
9. Tim Carroll, *The Great Escapers: The full story of the Second World War's most remarkable mass escape*, Bath, UK: Windsor, 2005
10. Walters, *The Real Great Escape*, p. 220

6 Introducing Michal

1. 'History of the air battle on September 11th, 1944', Museum of Air, *Battle over the Ore Mountains on September 11th, 1944 in Kovárská*, <http://new.museum119.cz/battle-history/>, accessed 29 June 2014; *Remembering World War Two Airmen*, <www..100thbg.com/mainpages/history/history3/christopher1.htm>, 2014, accessed 1 June 2014
2. *Remembering World War Two Airmen*

7 Paradise on Sea

1. Paula Hamilton, *Cracking Awaba: Stories of Mosman and Northern Beaches Communities during the Depression*, Sydney: SHOROC Council of Libraries, 2013, p. 50
2. Hamilton, *Cracking Awaba*, p. 131
3. Pauline Curby, *Seven Miles from Sydney: A History of Manly*, Sydney: Manly Council, 2001, p. 226
4. Hamilton, *Cracking Awaba*, p. 129

5   John Ramsland, *Brave and Bold: Manly Village Public School 1858–2008*, Melbourne: Brolga Publishing, 2008, p. 131
6   Ramsland, *Brave and Bold*, pp. 133, 121
7   Although Manly Beach owed its name to the confidence and 'manly' behaviour of the Aboriginal people of the Cannalgal and Kayimai clans who waded out to meet the first white British settlers in 1788, this masculine subculture was exclusively racially white: 'Manly heritage and history', Manly Council, <www.manly.nsw.gov.au/council/about-manly/manly-heritage--history/>, 2014, accessed 12 December 2014

8 In Search of a Decent Education

1   Ramsland, *Brave and Bold*, p. 121
2   Ramsland, *Brave and Bold*, p. 121
3   Shore Foundation Charter, <www.shore.nsw.edu.au/about/foundation-charter,> 2014, accessed 12 December, 2014
4   Geoffrey Sherington, *Shore: A History of Sydney Church of England Grammar School*, Sydney: Allen & Unwin, 1983, pp. 63, 102
5   Peter Taylor, *A Celebration of Shore*, Sydney: Allen & Unwin, 1988, p. 75
6   Sherington, *Shore*, p. 111
7   Sherington, *Shore*, p. 114
8   Sherington, *Shore*, p. 136
9   Sherington, *Shore*, p. 136
10 *The Torchbearer*, 1 September 1936, pp. 90, 88
11 'Sharks: Mr. Stead's warning—The ferocious "whaler"', *Sydney Morning Herald*, 7 January 1931, p. 13; 'Sharks in harbour: warning to bathers', *Sydney Morning Herald*, 9 January 1932, p. 12
12 Rhonda Blut, 'Middle Harbour Public School', *Mosman Memories of Your Street*, <http://mosmanmemories.net/story/163/middle-harbour-public-school>, 2015, accessed 23 March 2015
13 Mark McGinniss, 'A non-stop boy's own adventure: Snow Swift, 1915–2007', *Sydney Morning Herald*, 8 October 2007, <www.smh.com.au/news/obituaries/a-nonstop-boys-own-adventure/2007/10/07/1191695733133.html?page=fullpage>, 2014, accessed 9 December 2014
14 *The Torchbearer*, 1 May 1934, 1 May 1935
15 *The Torchbearer*, 1 September 1932, p. 111

9 The Arrest

1. National Archives, Kew, photos KPSt-Reichenberg 45/44, 44/44, 48/44, 50/44
2. Burgess, *The Longest Tunnel*, p. 183. The original American spelling is used
3. Tim Carroll, *The Great Escape from Stalag Luft III: the full story of how 76 Allied officers carried out World War II's most remarkable mass escape*, New York: Pocket Books, 2005, p. 236
4. Interview with Jimmy James, June and October 2006.

10 The Rise of an Aussie Icon

1. Hamilton, *Cracking Awaba*, p. 72
2. Manly Warringah Tourism Bureau advertisement, 1942
3. Tim Baker, *Australia's Century of Surf: how a big island at the bottom of the world became the greatest surfing nation on earth*, Sydney: Random House, 2013, p. 36
4. Baker, *Australia's Century of Surf*, p. 36
5. Baker, *Australia's Century of Surf*, p. 39
6. *Surf in Australia*, 1 September 1936, p. 28
7. *Surf in Australia*, 1 September 1936, p. 28
8. Ed Jaggard, *Between the Flags: One hundred summers of surf lifesaving*, Sydney: University of New South Wales Press, 2007, p. 11
9. Baker, *Australia's Century of Surf*, p. 39
10. Jaggard, E. *Between the Flags*, p. 7
11. John Wilkinson, *Alcohol and Tobacco in NSW: Consumption, revenue and concern*, Briefing Paper No. 7/97, Sydney: NSW Parliamentary Library Research Service, 1997
12. *History of Manly Life Saving Club*, Manly Library, Local History Collection, 1957
13. Jaggard, *Between the Flags*, p. 82
14. *Surf in Australia*, 1 September 1936, p. 30
15. Malcolm Gault-Williams, *Legendary Surfers*, vol. 3, *The 1930s*, Raleigh, NC: Lulu.com/Malcolm Gault-Williams, 2012, pp. 17–18
16. '1985 Snow McAllister (dec) NSW', *Australian Surfing Awards incorporating the Hall of Fame*, <www.australiansurfingawards.com/#!hall-of-fame-inductees>, 2014, accessed 2 December 2014
17. Interview with Hans 'Harry' Wicke, 18 May 2012

18 Baker, *Australia's Century of Surf*, p. 68
19 *Sydney Morning Herald*, 30 December 1935, p. 1

11 Choosing the Future

1 *Sydney Morning Herald*, 14 March 1936, p. 17
2 'Life Savers and Hitler Youth', Manly Library Local Studies blog, posted 28 February 2010, <http://manlylocalstudies.blogspot.com.au/2010_02_01_archive.html>, 2015, accessed 24 March 2015
3 'Life Savers and Hitler Youth', Manly Library Local Studies blog, posted 28 February 2010, <http://manlylocalstudies.blogspot.com.au/2010_02_01_archive.html>, 2015, accessed 24 March 2015
4 *Surf in Australia*, 1 September 1936, p. 28
5 D. Aubert-Marson, 'Sir Francis Galton: the father of eugenics', *PubMed.gov*, <www.ncbi.nlm.nih.gov/pubmed/19602363>, 2014, accessed 31 December 2014
6 Australasian Society for Advancement of Science, 'The Adaptation of Man to Australian Conditions,' Presidential address, Prof. H.G. Chapman, University of Sydney, January 1928, Hobart

12 The Mother Country

1 'Selecting air crews', *Newcastle Morning Herald*, 2 August 1940, p. 7
2 Edward Sly, *The Luck of the Draw: Horses, Spitfires and Kittyhawks*, Sydney: author, 2003
3 Matt Novak, 'What international air travel was like in the 1930s', *Paleofuture*, http://paleofuture.gizmodo.com/what-international-air-travel-was-like-in-the-1930s-1471258414, 2014, accessed 21 November 2014
4 *Sunday Mail* (Brisbane), 29 March 1936, p. 25
5 *Sydney Morning Herald*, 27 June 1938, p. 8
6 *The Advertiser* (Adelaide), 25 May 1939, p. 20
7 *Sydney Morning Herald*, 20 January 1937, p. 13
8 *The Daily News* (Perth), 27 November 1937, p. 12
9 'Doctors on qualities needed by war pilots', *Northern Star* (Lismore), 22 October 1940, p. 1
10 'Collins, William Patrick (IWM interview)', *Imperial War Museum*, audio file, catalogue no. 6673, 1983, <http://www.iwm.org.uk/collections/item/object/80006493>, 2014, accessed 20 December 2014

11 *The Advertiser*, 12 October 1939, p. 17
12 John Golley, *Aircrew Unlimited: The Commonwealth Air Training Plan during World War 2*, Sparkford, UK: Patrick Stephens, 1993
13 Illington, 'Aircraftsman in RAF, 1939 to 1940', *WW2 People's War: an archive of World War Two memories—written by the public, gathered by the BBC*, BBC Oral History project, Article ID A2307908, contributed on 18 February 2004, <www.bbc.co.uk/history/ww2peopleswar/stories/08/a2307908.shtml>, 2014, accessed 16 March 2014

13 Ivo Tonder—the Last Glimpse

1 Statement of Ivo Tonder, United Kingdom Charges Against German War Criminals, Charge no UK–G/B 70, p. 8, File AIR40/2275, National Archives (Britain), Kew
2 Mike Meserole, *The Great Escape: the longest tunnel*, New York: Sterling Publishing, 2008, p. 179
3 Statement of Ivo Tonder
4 Statement of Ivo Tonder
5 Statement of Ivo Tonder

14 In Search of the Elusive English Gentleman

1 'Helm, Robert French (IWM interview)', *Imperial War Museum*, audio file, catalogue no. 4583, 1980, <www.iwm.org.uk/collections/item/object/80004543>, 2014, accessed 23 November 2014
2 Francis, *The Flyer*, p. 16
3 Francis, *The Flyer*, p. 6
4 Drake, Billy (IWM interview), catalogue number 27073
5 *Manning—Plans and Policy, The Royal Air Force, 1934–38*, monograph held by the RAF Museum, Hendon, p. 5
6 *The Second World War, 1939–1945*, Royal Air Force, monograph, *Flying Training*, vol. II, p. 91, File AIR41/69, National Archives
7 'The rise of the Luftwaffe', *Royal Air Force Museum*, <www.rafmuseum.org.uk/research/online-exhibitions/history-of-the-battle-of-britain/the-rise-of-the-luftwaffe.aspx>, 2014, accessed 2 November 2014
8 Peter H. Oppenheimer, 'From the Spanish Civil War to the fall of France: Luftwaffe lessons learned and applied', *Journal of Historical Review*, 1986, vol. 7, no. 2, pp. 133–74

9   Sir Archibald Sinclair, *Hansard*, paragraph 1270, <http://hansard.millbanksystems.com/commons/1938/may/25/air-defences#S5CV0336P0_19380525_HOC_342>, accessed 12 October 2014
10 Billy Drake with Christopher Shores, *Billy Drake, Fighter Leader: The autobiography of Group Captain B. Drake DSO, DFC & Bar, US DFC*, London: Grub Street, 2002, p. 19
11 *Manning—Plans and Policy*, p. 44
12 'Drake, Billy (IWM interview), *Imperial War Museum*, audio file, catalogue no. 27073, 2004, <www.iwm.org.uk/collections/item/object/80024303>, 2014, accessed 17 November 2014
13 'Monk, John Walter (IWM interview)', *Imperial War Museum*, audio file, catalogue no. 3169, 1978, <www.iwm.org.uk/collections/item/object/80003155>, accessed 17 November 2014
14 'Rose, Nigel (IWM interview)', *Imperial War Museum*, audio file, catalogue no. 29076, 2006, <www.iwm.org.uk/collections/item/object/80027124>, 2014, accessed 17 November 2014
15 Williams Family collection, sourced from: The Royal Air Force, Headquarters Air Command, Trenchard Hall, Royal Air Force Cranwell, Sleaford, NG34 8HB, England (Records are available only to next of kin through proof of relationship, so there is no publicly available record of these documents.)
16 Drake, Billy (IWM interview)
17 F.A. de V. Robertson, 'The Central Flying School', *Flight*, 10 March 1938, <www.flightglobal.com/pdfarchive/view/1938/1938%20-%202331.html?search=Central%20Flying%20School>, 2014, accessed 13 December 2014
18 Tony Mansell, 'The Royal Airforce Volunteer Reserve, 1936–39', *Royal Airforce Reserve and Auxiliary Forces*, Oxford: Royal Air Force Historical Society, 2003, p. 31
19 Simon Pearson, *The Great Escaper: the life and death of Roger Bushell—love, betrayal, Big X and the great escape*, London: Hodder & Stoughton, 2013, pp. 34–73
20 Mansell, 'Royal Airforce Volunteer Reserve', p. 30
21 Mansell, 'Royal Airforce Volunteer Reserve', p. 32
22 'Surf Lifesaving Australia: Surf in Australia, 1938', *surfresearch.com.au*, <www.surfresearch.com.au/1939_SLSA_Surf_Australia.html>, accessed 2 January 1939

23 'The University of Cambridge: The modern university (1882–1939)', in J.P.C. Roach (ed.), *A History of the County of Cambridge and the Isle of Ely: Volume 3, The City and University of Cambridge*, London: Victoria County History, 1959, pp. 266–306, <www.british-history.ac.uk/vch/cambs/vol3/pp266-306>, 2014, accessed 31 December 2014

24 Collins, William Patrick (IWM interview), Imperial War Museum audio file, catalogue number 6673, 1983, http://www.iwm.org.uk/collections/item/object/80006493, accessed 9 June 2014

25 Richard Hillary, *The Last Enemy*, Kindle edn, London: Michael O'Mara Books, 2014, locations 163, 126, 132 and 170

15 Scotland, and the Brave

1 Arnd Bernaerts, 'D-6 The second cold wave and not only Denmark was shivering', *A large-scale experiement with climate—the extreme winter of 1939/40 and climate research*, <http://www.1ocean-1climate.com/193940.php>, accessed 2 December 2014

2 'Helm, Robert French (IWM interview)'

3 Hillary, *The Last Enemy*, location 428

4 'World War II in Europe: timeline with photos and text', *The History Place*, <http://www.historyplace.com/worldwar2/timeline/ww2time.htm#1939>, accessed 2 December 2014

5 Beevor, *The Second World War*, p. 42

6 John Herington, *Air War against Germany and Italy, 1939–43*, Canberra: Australian War Memorial, 1954, p. 9

7 'Collins, William Patrick (IWM interview)'

8 'Rose, Nigel (IWM interview)'

9 'Kinloss, Moray, Scotland genealogy', *FamilySearch*, <https://familysearch.org/learn/wiki/en/Kinloss,_Moray,_Scotland>, accessed 3 January 2015

10 Hillary, *The Last Enemy*, location 437; 'Kinloss, Moray, Scotland genealogy'

11 Hillary, *The Last Enemy*, location 427

12 Hillary, *The Last Enemy*, location 571

13 Hillary, *The Last Enemy*, locations 571, 610

14 Cecil Beaton, *Winged Squadrons ... with Photographs by the Author*, London: Hutchinson, 1942, pp. 17–18

15 Francis, *The Flyer*, p. 64

16 Both quotes from Francis, *The Flyer*, p. 64
17 Francis, *The Flyer*, p. 65
18 Beevor, *The Second World War*, p. 128
19 Herington, *Air War*, p. 9
20 Herington, *Air War*, p. 2
21 Peter Ilberry, *Empire Airmen Strike Back: The Empire Air Training Scheme and 5 SFTS, Uranquinty*, Maryborough, Qld: Banner Books, 1999, p. 7
22 Australians at War, Film Archive, Empire Training Scheme overview, <www.australiansatwarfilmarchive.gov.au/aawfa/campaigns/Empire_Air_Training_Schem.html>, accessed 12 January 2015
23 Davies, *Europe*, p. 1008
24 Davies, *Europe*, p. 1008

16 The First POW

1 Joan Beaumont, Ilma Martinuzzi O'Brien & Mathew Trinca (eds), *Under Suspicion: Citizenship and internment in Australia during the Second World War*, Canberra: National Museum of Australia Press, 2008, p. 2
2 Beaumont, *Under Suspicion*, p. 2
3 Beaumont, *Under Suspicion*, p. 7

17 The Australians Are Coming

1 'Highlander honour players who fought and fell in the toughest match of all', *Sydney Morning Herald*, 5 May 1968
2 *Sydney Morning Herald*, 19 August 1940, p. 8
3 Interview with Peter Kierath, Narromine, 1 December 2014
4 Holburn, Hajo, *A History of Modern Germany, 1840–1945, Volume 3*, Princeton, NJ, USA: Princeton University Press, 1969, p. 123
5 F.O.M., 'The Sketcher: Memories of Bourke', *Sydney Mail*, 28 November 1896, recounting a trip made in 1881, <http://trove.nla.gov.au/ndp/del/article/163783016?searchTerm=narramine%20inn&searchLimits=l-state=New+South+Wales|||l-title=698|||l-decade=189|||l-year=1896|||l-month=11>, accessed 9 January 2015
6 Matthew Colloff, *Flooded Forest and Desert Creek: Ecology and history of the river red gum*, Melbourne: CSIRO Publications, 2014, pp. 25, xvii
7 Philip King, *A History of Narromine District, Timbrebongie Shire Council and Narromine Municipal Council*, 1980, pp. 7-9

8   'Narromine timeline', Macquarie Regional Library, <www.mrl.nsw.gov. au/LocalHeritage/narromine-timeline>, accessed 21 December 2014
9   'Pre-war era', Narromine Aviation Museum, <www.narromineaviation museum.org.au/index.php?option=com_content&view=category&layout=blog&id=1&Itemid=7>, accessed 9 January 2015

18 Out in Africa

1   'Fenton, Alfred Earnest "Church" (IWM interview)', Imperial War Museum, audio file, catalogue number 17543, 1997, <www.iwm.org.uk/collections/item/object/80016880>, accessed 24 March 2015
2   Beevor, *The Second World War*, p. 143
3   Mark Johnston & Peter Stanley, *Alamein: The Australian story*, Melbourne: Oxford University Press, 2002, p. 10
4   Beevor, *The Second World War*, p. 150
5   Alan Moorehead, *The Desert War: The classic trilogy on the North African campaign, 1940–43*, London: Aurum Press, 2009, p. 5
6   Malcolm E. Barker, 'Memories of Durban', *Facts about Durban*, <www.fad.co.za/Resources/memoirs/barker/>, accessed 15 January 2014
7   'Collier, Patrick Victor (IWM interview)', Imperial War Museum, audio file, catalogue number 22391, 2001, <www.iwm.org.uk/collections/item/object/80021215>, accessed 24 March 2015
8   Photos in Letters to Mother, Len Williams RAAF pilot, edited by Keith Williams (no relation to author), private collection
9   Rusty's private letter home, 15 December 1940, letters of Reginald 'Rusty' Kierath, private collection/held by Peter Kierath
10 'The Heritage Gallery: Point Cook', RAAF Museum: Point Cook, <www.airforce.gov.au/raafmuseum/exhibitions/heritage.htm>, accessed 16 January 2015; *Sydney Morning Herald*, 31 December 1940, p. 7
11 Interview with Ted Sly, Sydney, 27 September 2006; Sly, *Luck of the Draw*
12 Letters to Mother, the letters of Len Williams
13 Joyce A. Quinn & Susan L. Woodward (eds), *Earth's Landscape: An Encyclopedia of the World's Geographic Features [2 volumes]* (Google eBook), Nature, 2015, pp. 213–14 <https://books.google.com.au/books?id=ErkxBgAAQBAJ&pg=PA213&dq=drakensberg+mountains&hl=en&sa=X&ei=YDojVcnEA87V8gWayIH4CA&ved=0CFUQ6AEwBw#v=onepage&q=drakensberg%20mountains&f=false.>, accessed 7 April 2015
14 'Collier, Patrick Victor (IWM interview)'
15 'Collier, Patrick Victor (IWM interview)'

16 Various oral histories of this same trip
17 'History', *Bulawayo Images*, <www.bulawayomemories.com/defaultbyo.html>, accessed 2 January 2015
18 Rhodesian Air Training Group, *Rhodesian Air Training Group Royal Air Force*, 1945, p. 21, <http://rhodesiaandtheraf.blogspot.com.au/>, accessed 24 March 2015.
19 Wilkins, Derek, 'RAF training in southern Africa', *WW2 People's War: an archive of World War Two memories—written by the public, gathered by the BBC*, BBC Oral History project, Article ID A1122337, contributed on 25 July 2003, <www.bbc.co.uk/history/ww2peopleswar/stories/37/a1122337.shtml>, accessed 14 April 2014
20 '31 August 1944: Peak wartime strength reached', *History Record Time Line*, <http://airpower.airforce.gov.au/HistoryRecord/HistoryRecordDetail.aspx?rid=590>, accessed 4 January 2015; 'Point Cook'
21 'English, John (IWM interview)', Imperial War Museum, audio file, catalogue number 29040, 2006, <www.iwm.org.uk/collections/item/object/80027126>, accessed 24 March 2015
22 The Skull of Lobengula', *Time* magazine, vol. 43, no. 2, 10 January/1 October 1944, p. 37
23 Geoff Wright, 'Part 3 RAF pilot training Geoff Wright—southern Rhodesia', *WW2 People's War: an archive of World War Two memories—written by the public, gathered by the BBC*, BBC Oral History project, Article ID A2778997, contributed 24 June 2004, <www.bbc.co.uk/history/ww2peopleswar/stories/97/a2778997.shtml>, accessed 14 April 2014
24 Bill Bundock, 'Life as an RAF pilot: Chapter 2: To southern Africa', *WW2 People's War: an archive of World War Two memories—written by the public, gathered by the BBC*, BBC Oral History project, Article ID A2540837, <www.bbc.co.uk/history/ww2peopleswar/stories/37/a2540837.shtml>, accessed 2 December 2014
25 'Point Cook'; 'Air war Europe 1939–1945', *Australia's War 1939–1945*, <www.ww2australia.gov.au/raaf/>, accessed 24 March 2015
26 'English, John (IWM interview)'
27 'English, John (IWM interview)'
28 Rhodesian Air Training Group

19 A Tale of Two Men and Two Messes

1. Rhodesian Air Training Group, *Rhodesian Air Training Group*
2. Letters of Reginald Kierath
3. Herington, *Air War*, pp. 117, 120
4. Herington, *Air War*, p. 115
5. 'Siege of Tobruk', *Australian War Memorial*, <www.awm.gov.au/encyclopedia/tobruk/>, accessed 2 December 2014; Beevor, *The Second World War*, p. 176
6. Moorehead, *The Desert War*, p. 82

20 To War in the Desert

1. T. R. Moreman, *Desert Rats, British 8th Army in North Africa 1941–43*, Oxford, UK: Osprey Publishing, 2007, p. 9, Spelling variants of *khaseem* include *khasim* and *khasimin*. Quote from Moorehead, *The Desert War*, p. 7
2. Moorehead, *The Desert War*, p. 8
3. Winston Churchill, *The River War: An account of the reconquest of the Sudan*, Project Gutenberg edn, [1902] 2004, <www.gutenberg.org/files/4943/4943-h/4943-h.htm>, accessed 25 March 2015
4. Churchill, Winston, *The River War*
5. John Sadler, Desert Rats, Amberley Publishing Limited, 2013, accessed online, <https://books.google.com.au/books?id=xVaoAwAAQBAJ&pg=PT77&dq=here+there+are+not+the+masses+of+men+and+material.+Nobody+and+nothing+is+concealed&hl=en&sa=X&ei=gFwjVfGHEsbEmAXjz4G4Ag&ved=0CB0Q6AEwAA#v=onepage&q=Lieutenant%20Joachim%20Schorm&f=false>, location 37
6. Francis, *The Flyer*, p. 16
7. Johnston and Stanley, *Alamein*, p. 15
8. Herington, *Air War*, pp. 74–5
9. Herington, *Air War*, p. 52
10. 'Timeline: Australia in the First World War, 1914–1918', Australian War Memorial, <http://www.awm.gov.au/1914-1918/timeline/#>, accessed 31 January 2015
11. 'Wing Commander Robert Henry Maxwell (Bobby) Gibbes DSO DFC & Bar (Rtd), interviewed by Ken Llewelyn, about his service in the Royal Australian Air Force (RAAF) during the Second World War', Australian War Memorial, sound file, ID number S01646, 1993, <https://www.

awm.gov.au/collection/S01646/>, accessed 20 January 2015

12 Peter Dornan, *Nicky Barr, An Australian Air Ace: A story of courage and adventure*, Sydney: Allen & Unwin, 2002, p. 113
13 '402364—Kierath', *No. 450 Squadron RAAF: Honouring Our Heroes . . .*, <http://450squadronraaf.smugmug.com/gallery/23209860_KhLN4V#!i=1870949855&k=z3ZjvLg>, accessed 4 March 2014
14 Churchill, *The River War*
15 Williams Family collection, sourced from: The Royal Air Force, Headquarters Air Command, Trenchard Hall, Royal Air Force Cranwell, Sleaford, NG34 8HB, England (records available only to next of kin through proof of relationship, so there is no publicly available record of these documents)
16 'Down, Peter Derrick Macleod (IWM interview)', Imperial War Museum, audio file, catalogue number 11449, 1990, <www.iwm.org.uk/collections/item/object/80011204>, accessed 25 March 2014
17 Herington, *Air War*, p. 97
18 Herington, *Air War*, p. 97
19 'Short Empire, C Class Flying Boat', Museum Victoria, <http://museumvictoria.com.au/collections/themes/3671/short-empire-c-class-flying-boat>, accessed 27 January 2015

21 Reunion

1 'Down, Peter Derrick Macleod (IWM interview)'
2 Multiple accounts, plus Moorehead, *The Desert War*, p. 23
3 Letter of 29 April 1987 from J.D. 'Jack' Gleeson
4 Leonard L. Barton, *The Desert Harassers: Being memoirs of 450 (R.A.A.F.) Squadron, 1941–1945*, Sydney: Astor Publications, 1991, p. 7
5 Letters of Reginald 'Rusty' Kierath
6 *Surf in Australia*, 1 July 1941, 1 June 1940, p. 1
7 *Surf in Australia*, 8 July 1942, p. 8
8 'Wing Commander Robert Gibbes', Australian War Memorial sound file
9 Down, Peter Derrick Macleod (IWM interview)
10 Johnston & Stanley, *Alamein*, p. 18

22 Holding Your Nerve

1 Attributed to British Field Marshal George Francis Milne and others
2 'Burt, Francis Theadore Page (IWM interview)', Imperial War Museum, audio file, catalogue number 25056, 2003, <www.iwm.org.uk/

collections/item/object/80024284>, accessed 20 January 2015
3   Francis, *The Flyer*, p. 110
4   Francis, *The Flyer*, p. 120
5   Barton, *The Desert Harassers*, p. 1
6   Moorehead, *The Desert War*, p. 32
7   'Andrew William "Nicky" Barr as a squadron leader, 3 Squadron RAAF, interviewed by Edward Stokes for The Keith Murdoch Sound Archive of Australia in the War of 1939–1945', Australian War Memorial, sound file, ID number S00939, 1990, <https://www.awm.gov.au/collection/S00939/>, accessed 20 January 2015
8   David Cecil, 'The R.A.F.: A layman's glimpse', in W. Rothenstein, *Men of the R.A.F. (Forty portraits, with some account of life in the R.A.F.)*, London: Oxford University Press, 1942, p. 79
9   Pauline Curby, *Seven Miles from Sydney, A History of Manly*, Manly Council, 2001, pp. 243–4
10 'Wing Commander Robert Gibbes', Australian War Memorial sound file
11 Francis, *The Flyer*, p. 112
12 Edgar Jones, 'LMF: The use of psychiatric stigma in the Royal Air Force during the Second World War', *Journal of Military History*, vol. 70, no. 2, 2006, p. 449
13 Peter Monteath, *P.O.W.: Australian Prisoners of War in Hitler's Reich*, Sydney: Macmillan, 2011, p. 25
14 'Wing Commander Robert Gibbes', Australian War Memorial sound file
15 Francis, *The Flyer*, p. 112
16 Roald Dahl, *Over to You: Ten stories of flyers and flying*, Harmondsworth, UK: Penguin, 1973 pp. 12–13
17 Francis, *The Flyer*, p. 119

23 Flipping the Bird

1   Letters of Reginald 'Rusty' Kierath
2   Moorehead, *The Desert War*, p. 258
3   Beevor, *The Second World War*, p. 312
4   J.D. (Jack) Gleeson, 450 Squadron, letter (1987) containing personal recollections of John Williams in the Desert War, copy held by author
5   J.D. Gleeson, letter
6   Meeting with Gordon Steege, 2013; interview with Peter Kierath,

December 2014

24 A Big Flap

1. Russell Brown, *Desert Warriors: Australian P-40 pilots at war in the Middle East and North Africa 1941–1943*, Maryborough, Qld: Banner Books, 2000, p. 182
2. Joan Beaumont, 'Prisoners of war in the Australian national memory', in Bob Moore & Barbara Hately-Broad (eds), *Prisoners of War, Prisoners of Peace: Captivity, homecoming, and memory in World War II*, Oxford and New York: Berg, 2005, pp. 185–194
3. Dornan, *Nicky Barr*, p. 120
4. Declassified documents, 12 June 1942, file no. AIR 27/1887, National Archives, UK
5. Brown, *Desert Warriors*, p. 122
6. J.F. Edwards, *Kittyhawk Pilot*, Battleford, Canada: Turner-Warwick Publications, 1983, p. 73
7. Australian Associated Press, *Sydney Morning Herald*, published approx. 19 June 1942
8. Australia in the War of 1939–45, Air War Against Germany and Italy, Greece, Syria and the Western Desert, p. 140, John Herrington, Australian War Memorial, 1954
9. Australian War Memorial, Bobby Gibbes, interview, 28 April 1990 <https://www.awm.gov.au/collection/S00939/>
10. Australian War Memorial, Nicky Barr, interview, July 1990. <https://www.awm.gov.au/collection/S00939/>
11. 'Wing Commander Robert Gibbes', Australian War Memorial sound file; 'Andrew William "Nicky" Barr', interview, Australian War Memorial sound file
12. Pilot's logbook, J.E.A. Williams, Williams Family collection, entry 24 June 1942
13. J.D. (Jack) Gleeson, letter (1987) containing personal recollections of John Williams in the Desert War, copy held by author
14. Moorehead, *The Desert War*, pp. 368–9
15. Moorehead, *The Desert War*, pp. 368–9
16. Drake, with Shores, *Billy Drake*, p. 47
17. Sly, *Luck of the Draw*, p. 63 and interview with Sly, 27 September 2006
18. Edwards, *Kittyhawk Pilot*, p. 75

19   Sly, *Luck of the Draw*, pp. 85–6
20   Sly, *Luck of the Draw*, pp. 85–6
21   Operations Record Book, 450 Squadron, entry 26 June, File AIR 27/1884, National Archives, UK
22   Operations Record Book, 450 Squadron, entry 26 June 1942
23   Brown, *Desert Warriors* p. 135
24   'Drake, Billy (IWM interview)'

25   While We Still Have Breath in Our Bodies

1   Drake, with Shores, *Billy Drake*, p. 102
2   Drake, with Shores, *Billy Drake*, p. 102
3   Collection of private letters from members of 450 Squadron
4   Collection of private letters from members of 450 Squadron
5   Johnston & Stanley, *Alamein*, p. 131
6   Edwards, *Kittyhawk Pilot*, p. 133; quotes from Johnston & Stanley, *Alamein*, p. 131
7   I.C.B. Dear (ed.), *The Oxford Companion to the Second World War*, Oxford: Oxford University Press, 1995, p. 326
8   450 Squadron correspondence, 17 September 1942, File AIR 27/1887, National Archives, UK
9   File AIR 27/1887, National Archives, UK
10   450 Squadron correspondence, 17 September 1942
11   Christopher Shores & Hans Ring, *Fighters over the Desert: The air battles in the Western Desert, June 1940 to December 1942*, London: Spearman, 1969, p. 9
12   450 Squadron correspondence, September 1942, File AIR 27/1887, National Archives, UK
13   Pilot's logbook, J.E.A. Williams; Sly, *Luck of the Draw*, p. 63
14   450 Squadron correspondence, 23 October 1942
15   Madeline Chambers, 'The devil's general? German film seeks to debunk Rommel myth', Reuters, 1 November 2012, <www.reuters.com/article/2012/11/01/entertainment-us-germany-rommel-idUSBRE8A00RM20121101>, accessed 2 January 2015
16   Shores & Ring, *Fighters over the Desert*, p. 191; Beevor, *The Second World War*, p. 376; *Oxford Companion to the Second World War*, p. 326
17   J.D. Gleeson, letter (1987)
18   Brown, *Desert Warriors*, p. 188

26 Down But Not Out

1. 'Andrew William "Nicky" Barr', interview, Australian War Memorial sound file
2. 'Drake, Billy (IWM interview)'
3. 'El Alamein battles', Australian War Memorial, <https://www.awm.gov.au/encyclopedia/el_alamein/reading/>, accessed 2 January 2015
4. *Sydney Morning Herald*, 23 November 1942, p. 4
5. Francis, *The Flyer*, pp. 110–11
6. Brown, *Desert Warriors*, p. ix
7. Flying Officer Alex Markle, 450 Squadron, letter (1987) containing personal recollections of John Williams in the Desert War, copy held by author
8. Johnston & Stanley, *Alamein*, p. 264
9. *Sydney Morning Herald*, 23 November 1942, p. 4
10. Johnston & Stanley, *Alamein*, p. 258

27 The Face of the Enemy

1. 'Younger, Calton "Cal" (IWM interview)', Imperial War Museum, audio file, catalogue number 23329, 2002, <www.iwm.org.uk/collections/item/object/80025614>, accessed 25 March 2015
2. 'Younger, Calton "Cal" (IWM interview)'
3. Moorehead, Alan, *The Desert War*, 1946, p. 416
4. Moorehead, *The Desert War*, p. 416
5. Monteath, *P.O.W.*, pp. 56–7
6. George Odgers, 'Introduction', *Official History of Australia in the War of 1914–1918, Volume VIII: The Australian Flying Corps in the Western and Eastern Theatres of War, 1914–1918*, Australian War Memorial, <https://www.awm.gov.au/histories/first_world_war/volVIII_introduction/>, accessed 2 February 2015
7. 'Prisoner of war', Royal Air Force Museum, <www.rafmuseum.org.uk/research/online-exhibitions/douglas-bader-fighter-pilot/prisoner-of-war.aspx>, accessed 2 January 2015
8. Monteath, *P.O.W.*, p. 161
9. 'Younger, Calton "Cal" (IWM interview)'
10. 'Cassie, Alex (IWM interview)', Imperial War Museum, audio file, catalogue number 26558, 2004, <www.iwm.org.uk/collections/item/object/80024310>, accessed 2 February 2015
11. Monteath, *P.O.W.*, pp. 166–7

12 Charles Rollings, *Prisoner of War: Voices from behind the wire in the Second World War*, London: Ebury, 2008, p. 4
13 'Convention relative to the treatment of prisoners of war. Geneva, 27 July 1929', International Committee of the Red Cross, <https://www.icrc.org/applic/ihl/ihl.nsf/States.xsp?xp_viewStates=XPages_NORMStatesParties&xp_treatySelected=305>, accessed 25 March 2015
14 'Cassie, Alex (IWM interview)'; Detlef Siebert, 'British bombing strategy in World War Two', *BBC: History*, <www.bbc.co.uk/history/worldwars/wwtwo/area_bombing_01.shtml>, accessed 2 February 2015
15 Rollings, *Prisoner of War*, p. 4
16 Winston Churchill, *My Early Life*, Simon and Schuster, 2010 edition, p. 259, accessed online, 2 January 2015 <https://books.google.com.au/books?id=n2EK2khQWfsC&dq=Winston+Churchill,+My+Early+Life,&source=gbs_navlinks_s>
17 Rollings, *Prisoner of War*, p. 4
18 Monteath, *P.O.W.*, p. 349
19 Jonathan F. Vance, *A Gallant Company: The men of the great escape*, ibooks Inc, 2003, p. 9
20 'Nelson, Thomas Robert (IWM interview)', Imperial War Museum, audio file, catalogue number 8276, 1984, <www.iwm.org.uk/collections/item/object/80008076>, accessed 25 March 2015
21 'Calton "Cal" Younger (IWM interview)', Imperial War Museum, audio file, catalogue number 23320, 2002 <www.iwm.org.uk/collections/item/object/80025614>, accessed 6 February 2015
22 This is based on cross-referencing known POWs from his squadron with lists of prisoners at Stalag Luft III and cannot be confirmed

28 In the Bag

1 'Foinette, Eric Norman (IWM interview)', Imperial War Museum, audio file, catalogue number 6095, 1982, <www.iwm.org.uk/collections/item/object/80005923>, accessed 25 March 2015
2 Walters, *The Real Great Escape*, p. 85
3 Document K152, File AIR40/266, National Archives, UK
4 'Eric Foinette (IWM interview)', Imperial War Museum, audio file, catalogue number 6095, 1982 <www.iwm.org.uk/collections/item/object/80005923>, accessed 11 February 2015

5 Flockhart, C.B. (1945). Camp History of Stalag Luft III (Sagan), Air Force personnel reports, April 1942–January 1945. Bound, typescript book, original, RAF Museum Archives, RAF Museum, Hendon, p. 64
6 Rob Davis, personal website, <www.elsham.pwp.blueyonder.co.uk/gt_esc/>, accessed 4 April 2015
7 Rollings, *Prisoner of War*, p. 240
8 'Cassie, Alex (IWM interview)'; details from 'Foinette, Eric Norman (IWM interview)'
9 Walters, *The Real Great Escape*, pp. 78–79
10 MI9 sample lecture, in Monteath, *P.O.W.*, p. 345
11 Walters, *The Real Great Escape*, p. 73
12 War Office, International Red Cross and Protecting Powers (Geneva) Reports concerning Prisoner of War camps in Europe and the Far East, Stalag Luft III, 1941–45, File W0 224/63A, National Archives, UK
13 D.S. Mills & Jeremy N. Marchant-Forde (eds), *The Encyclopedia of Applied Animal Behaviour and Welfare*, Wallingford, UK: CABI, 2010, p. 125

29 Big X

1 Walters, *The Real Great Escape*, p. 53
2 Pearson, *The Great Escaper*, p. 262
3 Pearson, *The Great Escaper*, p. 255
4 Pearson, *The Great Escaper*, p. 261
5 Burgess, *The Longest Tunnel*, pp. 22–3
6 Private Williams family letter
7 Walters, *The Real Great Escape*, p. 101

30 Second Time Unlucky

1 'How should we remember Bomber Command?', *The Guardian*, 14 May 2010, <www.theguardian.com/commentisfree/2010/may/14/bomber-command-war-memorial>, accessed 2 January 2015

31 The Swimming Pool

1 'Cornish, Geoffrey (IWM interview)', Imperial War Museum, audio file, catalogue number 27054, 2004, <www.iwm.org.uk/collections/item/object/80024320>, accessed 26 March 2015
2 Flockhart, Camp History of Stalag Luft III, p. 12

3   Flockhart, Camp History of Stalag Luft III, p. 7
4   Imperial War Museum, interview with Walter Morison, 2003, <www.iwm.org.uk/collections/item/object/80023269>, as quoted in Walters, *The Real Great Escape*, p. 113
5   Walters, *The Real Great Escape*, p. 113
6   Interview with the author
7   Hal Arkowitz & Scott O. Lilienfeld, 'Why science tells us not to rely on eyewitness accounts', *Scientific American*, 8 January 2009, <www.scientificamerican.com/article/do-the-eyes-have-it/?page=2>, accessed 2 February 2015
8   I have tried to cross-reference written reports, letters and personal recollections to confirm details where possible. I realise no single account will ever satisfy everyone, especially the many experts and amateurs who have followed this story and its repercussions over many decades.
9   Meserole, *The Great Escape*, p. 47
10 Walters, *The Real Great Escape*, p. 111
11 'Dowse, Sydney Hastings (IWM interview)', Imperial War Museum, audio file, catalogue number 27731, 2004, <www.iwm.org.uk/collections/item/object/80024871>, accessed 3 March 2014
12 Walters, *The Real Great Escape*, p. 124
13 Scangriff, *Spotlight on Stalag Luft III*, UK: private publication, 1947, p. 27
14 Aidan Crawley, *Escape from Germany*, as quoted in Pearson, *The Great Escaper*, p. 269
15 Flockhart, *Camp History of Stalag Luft III*, p. 9

32 Another German Friend

1   *Spotlight on Stalag Luft III*, p. 17
2   Carroll, *The Great Escape from Stalag Luft III*, p. 118
3   Judge Advocate General's Office, Military Deputy's Department, and War Office, Directorates of Army Legal Services and Personal Services: War Crimes Files (MO/JAG/FS and other series). Escape from Stalag 357, Stalag Luft III and Stalag Luft VI, July 1942–September 1944, File WO311/759, National Archives, UK
4   File WO311/759

33 Cooking and Carpentry

1. *Spotlight on Stalag Luft III*, p. 19
2. *Spotlight on Stalag Luft III*, p. 19
3. 'Bernard, David (IWM interview)', Imperial War Museum, audio file, Reel 13, catalogue no. 26561, 2004, <www.iwm.org.uk/collections/item/object/80024321>, accessed 22 November 2014
4. Pearson, *The Great Escaper*, p. 263
5. Flockhart, *Camp History of Stalag Luft III*, p. 7
6. Paul Brickhill, *The Great Escape*, London: Faber & Faber, 1951, p. 110
7. Flockhart, *Camp History of Stalag Luft III*, p. 31
8. Sara B. Johnson, Robert W. Blum & Jay N. Giedd, 'Adolescent maturity and the brain: The promise and pitfalls of neuroscience research in adolescent health policy', *Journal of Adolescent Health*, vol. 45, no. 3, 2009, pp. 216–21, <www.ncbi.nlm.nih.gov/pmc/articles/PMC2892678/>, accessed 2 February 2015
9. Walters, *The Real Great Escape*, p. 170
10. Flockhart, *Camp History of Stalag Luft III*, p. 9
11. 'Dowse, Sydney Hastings (IWM interview)'
12. Walters, *The Real Great Escape*, pp. 125–6
13. Jasper Rees, 'The secrets of history's most daring escape', *The Telegraph* [UK], 28 November 2011, <www.telegraph.co.uk/culture/tvandradio/8916302/The-secrets-of-historys-most-daring-escape.html>, accessed 12 December 2014
14. Pearson, *The Great Escaper*, p. 95
15. 'World War II in Europe: Timeline with photos and text', *The History Place*, <www.historyplace.com/worldwar2/timeline/ww2time.htm>, accessed 2 January 2015
16. Pearson, *The Great Escaper*, pp. 323–4
17. Multiple accounts, including Rob Davis, 'The great escape: Stalag Luft III, Sagan, March 24/25th, 1944', <www.elsham.pwp.blueyonder.co.uk/gt_esc/>, accessed 3 January 2015
18. James, *Moonless Night*, p. 95
19. 'Dowse, Sydney Hastings (IWM interview)'

34 A Ticket in the Lottery

1. Flockhart, *Camp History of Stalag Luft III*, p. 45
2. 'Cornish, Geoffrey (IWM interview)'

3   Brickhill, *The Great Escape*, p. 163
4   James, interviews with the author, June and October 2006

35 Shuffling the Cards

1   Plotline can be found at 'The Great Escape (1963): Plotlines', *IMDb*, <www.imdb.com/title/tt0057115/plotsummary>, accessed 2 January 2015
2   Statement of Anton Sawerthal, administrative chief of the Brux crematorium, 28 March 1946, to the RAF Special Investigations Branch, File AIR40/2281, National Archives, UK
3   Simon Read, *Human Game: The true story of the 'Great Escape' murders and the hunt for the Gestapo gunmen*, New York: Penguin, 2012, p. 102
4   Statement by Ivo Tonder
5   Statement of Anton Sawerthal
6   File WO311/955, Appendix, National Archives, UK
7   Statement of Anton Sawerthal
8   'Cornish, Geoffrey, (IWM interview)'
9   A.P. Scotland, *The London Cage: An account of the author's experiences in intelligence and security work*, London: Evans Brothers, 1957, p. 132
10 Scotland, *The London Cage*, p. 132
11 Monteath, *P.O.W.*, pp. 279–80
12 Scotland, *The London Cage*, p. 132
13 Scotland, *The London Cage*, p. 131
14 Air Ministry, Directorate of Intelligence and related bodies, Prisoners of War, killing of 50 R.A.F. and other officers from Stalag Luft III, statement by Peter Mohr, File AIR40/2268, National Archives, UK
15 AIR/40 2268, National Archives, UK
16 Eden, Commons statement, 23 June 1944, FO 371 38998 c9292/14/62, Public Records Office, London

36 The Bereaved Mother's Badge

1   *Worst Place To Be a Pilot*, television mini-series, episode 4, 2014, <www.sbs.com.au/ondemand/video/383313475735/Worst-Place-To-Be-A-Pilot-S1-Ep4>, viewed on 16 February 2015
2   Australian Bureau of Statistics, 'Australian Services during World War II', *Year Book Australia, 1946–47*, catalogue no. 1301.0, <www.abs.gov.au/ausstats/abs@.nsf/featurearticlesbytitle/F19B5A51A60904F3CA2569DE0020331F?OpenDocument>, accessed 4 February 2015

3   Read, Simon, author of Human Game in article at <www.dailymail. co.uk/home/moslive/article-2285629/Nazi-killers-How-Great-Escape-murders-led-post-war-Europes-biggest-manhunts.html,> accessed 15 April 2015
4   Williams, J.E.A., Casualty File, copy held by author, accessed via National Archives of Australia, <http://recordsearch.naa. gov.au/SearchNRetrieve/Interface/DetailsReports/Item Detail. aspx?Barcode=1055660&isAv=N>
5   Based on the evidence given in other cases. No witnesses were ever found
6   Williams, J.E.A., Casualty File, 24/11/1944
7   Williams, J.E.A, Casualty File, 14/7/1944
8   Correspondence contained in Williams, J.E.A., Casualty File
9   Interview with author, June 2006
10 'The Long March history', Royal Air Force, <www.raf.mod.uk/history/TheLongMarchHistory.cfm>, accessed 12 February 2015

37 In Memoriam

1   Obituary: Ivo Tonder, 11 May 1995, <www.independent.co.uk/news/people/obituary--ivo-tonder-1619036.html,> accessed 16 April 2015
2   'Secret Army', feature, 6 July 2001<www.theguardian.com/film/2001/jul/06/artsfeatures> accessed 16 April 2015
3   File AIR 40/2281, National Archives, UK
4   Richard Cox, 'Archives, war, and memory: Building a framework', *Library and Archival Security*, vol. 25, no. 1, 2012, pp. 21–57, < http://dx.doi.org/10.1080/01960075.2012.657945>, accessed 26 March 2015
5   Molly S. Castelloe, 'The lives of monuments: How monuments and memorials tell our emotional temperature', *Psychology Today*, 28 May 2010, <www.psychologytoday.com/blog/the-me-in-we/201005/the-lives-monuments>, accessed 3 April 2014

38 Surfing at Manly

1   Australian press reports including *Sunday Times* (Perth), 28 May 1944, p. 1

BIBLIOGRAPHY

Baker, Tim, *Australia's Century of Surf: How a big island at the bottom of the world became the greatest surfing nation on earth*, Ebury Press, 2013.

Barton, Leonard, *The Desert Harassers, Memoirs of 450 (RAAF) Squadron*, Astor Publications, 1991.

Beevor, Anthony, *The Second World War*, Phoenix, 2012.

Brawley, Sean, *The Bondi lifesaver: a history of an Australian icon*, Bondi Surf Bathers' Life Saving Club, 2007.

Brickhill, Paul, *The Great Escape*, Cassell Military Paperbacks, 2000.

Brown, Russell, *Desert Warriors, Australian P-40 pilots at war in the Middle East and North Africa*, Banner Books, 2000.

Burgess, Alan, *The Longest Tunnel*, Pocket Books, Simon and Schuster, 1990.

Curby, Pauline, *Manly, Seven Miles from Sydney: A History of Manly*, Manly Council, 2001.

Davies, Norman, *Europe, A History*, Pimlico, Random House, 1996.

Dear, I.C.B., *The Oxford Companion to the Second World War*, Oxford University Press, 1995.

Drake, Billy with Shores, Christopher, *Fighter leader: the autobiography of Group Captain B. Drake DSO, DFC & BAR, DFC (US)*, Grub Street, 2002.

Dornan, Peter, *Nicky Barr, an Australian air ace: a story of courage and adventure*, Allen & Unwin, 2005.

Edwards, Jimmy 'Stocky', *Kittyhawk Pilot: Wing Commander J. F. (Stocky) Edwards, Canadian Fighter Pilot*, Turner-Warwick Publications, Inc, North Battleford, Canada, 1983.

Fenton, Peter, *They called him Boy*, Random House, 2006.

FitzSimons, Peter, *Tobruk*, HarperCollins, 2009.

Flockhart, C.B. (1945), *Camp History of Stalag Luft III (Sagan)*, Air Force personnel reports, April 1942–January 1945. Bound, typescript book, original, RAF Museum Archives, RAF Museum.

Francis, Martin, *The Flyer: British Culture and the Royal Air Force, 1939–45*, Oxford University Press, 2008.
Gill, Anton, *The Great Escape: the full dramatic story with contributions from survivors and their families*, Review, 2002.
Gorham J.R & Hewett C.J.L. (eds.), *The Torch Bearers: War Service of the Shore Old Boys*, Shore, Sydney Church of England Grammar School, 1999.
Hamilton, Paula, *Cracking Awaba: Stories of Mosman and Northern Beaches Communities during the Depression*, SHOROC Council Libraries, 2005.
Hillary, Richard, *The Last Enemy*, Macmillan & Co, London, 1942, e-book, Michael O'Mara Books Limited, London, 2014.
Herington, John, *Air War Against Germany and Italy, 1939–1943*, Australian War Memorial, 1954.
Holmes, Tony and Thomas, Andrew, *Tomahawk and Kittyhawk Aces of the RAF and Commonwealth*, Osprey Publishing Ltd, Oxford, 2002.
Ilbery, Peter, *Empire Airmen Strike Back: the Empire Air Training Scheme and 5SFTS, Uranquinty*, Banner Books, 1999.
Jaggard E. (ed.), *Between the Flags, One Hundred Summers of Australian Surf Lifesaving*, UNSW Press, 2006.
James, B.A. 'Jimmy', *Moonless Night: The Second World War Escape Epic*, Pen & Sword, Military, 1983.
Johnston, Mark & Stanley, Peter, *Alamein: the Australian story*, Oxford University Press, 2002.
Lyall, Gavin (ed.), *The war in the air, 1939–1945 : an anthology of personal experiences*, Hutchinson, 1968.
Lucas, Laddie (ed), *Voices in the Air, 1939–1945, Incredible stories of World War II airmen in their own words*, Arrow Books, 2003.
Monteath, Peter, *POW, Australian prisoners of war in Hitler's Reich*, Macmillan, 2011.
Moorehead, Alan, *The Desert War: The classic trilogy on the North African campaign, 1940–43*, Aurum Press, 2009 edition (first published 1944).
Morgan, Hugh, *By the Seat of Your Pants*, Newton Books, 1990.
Pearson, Simon, *The Great Escaper: The Life and Death of Roger Bushell*, Hodder and Stoughton, 2013.
Ramsland, John, *Brave and Bold, Manly Village Public School, 1858–2008*, Brolga Publishing, 2008.
Read, Simon, *Human Game: Hunting the Great Escape Murderers*, Constable and Robinson Ltd, London, 2012.

Rollings, Charles, *Prisoner of War: Voices from Behind the Wire in the Second World War*, Ebury Press, 2008.
'Scangriff' (POWs' pen name), *Spotlight on Stalag Luft III*, published privately by the POWs' editorial team, 1947.
Scotland, A.P. Lt. Col., *The London Cage*, Evans Brothers Ltd, London, 1957.
Sherington, Geoffrey, *Shore: A History of SCEGS*, Sydney Church of England Grammar School, 1983.
Shores, Christopher & Ring, Hans, *Fighters over the Desert: Air Battles in the Western Desert, June 1940 to December 1942*, Neville Spearman, 1969.
Sly, Edward 'Ted', *The Luck of the Draw*, Spitfire Books, 2003.
Souter, Gavin, *Mosman: A History*, Melbourne University Press, 1994.
Taylor, Peter, *A Celebration of Shore*, Sydney Church of England Grammar School, 1988.
Vance, Jonathan, *A Gallant Company: The Men of The Great Escape*, Pacifica Military History, 2001.
Walters, Guy, *The Real Great Escape*, Bantam Books, 2013.
Watson, John W./Cmdr & Jones, Louis, *3 Squadron at War*, D.A.F. 3 Squadron Association, 1959.
Williams, Keith (ed.), *Letters to Mother, from a WWII RAAF Pilot*, Keith Williams, 1990.
Winter, Vincent, *Noble Six Hundred: the story of the Empire Training Scheme*, Vincent Winter, 1982.

ACKNOWLEDGEMENTS

There are so people to thank who have helped me, in many different ways and over many years, in piecing this story together. First, of course, is my late father, Owen Ashley Williams, who told us John's story as children. Then, my late uncle, David Ashley Williams, and aunt, Barbara Williams, who entrusted me with the family files that David had carefully compiled over the years. My wonderful mother, Margaret, has been a tireless and generous supporter and willing reader, backed by her husband, Bob, and my daughter, Clara. My siblings, Megan, Richard and David, all made invaluable contributions as did my mother-in-law, Ruth Baxter. And, my great friend, Cathy Griffin, has long been my much valued champion and a patient and helpful sounding board.

I am indebted to Peter Kierath for sharing his own knowledge and his family's precious memories and letters with me, and for his friendship and generosity. John's story would not be complete without 'Rusty' Kierath by his side. That the Kieraths and the Williams family met is thanks to the generosity and tenacity of Michal Holy, who set in train a series of extraordinary events when he decided to honour the men with a permanent memorial in the Czech Republic.

I would also like to thank Harry Wicke who, despite his own difficult wartime experiences, talked to me frankly and openly, enabling me to fill in many gaps. My father's cousin, Judy Eastway, was also able to help with family details. I was similarly fortunate to have been able to talk at length to Jimmy James and Edward 'Ted' Sly about John and their shared experiences and to meet and talk with Air Commodore Gordon Steege about the No. 450 Squadron RAAF. All three WWII fliers have since passed away.

Much of the material for the book was sourced from declassified documents held in the United Kingdom, the Czech Republic and Poland. Peter Devitt, from the RAF Museum in London, was especially supportive and helpful from my first inquiry. Marek Lazarz, from the Stalag Luft III Museum in Zagan, Poland, was likewise willing to share his time and considerable knowledge. In Australia, Sandi Nipperess and Doug Norrie, of the No. 450 Squadron RAAF Association have done a great job in keeping the Squadron's history and memory alive. John MacRitchie, from Manly Library's Local Studies Centre, was an invaluable source of knowledge about the history of Manly. Canadian military historian, Professor Jonathan Vance, generously shared some of his own research with me, including letters from pilots who served with John. Jonathan Grow kindly shared his understanding of aircraft, including World War II Kittyhawks. I also owe a great deal to the many researchers and curators in the United Kingdom and Australia who had the foresight to capture the voices and stories of a generation of John's contemporaries on tape and to make their vibrant and fascinating oral histories available, often online.

There are many more people whose interest and encouragement and belief in this project have made so much difference (you know who you are).

My biggest thanks goes to my husband, Craig, whose untiring support has made the project such a joy.

INDEX

Africa 119–22
　North *see* North Africa
　South *see* South Africa
Afrika Korps 132, 148
aircraft
　Blenheim bombers 180
　Empire Boat C Class 144
　Hurricanes 140, 150–1
　Junkers 151, 175
　Kittyhawks 38, 139, 150–1, 162–3, 165, 168, 174, 199
　Messerschmitts 37, 38, 84, 100, 141, 150–1, 163, 166, 175
　P40s 150
　Spitfires 150–1, 179, 193, 208, 219
　Tomahawks 150
airforce personnel 27–8, 82, 137, 146, 154, 171, 183–4
　casualties 101, 120–1, 122, 165–6, 177, 230–3
　fear 152–7, 176
　mental fatigue 155–6, 167, 176
　officers 168–9
　POWs, as 179–80, 183, 187–92
Alexandria 167, 170
Attenborough, Richard 10
Australian Flying Corps 72
Australian soldiers 4–5

Australian Surf Lifesaving Association 60, 70
Auxiliary Air Force (AAF) 87–9
　No. 601 Squadron (Millionaires Club) 88, 193
aviation 72–3, 113–14 *see also* Royal Air Force (RAF); Royal Australian Air Force (RAAF)
　WWI 72, 83–4, 87

Baatz, Bernhard 241
Bader, Wing Commander Douglas 179–80
Barr, Squadron Leader Nicky 149–50, 155, 162
Battle of Britain 102, 103, 108, 116
Belgium 96
Berchtesgaden 227
Berlin Olympics 1936 68–9
Bloody Hundredth (100th Bomb Group) 36
Boberröhrsdorf 32
Borneo 232
Bowes, Wing Commander Wilfred 241–2
bribing the guards 207–8
Brickhill, Paul 194, 203, 206
Brux (Most) 223, 225, 238–9
　Most memorial 236–8, 247

Bulawayo 120–3, 125, 126, 133
Bull, Flight Lieutenant Leslie 'Johnny' 8–9, 11, 32–3, 35, 38, 215
   cremation 224
   Czechoslovakia, in 55–6, 79
   death 232
   family 237–8
'Bullet Order' 218
Bushell, Squadron Leader Roger 10, 88, 193–6, 204, 205, 213–15, 219, 220

Cairo 139, 141, 144–5, 147–8, 167
Cambridge University Squadron (CUS) 91–2, 94, 99
Cassis, Alex 180
Catanach, Squadron Leader James 231
censorship
   letters home 140, 141
   letters to POWs 4
Central Flying School 87
Chamberlain, Neville 56, 84–5
Changi 5
Charlton, Andrew 'Boy' 58
Christensen, Flight Lieutenant Arnold 231
Churchill, Winston 136, 142, 147, 169, 182, 185, 218
Cold War 2, 34, 237–9
Condor Legion 84
Cornish, Geoff 200, 221, 225
cowardice 155–6
Czech Republic 34–5, 238
   Most memorial 236–8
Czechoslovakia 30, 32, 36, 37, 56, 85, 224, 237–9
   communists 36, 238–40, 242

Dachau concentration camp 29
Dahl, Roald 156
Darwin
   bombing 159
Darwin, Charles 70

Day, Group Captain Harry 'Wings' 214, 221
Dean, Professor H.R. 91
Denmark 96
Desert Air Force 147, 153–5, 164, 166, 169, 172
   239 Wing 147, 155, 161, 163, 166, 199
   Caterpillar Club 153
   Goldfish Club 153
   Late Arrivals Club 153
   slang 153
Desert Harassers (No. 450 Squadron) 10, 143–4, 147–8, 153, 159–66, 168, 176, 198, 235
desert warfare 135–9, 154, 176
'Dick' 194–5, 204, 206, 213–14
Digby, Lieutenant 170
Dodge, Major Johnny 32
Down, Squadron Leader Peter 143, 147, 150–1
Dowse, Sydney 208, 209, 215–16, 219, 222
Drake, Squadron Leader Billy 83, 85, 165, 167, 168
Drakensberg Mountains 119
Duke of Gloucester, Prince Henry 159
Dulag Luft 180–1, 199, 234
Dundock, Bill 122
Dunkirk 101
Durban 133–4

Eden, Foreign Secretary Anthony 229
Egypt 116, 132, 136–8, 158, 169, 171, 198
Eighth Army 169, 177, 198
El Alamein 167, 168, 172, 174, 196, 197
El Daba 175
Empire Training Scheme 102, 114, 117, 119–21, 130, 159
English, John 121, 126

English gentlemen 81, 93
Enigma 169
escape
  duty to 183, 190, 193–4, 201
  lottery 220–1
  rations 205
eugenics 70

Fairy Bower 44
fascism 70–1, 84
fear 152–7
Ferguson, Sir Charles 24–5
Ferguson, Squadron Leader Alan 169
Floody, Wally 219
Foinette, Eric 189
food 207, 211–13
Foodaco 212
Forbes 18
France 96, 101
Fullerton, Hector 169

Gable, Clark 73
Gallipoli 21, 139
Galton, Sir Francis 70
Gaza 148–9
Gazala line 158, 162–3, 166
Geneva Convention 179, 181, 217
German Air Force *see* Luftwaffe
German Army
  Africa, in 132, 146, 150, 158, 162, 164, 166–7, 169–72, 175, 178
  casualties 177
  Europe, move across 96, 101–2
  Panzer regiments 96, 137, 163, 172
  POWs, treatment of 178–9
Gestapo 78–9, 180, 193, 194, 218, 224, 228, 241–2
Gibbes, Squadron Leader Bobby 154–5, 176
Gibson, Perla 116–17
Gleeson, J.D. 'Jack' 147–8, 159
Glemnitz, Sergeant-Major Hermann 213

Gocher, William 59
Goodman, Charles 41
Göring, Hermann 84, 179–80, 184, 227, 234
Great Depression 26, 39–43, 61
  education during 47–8, 49, 75
Great Escape
  interpretations of 201–2
The Great Escape 1, 10, 13, 223, 236–7
Great War *see* World War I
Green, Flight Lieutenant Bernard 'Pop' 11
Green, Thomas Kirby 238
Greenaway, William 190
grief 230–3, 243
Guernica
  massacre 84

Hake, Flight Officer Al 33, 231
Hall, Charles 226
Hall, Leonard 191
Harare (Salisbury) 130–1
'Harry' 1, 8–9, 33, 194, 204, 206, 215, 219, 220
  underground cavern 215
  ventilation 211, 216
Hay 106
Hay, Harry 58, 69
Helm, Wing Commander Robert 81–2, 83, 86
Hesse, Corporal Eberhard 'Nicky' 208–9
hierarchy of loss 226
Hillary, Richard 92–3, 97–9, 103, 157
Hilts, Virgil 13, 223
Himmler, Heinrich 217, 227–8
Hitler, Adolf 30, 43, 66, 68–9, 84–5, 96, 159, 172, 175, 181, 234
  response to escape 227–8
Hitler Youth 69, 78
Holy, Michal 35–8, 78, 238–41, 243, 244

Howie's Way 73
Hughes, Billy 113

ideals 24–5, 51–2, 81
Induna 121
Italians 70, 84, 116, 132, 146, 177, 198, 218
  POWs, treatment of 179

James, Jimmy 32, 56, 201, 209, 219, 220–1, 234–5
Japanese 4–6, 106, 116, 149, 159, 162, 182, 232
  POWs, treatment of 182
Jefferson, Carl 149
Jeffrey, Squadron Leader Peter 140
Jenkins, Sergeant Max 173, 174–5
Jizera mountains 32

Kahanamoku, Duke 63
Keitel, Field Marshal Wilhelm 227
Kidder, Gordon 238
Kierath, Ada 112–14, 147–8, 197–9, 200, 211, 213, 221, 233
  death of Rusty 230
Kierath, Albert William (William) 110–13
Kierath, Captain Greg 114, 129–30, 233
Kierath, Charles 109–10
Kierath, Flight Lieutenant Reginald 'Rusty' 9, 10, 54, 113, 154, 215, 246
  Africa, in 117–18, 127–33, 137, 139–42, 147–8, 158–60, 197–8
  air force career 114, 117–18, 127–33
  character 108, 128, 159
  cremation 224
  Czechoslovakia, in 55–6, 79, 84
  death 224, 226, 230–2
  escape from Stalag Luft III 9, 11, 31–3, 38, 202, 220, 222
  flight instructor, as 159, 197
  prisoner of war 199, 211, 214, 221
  sport 108–9, 205–6
  Stalag Luft III, in 199
Kierath, Henrietta 109
Kierath, Herbert William 114
Kierath, Karl 109
Kierath, Louise 110
Kierath, Peter 34–5, 111, 113, 114, 226, 233, 237, 240
Kingsford Smith, Charles 73
Kinloss 95, 97–8, 102, 103
Klim tins 211, 216
Kohlfurt (Wegliniec) 79
Kovarska 36
Kumalo 120–1, 122, 125

Landau, Rom 100
larrikin tradition 61, 62
Lebensraum 30, 116
Leicester Square 9
Leigh, Thomas 231
Liberec (Reichenberg) 56, 79, 223, 240, 241
Libya 116, 138, 146, 158, 179, 198
Lion's Walk 191
Lobengula, King 121
Lubbock, Lieutenant David 211, 212
Luftwaffe 83–4, 96, 102–3, 108, 122, 142, 149–51, 162–3, 175, 180, 217
Luxembourg 96

McAlister, Charles 'Snow' 62, 63, 90
MacMalcolm, Duff 97
Macquarie River 111, 112
McQueen, Steve 13, 14, 223
Manly Beach 1, 39–45, 49, 58–9, 64, 68
Manly Life Saving Club 59, 62, 90, 105, 244
Manly Village Public School 47–8
Markle, Al 176, 242
Marshall, Flight Lieutenant Henry 'Johnny' 9

Massey, Group Captain Herbert 194
mateship 61, 153–4, 171
Mauthausen concentration camp 218
memorials 13, 36, 116, 235, 236–8, 241, 243, 247
mental fatigue 155–6, 167, 176
Menzies, Robert 102, 104, 147
MI9 183, 191, 193
MI19 War Crimes Investigation Unit 227
Middle East 83, 129, 139, 143, 159
Middle Harbour 52–3
Mondschein, Flying Officer Jerzy 12, 31, 32, 35, 38, 215
   cremation 224
   Czechoslovakia, in 55–6, 79
   death 232
   memorial 237
Mondschein, Malgorzata (Margaret) 32, 237
Montgomery, Lieutenant-General B.L. 169, 171–2, 176
Moorehead, Alan 133, 138, 153
Morison, Walter 201
Most (Brux) 223, 225, 238–9
   Most memorial 236–8, 247
Mussolini, Benito 70, 116
MV *Durban Castle* 115, 116

Narromine 110–14, 128, 140, 200
Nazis 5, 29, 30, 36, 55–6, 69, 84, 224, 235
   'Aryan race' theory 70
   German anti-Nazi feeling 208
   German Army *see* German Army
   Lord Haw-Haw 161
   SS (Schutzstaffel) 29, 217, 240
   Tripartite Pact 116
Nebe, Police General Arthur 228
Nelson, Thomas 184
Netherlands 96
New Zealand 23

North Africa 116
North Head 44, 45
Norway 96, 98, 102
Nuremburg trials 29

O'Brien, Tim 15, 16
Odurman Campaign 136
O'Neill, William 110, 112
Orange 106
Ore Mountains, Battle of 36
Ostrava 238
Oxford University Squadron 97

Packer, Frank 90, 109
'The Palms' Benghazi 179
Parker, Dudley 150, 179
Paus, Leslie 237–8
Pavlíček, Colonel Jan 238
Pearl Harbour 149
'penguins' 216
Picasso, Pablo 84
Piccadilly Circus 9
Pohe, Johnny 231
Poland 2, 29–30, 33, 36, 96, 218, 237–8
Poznan 182
Prague 34, 35–6, 78, 193
Prestwick 81, 86
prisoners of war (POWs) 30, 178–85
   airmen 179–80, 183, 187–92
   Australia, in 104–7
   bribing the guards 207–8
   coded messages to Allies 189
   educational opportunities 190
   escape, duty to 183, 190, 193–4, 201
   food 207, 211–13
   friendly guards 208–9
   German treatment of 178–9
   Japanese treatment of 182
   letters to 4, 247
   life inside camp 187–92

prisoners of war (POWs) (cont.)
  officers 28, 190–1
  senior British officer (SBO) 188–9, 194, 218
  sport 190–1, 201, 205–6

Qattara Depression 167, 172

Ratzel, Freidrich 30
Reavell-Carter, Squadron Leader Laurence 33
Red Cross 170, 181, 190, 192, 204, 207, 211–12, 240
Rees, Ken 216
Reichenberg (Liberec) 56, 79, 223, 240, 241
Rhodes, Cecil 127
Rhodesia 114, 119–20, 123, 127, 143, 159
Robson, L.C. 51
Rommel, Field Marshal Erwin 132, 146, 150, 158, 162–7, 169–72, 175, 181, 196
Roosevelt, Theodore 218
Rose, Nigel 97
Royal Air Force (RAF) 5, 83–4, 124–5
  Australian pilots 73–5, 130–1
  changing culture 98–9, 140
  Investigation Branch 241
  No. 33 Squadron 133, 140
  No. 112 Squadron 143, 146–7
  No. 250 Squadron 147
  No. 260 Squadron 144
  training 81–2, 83, 85–7, 95–9, 102, 123, 126–7
Royal Australian Air Force (RAAF) 5, 73–4
  aircrew 7–8
  Desert Harassers (No. 450 Squadron) 10, 143–4, 147–8, 153, 159–66, 168, 176, 198, 235
  Middle East, in 143–4
  No. 3 Squadron 140, 143, 147, 149, 162
  training 120–1
Royle, Paul 234
'Rubberneck' 204, 219, 220
Russia 185

Sachsenhausen concentration camp 235
Sagan (Zagan) 10–11, 27–31, 77–9, 184
Sagan Order 228
Sawerthal, Anton 224
Scangriff 202–3, 205–6, 211
Schorm, Lieutenant Joachim 137
Scotland, Lieutenant Colonel A.P. 227
service and sacrifice 24, 25, 51, 52, 63
Sidi Aziez 163
Sidi Battani 175
Silesia 27–30, 36, 38, 184, 189, 203, 235
Sinclair, Sir Archibald 84
Singapore 149, 159
Slessor, Keith 175
Sly, Ted 118, 126, 165–6, 225, 235
Smith, Martha Eleanor 'Nellie' 18–19
Smith, Ross and Keith 113
South Africa 116–17, 121–2, 134
Spanish Civil War 70, 84
Spit Baths 53
Stalag Luft III 1, 2, 6, 8, 11, 30, 36–7, 180, 182, 184, 190
  70th anniversary of the escape 77–8, 240
  bribing the guards 207–8
  Bunk Room 23 8, 13
  death of POWs 224, 226, 230–1
  educational opportunities 190
  escape lottery 220–1
  execution order 227–8, 234–5, 240, 241
  ferrets 195, 204, 206–7, 213, 219, 220

final preparations 221–2
food 207, 211–13
friendly guards 208–9
Hut 104 8, 13, 195, 220
life inside 187–92
march 203, 235
memorials 236–7, 238
nationalities 187–8
post-war investigation 229, 241–2
purpose of camp 27–8, 191–2
recreation of tunnel 217
sport 190–1
swimming pool 200
tunnels *see* tunnels
Steege, Squadron Leader Gordon 160
Stower, Flying Officer John 'Johnny' 78–9, 241
Sudetenland 85
Suez Canal 116, 132, 139, 158
surf-lifesaving 59, 61–3, 65, 69–70
   Africa, in 148–9
surfboats 65
surfing 59–61, 63–6, 187
Swift, Snow 53–4, 108–9, 114, 199
   Africa, in 117–18, 127–9, 131
Sydney Church of England Grammar School (Shore) 48–54, 61, 62, 108, 113

Tatura 106, 234
Test Pilot 73
Tobruk 132, 137, 158, 161, 166
'Tom' 194, 195, 204, 206, 213–14
Tonder, Flight Lieutenant Ivo 78–80, 223–4, 240
Tonder, Jirina 240
Tonder, Petra 78–9, 240
travel documents
   forging 13–14, 189, 205, 209
Treaty of Versailles 30
Trenchard, Lord 87
Tripartite Pact 116
Tschiebsdorf 12, 31

Tuck, Bob 214
Tunisia 198–9
tunnels 194–5, 203–6, 213, 215–19
   'Dick' 194–5, 204, 206, 213–14
   'Harry' 1, 8–9, 33, 194, 204, 206, 211, 215–16, 219, 220
   recreation 217
   'Tom' 194, 195, 204, 206, 213–14
   underground cavern 215
   ventilation 211, 216

ULTRA 169
United States Air Force 36–7
Uxbridge 86

Valley of a Thousand Hills 119
Victoria Falls 127
Vietnam War 2, 15
Volk 30
Volunteer Reserve Force 87, 88
von Lindeiner, Kommandant Colonel 188, 189, 218

Walters, Guy 216
war stories, telling 15–16, 207, 242–3
Wegliniec (Kohlfurt) 79
Weissman, Robert 241
Wellesley College, Wellington 24–5
Wellington, New Zealand 21
Western Desert 131, 133, 135, 144, 147, 149, 185, 198
Weyland, Robert 241
Wicke, Hans (Harry) 42–3, 67–8, 70–1, 76, 187, 244–5
   death of John 234
   German heritage, problems with 93, 104–7
   surfing and surf-lifesaving 58–66, 90
   Suzie Williams, and 67–8, 93
Wilkins, Derek 120
Williams, Barry 5, 25, 76, 232

Williams, David 5, 22, 25, 39, 48, 49, 71, 76, 202, 221, 232
Williams, Edwin 19–20
Williams, Fanny 20
Williams, Llewellyn (Len) 5, 19, 20–1, 67, 90, 91, 124, 134, 195
  character 19
  death of John 232
  Great Depression 39–41, 48
  New Zealand, in 21–3, 25–6
Williams, Mildred 10, 67–8, 90, 100, 124, 134, 195, 200
  background 17–19
  Bereaved Mother's Badge 233
  character 17, 19, 47, 75–6, 101, 177, 245
  death of John 230–3, 245
  Great Depression 39, 43, 47–8
  Hans, court case against 104, 106
  letters to John 3–6, 247
  New Zealand, in 22, 23, 25–6
Williams, Owen 5, 26, 76, 186, 231, 245
Williams, Sarah 19, 20
Williams, Squadron Leader John Edwin Ashley 6, 12, 154
  Africa 114, 115–20, 122, 124–6, 142–5, 147–8, 155, 161–5, 167–76
  air force career 71–5, 81–2, 89–93
  birth 22
  carpentry 66, 213–15
  character 6, 7, 54, 157, 169, 186–7
  cremation 224
  Czechoslovakia, in 55–6, 79–80
  death 224, 226, 230–2
  Distinguished Flying Cross (DFC) 5, 175, 213, 232, 245
  Doreen 99–101
  Dulag Luft 180–1, 234
  education 24, 48–9, 53–4, 75
  El Alamein 167, 168, 172–4
  Escape Committee 195–6, 205, 208–9, 214
  escape from Stalag Luft III 9, 11, 13–14, 32–3, 38, 202, 222
  flight instructor, as 87, 91, 95–6, 103, 118, 122, 123–5, 245–6
  illness 134, 143
  letters home 4, 89–93, 99–100, 124, 134, 221
  Manly, in 41, 42–3, 49
  pilot training 81–2, 85–7, 93
  prisoner of war 178–80, 184–5, 187
  shot down 173, 174–7
  squadron leader 168–9
  Stalag Luft III, in 184–5, 199
  surf-lifesaving 59, 60–4, 66
  surfing 1, 59
  swimming 53–4, 58–9, 64–5
  test pilot, as 133–4
  train journey to Czechoslovakia 31–2
Williams, Susanna 20, 48–9
Williams, Suzie 5, 22, 48, 67–8, 76, 93, 107, 231
  Hans, court case against 104, 106
World War I 21–2, 27, 30, 42, 50, 60, 72, 114
  aviation 72, 83–4, 87, 155, 179

X Organisation 193, 196, 208, 213, 219, 220

Younger, Cal 180, 185